A do-it-yourself retreat

JOSEPH F. HOGAN, S.J., born in 1910, received his M.A. degree from St. Louis University followed by a licentiate in Philosophy and Theology. He was ordained in 1941. He served as chaplain with the U.S. Third Army for four years and is a lieutenant colonel in the Army reserve. From 1946 to 1959 he was student counselor at Loyola University, Chicago. At present he is Regional Director of the Apostleship of Prayer. Father Hogan has given retreats to men and women, professional groups both Catholic and non-Catholic, and to high school and university students.

JOSEPH F. HOGAN, S.J.

A do-it-yourself retreat

How to bring out the real good in you

LOYOLA UNIVERSITY PRESS

Chicago, Illinois

Illustrations on pages 178-79 by
Edward J. Mandula, S.J.

PREFACE

This book is for . . .

Those who have never made a retreat, and those to whom the word may sound strange or even forbidding. I think you will like it, and though you start it as an experiment, you may find it so interesting and worth-while that you will want the fuller and richer experience at a retreat house.

those who would like to make a closed retreat but cannot, especially God's beloved sick and suffering and those in the evening of life.

those who have made a retreat and who would like to retain the clarity of vision and the peace of soul it gave them.

husbands and wives who would like to make a retreat at home, either together or individually. It can help to oneness in outlook.

Finally, but finally only for emphasis, this book is for students who are making an open retreat and want a companion book—collateral reading—to keep them in the spirit of the retreat.

INTRODUCTION

The do-it-yourself appeal which is somewhat popular today is not just a fad. It meets the basic need in man to be creative.

This DO-IT-YOURSELF RETREAT makes the same appeal to your highest creative instincts.

However, in this case, you are shown not how to make some *thing*, but HOW TO BRING OUT THE REAL GOOD IN YOU and make yourself into the truly great person that God intended you to be. These pages will help you to discover who you really are, and the discovery will prove to be encouraging and consoling.

Although you are doing-it-yourself, this retreat follows a time-tested and approved method. It is progressive. Step by step it helps you to bring out the potential for all the goodness and greatness which is present in you.

You are also following a mystery story—these are God's mysteries—so you do not peek at the chapters ahead. One step at a time is best, and God be with you on the way.

CONTENTS

◆◆◆◆◆◆◆◆◆◆◆◆◆

1 A problem and an answer   1

2 I didn't know I had it in me   20

3 My mission   43

4 In case of emergency   65

5 Bless me, Father, for I have sinned   89

6 They're married   106

7 They're engaged—or on the way   128

8 A more excellent way   158

9 Christ with us   180

10 A mystery of love   199

11 Victory with peace   218

12 Learn to love   240

13 Planning for life   257

14 Prayers and examen   259

◆◆◆◆◆◆◆◆◆◆◆◆◆◆◆

A problem
and an answer

I wish to welcome you to this retreat. I am very glad that you have decided to make it. You aren't off in the silence of a retreat house. You aren't completely isolated from distractions as you would be there; but you can create little islands of quiet for yourself in the midst of a busy day—the half hour commuting on the train or riding the bus in the morning, the forty-five minutes after the kids have gone to bed, the free period in your school schedule. Admittedly, a do-it-yourself retreat takes some planning and arranging, but your effort will be well worth while. God is never outdone in generosity. So now lean back and relax, because it is in the atmosphere of peace and quiet and tranquility that you will get the most out of your retreat. I welcome you; and remember, easy does it.

More important, however, than my welcome to your retreat, would be the welcome from our Lord Himself. When you recall that He is human as well as divine, He is the son of man as well as the Son of God, we can say without exaggeration that He looks forward to spending these extra hours with you, His friends, as eagerly as you look forward to spending time with those dearest to you. In this atmosphere, then, you should be quite relaxed and at peace. Our Lord's favorite greeting is, "Peace. It is I. Fear not."

Now there are a couple of by-products which you can get from a retreat which might not appear on the surface. One is physical rest. You are making plans to be a bit more leisurely and to set aside some time for quiet reading and reflection. In this atmosphere of peace you will find yourself returning to the day's routine more serene and physically rested. There is also the by-product of mental refreshment. I don't care how interesting your job or studies may be; we all discover that in staying with a job day after day, day after day, the mind loses its edge, the memory loses its retentiveness, and we begin to get diminishing returns on our work. However, if we get away from it even for a brief time and think along slightly different lines, we will find ourselves going back mentally refreshed. Of course the most important aim and goal in a retreat is spiritual strength, courage, peace, and closeness to Christ which are best achieved in this atmosphere of peace and serenity. If we but touch the hem of His garment, we will be healed.

Perhaps some of you are making a retreat for the first time. Others have made many retreats and you can draw from your memories and experiences. But in either case, a good question to ask is: "What is a retreat?" Obviously there are any number of answers that can be given to this question. But I would like to propose it to you as a problem. I will give you a thumbnail sketch of the lives of four people and I will ask you to decide whether their lives are a success or a failure according to God's plan, and on what principles you would base your judgment.

The first life I offer for your consideration is from a Chicago *Tribune* story back a few years ago. The headline reads: "Tired and Alone, Famed Playboy . . . Suicide." And the subtitle, "Spent Millions Trying to Have a Good Time." Palm Beach, Florida. "Forgotten and alone, Byron . . . , who spent several million dollars during 63 years of life trying to have a good time, decided today that he couldn't take it any more.

"He wrote a note to his fourth wife, Betty Jean, . . . who divorced him a year ago, and another note to his lawyer. There wasn't anyone in his big white house, a Palm Beach showplace, for him to say goodbye to. He walked out on his private pier, fired a bullet into his breast, and his body toppled into Lake Wales.

"His death ended a spectacular spendthrift saga which began . . . when he burst forth on Broadway at 23, fresh from college, with $2,000,000 in his pockets, which he had just inherited from his father, a banker. He became the best known playboy of that thorofare's most glamorous era . . . His four wives, all of whom divorced him, were Broadway beauties. He never ran out of money, despite his lavishness. He testified once that he was down to his last $10,000, but another 1 million dollar inheritance tided him over." Now there was a man who had social position, wealth, a luxurious home. There were beautiful women in his life. He had the world, a trinket at his wrist. And I ask was his life a success according to God's plan, or was it a failure, and how would you decide?

The second life I offer for your thought is the life of a good friend of mine, Captain Morrison. The last time I saw him as a completely healthy man was one rainy Sunday in France. I had said Mass and he came up afterwards for a quick "Hello." That afternoon his glider was shot down. In the crash his neck was broken. He was captured, did not receive adequate medical attention, and went permanently blind. He wrote me: "If it were not for my Catholic faith, I would commit suicide." He had only a lifetime of darkness, helplessness, and dependency to look forward to. And I ask could such a life be a success according to God's plan, or would it be a failure, and how would you decide?

A third life I offer for your consideration is, again, a close friend of mine. He was a corporal in our outfit and that same Sunday morning after Mass he stopped for a cigarette. The next day I was called to his foxhole where he was lying with a piece of shrapnel in his back. He gave me a note for his wife and his little one-year-old daughter, and he died. Dead at twenty-three. We might say that life was just beginning. And I ask could such a life be a success according to God's plan, or was it a failure, and on what principle would you decide? Is there a certain number of years a man must live to be a success according to God's plan? If so, what is that magic number— eighteen, twenty-five, ninety-four? Should we demand or expect of God a long life or a short one?

3

The fourth life I offer for your reflection is your own. You know what goes to make it up. There is the obligation of working and earning a living, keeping a home, teaching or going to school, advancing in your profession. There is your happiness at home or lack of happiness. There are your social life, your successes, your failures, your unfulfilled hopes and ambitions, your prayer, your sufferings, your entertainment—all the little and big things that go to make up your life. And I ask is that life being led successfully according to God's plan, and how would you decide?

So here is one answer to "What is a retreat?"— A retreat is an opportunity to look over life once again and see where the values lie. This is needed because in the process of living we can get confused —all of us. We may start off with good direction, but we can begin to angle off and find ourselves "whither we wouldst not." Also, it can happen that something of first importance slips down to third place and some second- or third-rate value edges up to first. So a retreat is an opportunity to put first things first.

There is another answer to "What is a retreat?" I remember when I was in high school, back about a hundred years ago, a lay professor of ours made a remark which has stuck with me ever since. It was a warm spring day and we were seniors, tired of the textbook and anxious to get the professor away from it. He evidently had tired blood too, because when we threw out a baited question he rose to it, closed the textbook, and began to philosophize about life. The remark that he made then I can still quote word for word. It was: "This business of living is a lonely business; no one can do it for you." I remember thinking at the time: "Why did he say that? He is married and has three children. He has a classroom full of high-school students who would keep any man busy and occupied. There are lots of people in his life! Why, then, a 'lonely business'?" Yet, how true that statement is. "No one can do it for us." No matter how close we may be to wife, family, and friends, they cannot, either singly or collectively, lead our lives for us. Thank God for their companionship, and warmth, and love in our lives; but ultimately we are on our own. You can see that in a little child who will stand in front of his parents, stamp his foot, and say: "I won't!" Of course when he is small you can hustle him along and make him do it. But that first, "I won't," is a declaration of independence and a declaration of loneliness. He is on his own. No matter how parents may wish to lead his life for him and protect him, they can do so only up to a point. For there is an essential loneliness within every person. Strangely enough, we cannot be possessed nor understood in any totally satisfying way except by God. So a retreat is an opportunity to spend some extra time with our Lord, seeing how well I am conducting the business of life which He and I alone can conduct.

I have made out life to be lonely, and it is. However it is not quite so lonely as I have indicated because there is that other Person who knows us through and through. He knows us with our sins and faults, our virtues, our unfulfilled hopes and ambitions; and knowing us through and through He still likes us. He knows intimately all that goes to make up that unique person which is you. "All things were made through him, and without him was made nothing that has been made." Consequently, in His presence we do not have to put up a respectable front and appear to be something we are not. The eyes that look into our mind and heart and the depths of our being are more gentle and understanding in their judgments than the judgments which we make upon ourselves. Here we can love and trust completely and never be betrayed. So then, a retreat is spending a few days with our Lord talking about the two most interesting things in life—Himself and myself. It is consoling to recall that our Lord never made anyone unhappy.

If we want a picture of this, it is given to us in the Gospels. The day our Lord began His public life He walked down the road which wound along the banks of the river Jordan. John was baptizing there and proclaiming that the Messiah was coming soon. When our Lord passed by, John triumphantly and joyously pointed to Him and said: "Behold, the lamb of God" and ". . . this is the Son of God" (John 1:29, 34). Immediately two of the men who were with John detached themselves and followed our Lord down the road. Obviously they wanted to talk to Him. After a few paces our Lord stopped and turned around to look at them. There was a welcome in His eyes. There was friendship. Then He asked them a question, a question which our Lord asks every man. He said to them, "What is it you seek?" What do you really want? And like two good Irishmen, which they weren't, instead of answering the question they asked Him a question in return. "Master, where dwellest thou?" He answered: "Come and see." And it is recorded that they spent all that day with Him. "They came and saw where he was staying; and they stayed with him that day. It was about the tenth hour" (John 1:39). They found the meeting so important and significant that they noted the exact hour they met Him, the same way we might remember an event of great importance in our lives. So a retreat, then, is spending extra hours with our Lord talking about the two most interesting and important things in life—Himself and myself. Perhaps we, too, will find it so significant that we will record the day and the hour we really got to know Him better. It was during my do-it-yourself retreat that I got to know Him. Christ still goes seeking men and still asks them encouragingly, "What is it you seek?"

Another answer to "What is a retreat?"—a retreat is a very realistic thing. It doesn't pretend that we are perfect. In fact it supposes the opposite. If one of you making this retreat has not sinned ever, you should report in to your local Chancery office immediately. If you have never committed a sin, then undoubtedly they will stuff you, mount you, and put you in a museum. A retreat presumes that we are not perfect and realistically suggests that whatever we are we go forward from here. Now that is a reasonable thing to propose because we well know that with God's grace and help, and with intelligent planning on our part we can do better. We can live a fuller, happier life of closer union with God. The retreat is realistic in this sense, too: I am helping you to make it; but in the end, you are the one who does it—you and God. For it is true that in a few minutes of quiet prayer and thinking, God, who is the master of your soul, can give you more insight and courage and strength than you can get by much reading of these pages. St. Ignatius points out that a single thought, grasped and realized for oneself, is more important than a vast quantity of information. Therefore, the time of meditation, fifteen minutes or so, which is suggested at the end of each conference, is of extreme importance. It is the do-it-yourself part of the retreat. As a little help to this prayerful thinking there is a brief outline at the end of each conference. It is not an analytical outline, but rather pegs on which you can hang your prayerful thinking.

Finally, a retreat is a very hopeful thing. Our Lord's promise is: "I came that they may have life, and have it more abundantly" (John 10:10). And how we long for life and want it in its fullness and its completeness! So reviewing briefly, then, a retreat is an opportunity to see the real values in life. We have lived long enough and we have experience, so we can make a mature and balanced judgment. A retreat is an opportunity to see how well we are conducting the business of life which we alone can conduct. A retreat is spending some extra time with our Lord in intimate personal conversation. A retreat is a realistic thing, "We can go forward from here." It is a hopeful thing, "I came that they may have life, and have it more abundantly."

Now to get back to our original problem: the lives of four men. There was the millionaire playboy, the blind captain, the corporal dead at twenty-three, and my own life. What measuring rod will we use to determine whether these lives are a success or a failure according to God's plan? To get at that measuring rod suppose each one of us goes back in memory ten years. Make a quick flash back, using a kind of movie technique. Lean back, relax, and see the house and the neighborhood where you lived ten years ago—just a quick picture of it. Now go back twenty years and see the place where you were living.

Make it forty. Flash back to sixty years ago and see where you were living. Make it eighty-five years, just to be on the safe side. At this point I think possibly you are saying: "You dropped me back there about twenty or thirty years ago. I can only go back in memory a certain number of years and then I come to a blank. I cannot see the house or the neighborhood where I was living because I didn't exist. I was nothing." You could look for your name in the telephone book—not there. Knock on the door of the home where you lived, mention your name, and they would say: "There is no such person." It is an obvious fact that some twenty-five, thirty, sixty years ago we did not exist. A reasonable and basic question to ask is: "Well, then, where did I come from?" And an equally obvious answer is, "I came from my parents." And that is true.

Our parents cooperated in the production of the new life that was to come into existence. That is one of the great dignities of parenthood—a share in God's creative power. But parents provided only the matter for new life, and we know that we are something more than mere matter. Where did my soul come from? The principle within me which enables me to think and to will, and which, when it departs, leaves the body cold, inert, dead clay. Where did it come from? Well, we know both from philosophy and from religion that it could not evolve from the matter provided by our parents. You cannot get blood out of a turnip because there is no blood in a turnip, and you cannot get matter to evolve into a spiritual soul. But perhaps my parents gave me a part of their souls? We know this cannot be. The soul is a spiritual substance. It is simple and has no parts. Maybe one of them gave me his soul? Obviously this could not be, or he would have none left. This is simply a reminder that both from philosophy and from the clear teaching of the Church we know that God had to create that soul of mine and infuse it into the matter provided by my parents. His act of creation was deliberate; it was planned from all eternity; it was an act of infinite love. ". . . I have loved thee with an everlasting love: therefore have I drawn thee" (Jeremias 31:3).

Coming face to face with God in this fashion is almost frightening: it is so personal and intimate. It is also immensely consoling because at times, I think, all of us have the feeling that we are lost in the crowd. As we go out into the street at rush hour, as the buildings are emptying out the crowds, and cars are jamming the streets, we feel almost as though we have lost our identity, like a grain of sand on the seashore. Soldiers experience this when they look down a line and see five thousand men dressed identically. "I'm just a serial number," they say. But with God we are never lost in a crowd. There is no such thing as humanity, a multitude, a crowd. Only persons—Mary, Joseph, Joan, Jim, Henri, Kurt, Ruth, Miguel, Laurie, and you—each unique, whom He knows, understands completely, and loves. God saw other persons he might have created—say your identical twin—but he didn't create him. When He came to you and when He came to me He saw there was something that He loved, something that He wanted, and He created our souls, infusing them into the matter provided by our parents. After God made you He broke the mold and there will never be another quite like you. He has given each one of us a work to do that He has given to no other person. Each one of us is as important in his place as the Blessed Virgin in her glorious place.

Cardinal Newman in a sermon "God's Will the End of Life" expresses this idea eloquently: ". . . everyone who breathes, high and low, educated and ignorant, young and old, man and woman, has a mission, has a work. We are not sent into this world for nothing; we are not born at random . . . God sees every one of us; He creates every soul, He lodges it in the body, one by one, for a purpose. He needs, He deigns to need, every one of us. He has an end for each of us; we are all equal in His sight, and we are placed in our different ranks and stations, not to get what we can out of them for ourselves, but to labor in them for Him. As Christ has His work, we too have ours; as He rejoiced to do His work, we must rejoice in ours also." So if we say that we are unimportant, that we are nothing, a cipher, we are not looking at ourselves as God sees us. We are faced with this consoling fact: that God did lovingly create us and that our lives are significant.

Of course it follows that if God created me, then I belong to Him. I am His property and His possession. I belong to Him, mind, heart, body, hands, feet, eyes, talents, and lack of talent. I belong to Him as a child, as a young man or woman, in middle age; I belong to Him. In the evening of life, for all eternity, I am His property and His possession. I am completely dependent on Him. So, naturally, I turn to Him to ask: "My Lord, my God, my Creator, what do You want me to do? I am yours."

It is helpful to recall that there are a number of titles to ownership. One is through purchase, another is by finding a thing under certain conditions, and still another is by making something—all these can give one the right of ownership. In this last connection, I remember seeing a little boy sailing a boat whittled out of an orange crate. He had put a stick in it for a mast, added a little piece of paper for a sail, and was proudly pulling his boat up and down the lagoon with a string when some older boys began throwing rocks at it. The little fellow told them to stop, but they wouldn't. Finally, tearfully, he pulled it in by the string, hugged it to himself, and said: "Stop it. I made it. *It's mine!*" There was such an intensity of possession in his attitude and voice that the older boys left him alone. "I made it. *It's mine!*" That is the way God feels toward us. We are told in Scripture, "And now thus saith the Lord that created thee . . . and called thee by thy name. Thou art mine" (Isaias 43:1). Upon reflection, we are happy that there is someone who cares, someone who is possessive. Naturally, then, since we belong to Him, our lives are not our own to live as we see fit, independent of Him. We are not free to use life, talents, abilities, without reference to Him. He is Creator; He is Master; He is the almighty Lord; He is God!

We can see already where the millionaire playboy who fired a bullet into his breast made an essential mistake when he decided that he couldn't take it any more and chose that way out. He mistakenly presumed that his life was his own to terminate when he saw fit. We can see too, why the blind captain said what he did: "If it were not for my Catholic faith, I would commit suicide." What of the corporal dead at twenty-three. Is there a certain number of years we can demand of God that we should live? And if so, what is the mystical number? Is it twenty-five or fifty-two, nineteen or ninety-one?

If we want a picture of this great reality of creation and our total dependency on God, it can be beautifully summed up in the famous painting by Michelangelo called *Creation*. Adam is shown reclining and God is pictured coming in clouds of power and majesty, extending His omnipotent, creative finger, making contact with Adam's and communicating to him the spark of life. Adam is shown looking up at God with gratitude, love, adoration, and complete trust. But the picture does not merely portray the relationship of Creator and creature; rather it conveys the closer and gentler bond between Father and son, Father and daughter, which God Himself has chosen to establish. He tells us in Scripture: "I . . . will be a Father to you, and you shall be my sons and daughters, says the Lord almighty" (2 Corinthians 6:18). In fact, He claims for Himself a father's love blended with the love of a mother. "Can a woman forget her infant, so as not to have pity on the son of her womb? And if she should forget, yet will not I forget thee. Behold, I have graven thee in my hands" (Isaias 49:15-16). And did not our Lord Himself teach us to say: "Our *Father*, who art in heaven"?

So we have answered the question, "Where did I come from?" with "We came out from God by creation. We are God's children." And since He is our loving Father, we say trustingly: "My God, my Creator, my Father, what do You want me to do?" Like any loving father, He, of course, wants us to be successful. Our problem, then, is simple. It is to find His measuring rod for success. To do this we have to follow up "Where did I come from?" with the further question, "Where am I going? What is my destiny? What is the future my Father has planned for me?"

11

The answers to all these important questions are familiar to us from the first pages of the catechism; and they are what we would expect from so loving a Father. God plans for us an eternity of happiness with Himself. In our Father's providence, we are destined to enter into the inner life of the Trinity. We are to know and to love and to exist with the knowledge and love and existence which God Himself possesses and which makes Him perfectly happy through all eternity. This is almost too good to be true! We are to enter into the inner life of the Blessed Trinity! So if we recall that this is our goal and our destiny—to possess the infinite beauty, goodness, and love which is God—it will explain somewhat the divine discontent which is present in all of us. We are never totally satisfied in this life or with anything in it. God alone will satisfy. Yet, at times we think that somewhere around the corner there will be perfect happiness. We say, "When I get out of school then I will be perfectly happy." "When I get engaged." "When I get married." "When the children come." "When the house is paid for." "When I am ordained." Happy, perhaps, but not perfectly happy.

I recall, in this connection, one Christmas, I must have been four or five years old, and I had been looking forward to the day for months. Finally Christmas came. There were the tree and lights, the carols, the presents, the visitors, and the excitement of it all. It was a day full of wonder. But as it wore on, some of the toys were broken; the Christmas tree dropped some of its needles, and seemed to wilt a bit; I ate too much and got a little feverish and tired. The day ended and there was just a little sense of disappointment. I remember asking my mother, "Is that all?" And she said, "Yes, dear." Then, "Will Christmas come again soon?" "Next year." And still another question, "Is that a long time?" A first sense of "This is not enough." St. Augustine discovered this great truth the hard way. He sought for happiness in great learning and became a very learned man; but he found himself still unsatisfied. Then he sought for it in the arms of women and found himself not totally fulfilled. Finally, after a lifetime of searching and groping, he summed up his experiences in a statement which we recognize as oh, so true, "Our hearts were made for Thee, O God, and they will never be at rest until they rest in Thee." Strangely enough, no accumulation of temporal goods, no person, however dearly loved, can completely fill these hearts of ours. Our Lord insisted on that truth when He posed the question which has haunted the minds of men ever since He asked it! "For what does it profit a man, if he gain the whole world, but suffer the loss of his own soul? Or what will a man give in exchange for his soul" (Matthew 16:26)?

Our Lord here is not talking in terms of trifles. He is speaking in terms of great wealth. All the diamonds in Kimberley, the oil in Texas, the gold in the national vault, give that to one man; add to that all the honor and acclaim that have come to statesmen, scholars, generals, artists, at the great moment of their triumphs; add to that long days and nights of ecstasy. And our Lord said: "Having all that, what does it profit him if he does not save his soul?" Having all that, what if he failed to reach an eternity of happiness with God? Suppose we take our Lord's words and reverse them, "What difference would it make if a man lost the whole world so long as he saved his soul?" What difference will it make fifty years from now if I do not get that job I so desire, or the recognition I now crave, if I am eternally happy with God. If the end and purpose of life is to reach an eternity of happiness with God, then we can safely say that a man who does save his soul is a basic success, no matter how men may cry failure. If a man does not reach an eternity of happiness with God, he is a failure no matter how many lines he may have in *Who's Who*, no matter how many monuments may be erected to his name. Simply write down, "failure." So, if it is true that we came out from God by creation, and that we are destined for an eternity of happiness with Him; then we can evaluate more accurately the lives of the millionaire playboy, the blind captain, the corporal dead at twenty-three, and our own lives. The millionaire playboy, we might say of him that he gained the whole world: money, social position, luxurious living. But . . . The blind captain, we might say of him that he lost the whole world. But . . . And the corporal dead at twenty-three, we might say of him "Why his life was just beginning!" Yes, eternal life, eternal happiness. And our own life? Are we leading it successfully according to God's plan so that it will bring us to an eternity of happiness with Him? We came out from God by creation; we return to Him, completing the circle. He is the alpha and omega, the beginning and the end.

So now we have answered two questions: "Where did I come from and where am I going?" But obviously, too, we must answer the further question, "How am I going to get there?" I did not ask to be born. I found myself with this life given to me. Perhaps if I had been consulted in the matter, I might have said no. But here I am with this gift of life. How am I to spend it? Again the answer is simple and spelled out for us in the beginning of the catechism. A man is to spend his whole life praising God, reverencing God, and serving God. Life can be summed up that simply, says St. Ignatius. As we say those words it would sound almost as though we were to spend our lives in church. But on analysis we see that it is not so.

When do we praise God? When we speak well of Him. When we approve of His actions and admire His qualities. So also do we praise God by every act of thanksgiving, every act of contrition, by every genuflection, by the sign of the cross, by this retreat we are making. This is formal praise.

Especially do we praise Him at Mass. Say the Gloria of the Mass tomorrow and observe what a beautiful hymn of praise it is. It lifts us up and out of ourselves. "Glory to God in the highest . . . We praise You. We bless You. We adore You . . . We give You thanks for Your great glory. Lord God, heavenly King." So we praise God by prayer and especially by the Mass itself. But most of all we praise Him by what we are, not so much by what we say about Him. Isn't it true that a child reflects more credit on his parents by being a good child than by saying a lot of nice things about his parents? On graduation night the boy or girl is up on the stage receiving a diploma and has done well. The parents are proudly saying: "There is my girl, third from the left." At a football game, when a boy makes a good tackle, a long forward pass, the old gentleman, leaping up in the stands is saying to somebody, to everybody: "That's my boy, number twenty-four!" So also, if God, looking down at us and our lives, can point with pride and say: "There is my beloved son, in whom I am well pleased," that is one of the highest forms of praise we can offer God. We try to be worthy sons and daughters of so good a Father.

How do we show reverence of God? We might say that reverence, in our day, is a vanishing virtue. Reverence is a mixture of love and awe, respect and filial fear. Can you think of anything that is respected and reverenced in our day? Parental authority, civil authority, sex, God's name? In my experience I've heard God's name used more often as an expletive—to draw a laugh, to emphasize a point—than I have heard it used in prayer. Now, of course, we know that using God's name in this fashion is not serious sin, but it does show a lack of reverence and reflection. I remember that in the service, where His name was often used so carelessly, a chaplain finally turned to one man and said: "Don't you realize that man died for you?" And so, by our reverence we can make up for the irreverence that is all about us. I have seen tabernacles bayoneted, broken open, and everything sacred strewn around. What a field there is here for reparation to the Sacred Heart of Jesus that has loved men so much, but has received from men only coldness and indifference, especially in the sacrament of His love. Imagine! A Commie did a bawdy dance centered around the crowning of thorns. Reverence is a symbol of something deeper and higher and a sophisticated age such as ours finds it hard to reverence anything.

In his book *Luke Delmege*, Canon Sheehan describes the virtue of reverence with unforgettable simplicity and beauty: "Reverence is the secret of all religion and happiness. Without reverence, there is no faith, nor hope, nor love. Reverence is the motive of each of the Commandments of Sinai—reverence of God, reverence of our neighbour, reverence of ourselves. Humility is founded on it; piety is conserved by it; purity finds in it its shield and buckler. Reverence for God, and all that is associated with Him, His ministers, His temple, His services—that is *religion*. Reverence for our neighbour, his goods, his person, his chattles—that is *honesty*. Reverence for ourselves—clean bodies and pure souls —that is *chastity*. Satan is Satan because he is irreverent. There never yet was an infidel but he was irreverent and a mocker."

Service of God is most consoling. This we can do twenty-four hours a day, sixty minutes in the hour, and sixty seconds in the minute. Efficient business houses will sometimes put out a sign: "Service twenty-four hours a day." Each one of us can realistically make this the motto of his life: "Service of God twenty-four hours a day." A lifetime of service. Why? Because if we are in the state of sanctifying grace, and are doing the proper thing, at the proper time, in the proper way, with a good intention, we can serve God as well at the bridge table as we can at the communion rail. We can serve God as well over the dinner dishes, pounding a typewriter, raking the grass, minding the children, studying, turning out a term paper as we can at Mass. It is doing the proper thing, at the proper time, in the proper way, with a good intention. Our Lord, who led our life from birth to death, who slept and ate and attended marriage feasts, played with the children and earned His living, said of the Father: "I do always the things that are pleasing to him" (John 8:29). And we, like our Lord, can do the same. Sanctity, the service of God, is to be found in the daily routine in your home, at work, in the school, in the parish. If it cannot be found there, then sanctity is literally "out of this world." And this cannot be since God intends all of us to be saints and lovingly asks us for twenty-four hour service throughout our lives.

Now, if this is true that we are to spend our lives in God's praise, reverence, and service, then we can more accurately determine the success of the four lives we have proposed for consideration. The million-aire playboy? Did he reach an eternity of happiness with God? Was his life spent praising, reverencing, and serving God? The blind captain? Though blind and helpless, could he save his soul? Could his life be one of praise, reverence, and service? Do they also serve who only stand and wait? And the corporal dead at twenty-three? Aren't there canonized saints at eighteen? And my own life? This is all important. What of it? Am I on the way to reaching an eternity of happiness with God? Is my life one of praise, reverence, and service?

Review all of this and test it. See if it is true. I came out from God by creation, or I did not. Do I belong to Him? Am I His property and His posses-sion? Or am I a totally independent agent? Has He given me a work to do? A work given to no other person? Am I important in my place? Does He plan an eternity of happiness with Himself for me? Am I to spend my life in His praise, reverence, and service, or in my own? St. Ignatius calls the right answer to these questions a principle and a founda-tion. A principle because from these truths other, more detailed conclusions will follow. He calls it a foundation because it is rock bottom, and on this we can safely build the structure of a life that will last for eternity. This is the measuring rod for success—a life of praise, reverence, service, reaching an eter-nity of happiness with God.

How different this is from some of the philosophies of life around us. The beatniks, the atheists, the agnostics, the indifferent—these were summed up by Omar Khayyam: "Into this universe, and why not knowing; nor whence, like water willy-nilly flowing; And out of it, as wind along the waste, I know not whither, willy-nilly blowing." He doesn't know where he came from. He doesn't know where he is going. Obviously, he will not know how to get there. But we know where we came from. We came out from God by creation. We know where we are going. We are destined for an eternity of happiness with God. And we know how to get there—by a lifetime of praise, reverence, and service.

If you are reading this at night, it is suggested that you go on to the night prayers on page 261. All of the suggested prayers are in keeping with the spirit of the retreat. Or, if it is the morning hours, you might say the morning prayers on page 263.

The outline which follows is meant to help you in your fifteen-minute meditation. Also, tomorrow morning on arising your plan would be to say the prayers indicated (page 263 of the appendix), to go to Mass and Holy Communion, to say the prayers of thanksgiving after Communion (page 265), and then to move on to the next chapter, which will help you to discover the truly great person you are. This plan of a chapter a day with the fifteen minute meditation, a daily examination of conscience, and, if possible, Mass and Communion should keep your retreat moving along nicely. Keep up the good work.

Do it yourself!

Points for your prayerful thinking (15 minutes)

PREPARATORY PRAYER
to be said before beginning each meditation

My God, I wish to realize that I am in Your presence and that You are looking upon me with eyes of mercy and love. I adore You.

I offer You, O my God, my whole self, my body with all its senses, my soul with all its faculties, my heart with all its affections.

Bear with my weakness and misery and have mercy on me. Allow me to remain in the presence of Your infinite majesty and goodness with great reverence and with childlike confidence.

I offer You this meditation of mine. Enlighten my mind that I may know You more intimately. Inflame my heart that I may love You more ardently. Strengthen my will that I may better regulate my whole life according to Your most holy will.

A problem and an answer

1 *What is a retreat?*

It is a chance to evaluate life once again—to put first things first. It is a chance to see how we are conducting this business of living. No one can do it for you.

It is spending some extra time with our Lord: "Come and see." It is a realistic thing: we go forward from here. It is a hopeful thing: "I came that they may have life, and have it more abundantly."

2 *What of the life of these four men?*

| Millionaire playboy | Corporal dead at twenty-three | Blind captain | My own life |

To get a measuring rod for success these questions must be answered:
Where did I come from? Where am I going? How am I going to get there?

3 *Where did I come from?*

From my parents—but God created my soul. Therefore, I belong to Him. He is Master, Lord, Creator. He is also Father.

4 *Where am I going?*

To God. To an eternity of perfect happiness with Him. "Our hearts were made for You, O God, and will never be at rest until they rest in You."

5 *How am I going to get there?*

By a life of praise: prayer, and by what I am. By reverence: the vanishing virtue. By service: twenty-four hours a day. Whatever I do.

Conclude by saying one Our Father, a Hail Mary, and Glory Be to the Father.

◆◆◆◆◆◆◆◆◆◆◆

"I could never imagine anyone loving me—let alone God." Thus a man wrote to me. It is a cry of loneliness and emptiness filled with sadness. This experience of emptiness is not too uncommon. We ourselves may have felt it on occasion.

This next chapter should remove the insecurities and doubts that may come to us by showing how truly great we are, how lovable and how dearly beloved of God. There is a God-given beauty and charm in the innocent soul of a little child; in the sin-scarred soul of a person who has just returned to God; and in the souls of those who seem, to themselves, to be just plodding along after Christ.

"Blessed are ye," says our Lord to all His followers. So follow along to the next chapter, count your blessings, and admit admiringly, gratefully: "I didn't know I had it in me."

◆◆◆◆◆◆◆◆◆◆◆◆◆

I didn't know
I had it in me

Every once in a while we do something, either very good or very bad, which rather surprises us, and we are inclined to say: "I didn't know I had it in me." I think it is true that all of us do possess a capacity for both good and evil which does not always appear on the surface. For example, we may know a person over the years and figure that we have him rather well evaluated. Then he does something either very generous and heroic or the opposite, and we have to revise our opinion, usually with the accompanying thought: "I really didn't know him. I didn't know he had it in him." I recall a little boy at a summer camp who was somewhat small and a bit hostile. The other fellows used to kick him around before breakfast just for exercise, I think. I often wondered how he would ever be able to stand on his own two feet. Well, I didn't hear from him for about ten years. Then I got a letter from him saying: "I am a sergeant in the infantry! I am here in a hospital in Italy, and I'm wounded." Six months later I got another letter from him telling me that he was back in the hospital, wounded again. I certainly found it difficult to picture that little fellow as a rough, tough, infantry sergeant, a leader of men, and had to comment admiringly: "I didn't know he had it in him."

Now, if we look at ourselves carefully under the X ray of reason (what we can know about ourselves without divine revelation), and faith (what God tells us about ourselves), I think we will discover a dignity and a greatness and a beauty of soul which we did not anticipate, and we will be forced to say admiringly: "I didn't know I had it in *me*."

To get at this dignity and beauty which we do possess, suppose we become amateur scientists for the time being. As we look around this world of ours we see rocks, stones, minerals. Analyzing them we would say, "They don't have life." Chemistry and physics can explain them because they have only chemical and physical properties. But, as we gaze a little farther afield, we see trees and flowers. As we look at an oak tree, we observe that it has life. It can grow from a little oak tree into a big oak tree. It can bring little oak trees into existence. And if we carve our initials in its bark, in the course of time, the wound will be partially healed over. A plant or a tree can grow, reproduce, and repair injuries. It has life. As we look a bit further we see animals—a bird on the wing, a dog chasing a cat— and we study them. We note that the dog not only can grow and reproduce and repair injuries, but he has fivefold sensations. He can see, hear, taste, smell, and feel. Kick a tree and you get no response. Kick a dog and he will let you know that he can feel, see, hear, smell, and would like to sample you. He is a much higher form of life than a tree. And when we look still further, we see a fellow human being. Studying him, or ourselves, we recognize that we are minerals. We share their qualities, and I believe that with inflation, boiled down to our chemical constituents, we are worth more than a dollar. We are also vegetables: we grow hair, eyelashes, fingernails. And like the animals we have fivefold sensations. We can see, hear, taste, smell, and feel. But

21

something new has been added. Man has intelligence, and he can know—abstractly. He has a free will, like God, and he can choose; even God Himself cannot force man. And, like God, he will go on living forever because he has been built to last, not for just a lifetime, but for an eternity. Only man in this visible universe can look up to God and say: "You have intelligence. So have I. You have a free will and can do what You want. So can I. You will go on living forever. So will I." Only man in this visible world can look up at the blazing sun and say: "You were here before me, but when you are burned to a cinder, I will still be in existence." And to the calm stars: "When you are fallen from the heavens, I will be there to witness it." We are built for eternity and for an eternity of happiness because we are made in God's image and likeness.

Now this is as far as reason can take us. But even this much shows us our dignity and worth. I remember having to give a talk along these lines on television. It was to be filmed and used by the network for the opening program, early in the morning, and the signing-off program, late in the evening—a full three minutes worth. I thought at the time that it was something of a waste of effort. It was to be nondenominational, inspirational, and conversational. It certainly was perspirational! But strangely enough, it was well worth the effort. My Hooper rating consisted of one letter. The letter came from a college student in the East who wrote: "I don't know what possessed me to turn on the television at two in the morning, but there you were. I have had psychiatric treatment because of my emotional problems. I am tempted to go into them, but I will not inflict that on you. I was feeling unusually depressed. But when you said, 'God made us to His image and likeness,' then I concluded that God must love me or else why would He make me in His image and likeness. Before that I could never imagine anyone loving me, let alone God. When you added that God has given each of us a work to do, given to no other, and that in God's sight we are important and fit into His fatherly plans, I began to feel that I was not a total

and likeness. Some are carved in ebony, some in teakwood, others in ivory, but all are dearly beloved sons and daughters of God, our Father.

This, then, is as far as reason can take us; and we would not know that there can be a higher form of life in man, with still greater dignity, unless God chose to tell us about it. He has told us, however, that there is a higher life and a greater worth in man. We are certainly very secure accepting His word even though it makes us great and raises us up toward divinity. He tells us that those who have been baptized receive a whole new life added above the life of intellect and free will. "I came that they may have life, and have it more abundantly" (John 10:10). Through this God-given gift, freely bestowed without merit on our part, we are made to share in the divine nature. ". . . he has granted us the very great and precious promises, so that through them you may become partakers of the divine nature" (2 Peter 1:4). A whole new life is given to us. We are raised from creatures to sons and daughters of God; and possessing this gift, we are destined to enter into the inner life of the Blessed Trinity. We are to share in the knowledge and love and existence of God. This gift, as we know, is called sanctifying grace or supernatural life. Here is dignity and greatness for all.

The Church takes it for granted that we share in the divine nature. At the Mass when the priest pours a drop of water into the chalice, the prayer reads: ". . . grant that, . . . we may be made partakers of His Divinity who was pleased to become partaker of our humanity, Jesus Christ, Your Son, our Lord." In the last Gospel we read at Mass every day, St. John reminds us: "as many as received Him He gave the power of becoming sons of God." If we were to deny this fact, we would be heretics! However, at times, phrases such as this are used and their consoling reality is missed. We have a share in the divine nature!

Let's press the point. This would seem to make us God. If I have the nature of a tree, I am a tree. If I have the nature of a dog, I am a dog. If I have nature of a human being, I am a human being. If I share in the divine nature, it would seem that I would be God. And this would be true except for a number of differences between God and man. God possesses His nature of His own essence. He only communicates it to us. He has it in an infinite degree. We have it in a finite degree. He has it and cannot possibly lose it. We can lose it through sin. So these differences, among others, obviously keep us from being God. But that does not deny the great truth that we do share in His divine nature because we have sanctifying grace.

Now what does this do for us? First of all, it gives us internal beauty and light so appealing that if we were given a vision of it, we would gasp at the splendor of it all. A saint was given a glimpse of a soul in sanctifying grace and her first impulse was to get down and adore because it looked so much like God. The sanctifying grace in our souls makes us so compellingly attractive that God Himself has to love us. He has to love Himself and He has to love those who share in His divine nature. We know how physical attraction and charm, even with the use of nationally advertised products, reaches a limited perfection. We have to face that truth in the mirror every morning. But the internal beauty of sanctifying grace goes on increasing day after day, year after year. Physical beauty may fade, mental powers may diminish, but this supernatural life can reach its peak and its perfection as we draw our last breath. What a consolation for the elderly or sick who feel that life is fading. These later years are golden years in our Lord's sight and are really the fullness of life. Charlotte Gilman had no inkling of this great truth or she would not have "preferred chloroform to cancer."

To help us to understand all this better, our Lord, when He walked the earth, looked like any other man. His divinity did not usually shine through. On one or two occasions, however, he permitted it to do so; as on Mount Tabor when Christ "was transfigured before them. And his face shone as the sun, and his garments became white as snow" (Matthew

17:2). If we could see the beauty of our souls in grace as God does, we would be immensely consoled. Around each one who is in sanctifying grace there is a circle, like a halo. There is a man who stands out from the crowd! And God looking at him says, "How much he resembles My Only Begotten Son."

The second thing sanctifying grace does for us is to dignify the least actions which we perform. Our daily routine seems to be composed of actions which are not particularly significant. We get up. We wash. Go to work. Eat. Return. Read. Study. Look at TV. Say some prayers. There is our social life. We get tired. We go to bed. And we say, "Where is there greatness here?" For most of us there is nothing in our lives that would be worthy of notice, even in a very small neighborhood newspaper. We tend to feel insignificant and futile. Yet that is not God's view of us, our life, or our activities. Christ Himself who ate and slept and worked with His hands had His heavenly Father's minute-by-minute approval and love, "This is my beloved Son in whom I am well pleased." And our Lord, conscious of this, said of His Father, "I do always the things that are pleasing to him." Eating, sleeping, working. His least action had infinite value because it was done by an infinite Person. So our least action can have very great value because it is done by one who shares in the divine nature. We have, then, the capacity to dignify our life because in human living it is not so much the work done that counts as the workman who does it. I think you can see that this is true. Granted it is also true that if we possess talents and abilities, God will one day demand an accounting of them. One day He will ask: "What did you do with the three talents, the two, the one, I gave you?" But after that has been said, the fact remains that a street cleaner can be greater in God's sight than the pope. The girl at the typewriter can be greater in God's sight than the atomic scientist. A man in the evening of life, crippled with arthritis and a little vague in his thinking, can be more successful in God's sight than the dynamic, eloquent, young lawyer. It is not so much the work done as the workman that counts.

To get at this viewpoint and see that it is true, just suppose that you are God for the time being. As you look down at this world of ours and the men in it, going about their work and play, would you be particularly impressed by the engineering feats of men when they swing a bridge across the San Francisco Harbor, the magnificent Golden Gate Bridge? Would that impress you when you had set the universe in motion and poised and balanced it? If you were almighty God, would you be particularly impressed by the Explorers and Sputniks which men blast into orbit, when you had set the galaxies spinning, things of beauty and light and precision? If you were almighty God, would you be particularly impressed by the million dollars a man could accumulate in a lifetime, when you, as God, had put into the world all its riches and resources? I don't think so. However, historically we know when God was impressed. He looked down on this world of ours and the people in it and their achievements. He saw a little village hidden away in the hills and a little girl in a small cottage doing housework and He sent an angel to say to her: "Hail, full of grace, the Lord is with thee. Blessed art thou among women." Yet her work was as inconspicuous as that of any woman down the street, or as your own. St. Joseph is another of God's great ones, though his life was totally hidden. There is not a single recorded word of his left for our remembrance. We do not know exactly when he died, but millions testify to his greatness, so warmly expressed in the preface for the feast of St. Joseph: "It is truly fitting and proper . . . that we should . . . magnify, bless, and glorify You on the Feast of St. Joseph, who, as a just man, was given by You as spouse to the Virgin Mother of God, and as a faithful and prudent servant, was set over Your family, that with fatherly care he might guard Your only-begotten Son." So we can see that it is not so much the work we do as the workman that counts. Successful living according to God's plan is the degree to which we share in the divine nature.

This sharing in the divine nature dignifies the very least action that we perform. We get a hint of this when we see how nature transforms ordinary, even ugly things, into things of beauty. Take a pearl. It is formed by an irritant getting into an oyster. The oyster puts a secretion around it and under ideal conditions it develops into the lustrous thing of beauty which we prize and treasure as a pearl. An odd beginning for such a thing of beauty—an irritant. Or take a diamond. It is simply a piece of carbon. But this carbon, under great heat and pressure in the heart of the earth, is changed into the beautiful crystal encasing all the colors of the rainbow. What an odd beginning for such a thing of beauty—carbon. Or take a snowflake. It could be formed by the sun drawing dirty gutter water into the heavens by evaporation, crystallizing it there, and sending it down again as a pure, beautiful snowflake. Or take ourselves. When we are in the state of grace we, too, can take the irritants of daily living —financial worries, thorny personalities, the inconvenience of weather, sick headaches, failures, suffering—and turn them into pearls of great price. We can take the carbon of daily duties, of routine work or study, and we can take the "dishwater" which flows through our lives in such abundance, and transform them into things of beauty and value in God's sight. The day offered for "all the intentions of the Sacred Heart" becomes truly apostolic. It saves the souls of others and sanctifies us. There is dignity and greatness in the daily routine.

O Jesus, through the immaculate heart of Mary,
I offer You my prayers, works, joys, and
    sufferings of this day
For all the intentions of Your Sacred Heart,
In union with the holy sacrifice of the Mass
    throughout the world,
In reparation for my sins,
For the intentions of all our associates,
For the reunion of Christendom,
And in particular for the intentions of this month.

(This intention approved by the pope varies
    from month to month.)

When we say and try to live this morning offering, we are not offering God junk; we are offering Him our day and all that it contains. What a terrible miscalculation if we thought our day was a useless thing to be cast carelessly aside.

I remember in this connection, that as seminarians we were helping to build a little chapel at our country vacation spot. We didn't have enough materials so we went scrounging around the countryside. One farmer had a big heap of rocks that he had grubbed out of his field while plowing. His farm was in the glacier area and to him these rocks were a nuisance, just a backache, and utterly useless. When we asked for them, his reply had the tone of disgust: "You're welcome to them. Glad to get rid of them. They're useless." He even helped us haul them away. A couple of months later, when the beautiful little chapel was completed, thanks to his "useless" rocks, we had the dedication. There was a little dinner afterwards and since he had done so much to make it all possible, he was the guest of honor and was called on for a few words. He stood up, half smiling and half crying, and said simply: "Isn't it amazing. These rocks that I thought were useless and was throwing away—from all eternity God had planned to build a chapel with them." Wouldn't it be a terrible loss if we threw aside as useless the prayers, works, sufferings, and joys of our day, when from all eternity God had planned to sanctify us and save souls with them? The Morning Offering gives them to the Sacred Heart for His purposes—the salvation of souls, our own and those of others.

There is a third thing that sanctifying grace does for us. It provides the basis of our charity and love for one another. Now I think that we can take for granted that there is such a thing as chemical incompatibility. There are certain people we do not instinctively take to. To put it bluntly, we don't like them. We can be riding on the bus and see someone across from us and feel a surge of dislike. The hair almost stands up on the back of our necks. He may, as a matter of fact, be a very pleasant person, but our reaction to him is, "Ugh!" We can also observe these chemical or surface reactions in children. You've seen a child run to hide behind his mother's skirts and peek out fearfully when a certain person walks into the room. Actually, it might be Uncle Mike who is setting up a trust fund for him. Another person will come in (who might be a burglar) but the child will run up and embrace him. A dog shows the same reaction. To one he goes up wagging his tail, and this one may be a confidence man. To another he shows his teeth, and this one may be Santa Claus. This is known as chemical dislike. We can take it for granted. But charity is something deeper.

By charity I mean that regard we should have for one another because we share in the divine nature. We are brothers and sisters in Christ. This is not mere sentimentality. Christ clearly points it out to us. He tells us that on the last day, and surely He does not trifle when speaking of the Last Judgment, that He will turn to those on His left and say: "I was hungry and you gave Me not to eat. I was thirsty and you gave Me not to drink. I was in jail and you visited Me not." And they will say to Him: "Lord, when did we see *You* hungry, thirsty, in jail? If it had been You, surely we would have helped You out." And He will answer them saying: "when you refused it to one of the least of my brethren here, you refused it to me." Then on the positive side, which is most encouraging, He will turn to those on His right and say: "I was hungry, and you gave Me food. I was thirsty, and you gave Me drink. I was in jail, and you came to Me." And they will say to Him in surprise, "Lord, when did we see *You* hungry, thirsty, in jail?" He will answer them: "when you did it to one of the least of my brethren here, you did it to me" (Matthew 25:40, *Knox*). And these on the right hand will go into eternal life, the others into eternal punishment. But in spite of this warning, our Lord hints that we will tend to forget the great truth and be surprised, some pleasantly, and others unpleasantly. So there we have it all spelled out. Whenever there is an unkindness, whenever there is a kind act or bit of service, the eternal triangle is present: Christ, the other person, and myself.

Now as we listen to these words of Christ, we can be a little unrealistic and say: "I have not been to the jail recently. If I wish to receive Christ's commendation, I had better make a quick visit down there, like the pope does. I have not met too many starving people; perhaps I should go down to skid row to get Christ's approval." Or, we may be a bit more unrealistic and say: "Some day I will meet a starving, shivering wretch in the streets and, like St. Martin, I will draw my sword, because I always carry a sword, and I will cut a panel off my mink or my overcoat and give it to him. As I do this, Lo! I shall behold the features of Christ emerging from this poor wretch's face. Or maybe, some day, like Damien, I will meet a leper, embrace him, kiss him, and salute him: 'Fellow Leper!' and thus I will receive Christ's approval." But if it is true that Christ identifies Himself with the jailbird, doesn't He also identify Himself with your wife, your husband, your children, your father, your mother, your girlfriend, the person sitting next to you, the man in the office who has a few illusions of grandeur about his authority, the priest with whom you are not chemically compatible? Why should they be ignored and only the jailbird, the starving, and the naked receive the title "brother"?

To illustrate this, if you do not mind a personal reference, I have a relative who is a very interesting and charming woman. In one of her letters to me she asked how my retreats were going. Then she went on to say: "My only suggestion for your retreats [and I really didn't ask her for any] is that you give everyone two helpful, practical thoughts that they can take home and remember for a year. I was terribly impressed by the retreat I just made and found myself mulling it over in my mind for about two weeks afterwards, while it was still fresh. Then when it began to fade out, in the usualness and press of everyday things, I found that I still had two things to hang onto. Two very helpful things. One was a way to practice humility, I mean to be humble. And the second one was when the going gets tough, as it does, it makes it easier to try to see Christ in your husband and children and do the inferior, menial, maddening things about the house for Him. For example, Bill is as near perfect as a human being can be, but like all other people he has a few little ways of his own. Among them, a coy habit of throwing his socks and shoetrees on the floor. He used to throw his socks sort of under the bed so that I had to crawl on my hands and knees to retrieve them for the laundry. Now, he only drops them in the middle of the rug. Well, every once in a while, after fourteen years of married life, you go in to make the bed and see the darn socks and think, why can't he pick up his own socks? Why should I? Of course you can be reasonable and say to yourself, as I have, he does many other things he doesn't have to do, such as make his own breakfast when I am late getting up; and he doesn't complain about it too much. But sometimes, even sweet reason has no effect. And as the priest said: 'Why should you do all those disagreeable things for this man, when he could perfectly well do them for himself? Well, don't!' said he. 'Do them for Christ.' So it's easier. And that is what I think people are looking for when they go to a retreat. Something they can take home and work into their daily lives. The average person has little time or privacy in the day for praying on his knees, but if he can work it in like that, it seems to mean even more."

Now would you say that this is the overpious emoting of a woman who has gone on a retreat and come home with a spiritual jag on? Or is this the reality "When you did it to one of the least of my brethren here, you did it to me"? Are the thousands of meals that a woman makes for her family to be counted out? "I was hungry and you gave me to eat." Our Lord didn't say, "I was starving"—just "hungry." A man goes down to work in order to provide for his family. It's his duty. He loves his family. Yet doesn't Christ take that as done to Himself? A husband and wife are thoughtful hosts to their friends, and wine and dine them. Does not Christ take that as done to Himself? The Benedictine motto: "Venit hospes, venit Christus," as "Comes a guest, Christ comes," is very realistic. A student prepares for his future career so that he may do the work God has given him to do. Aren't these years of school a work done for Christ? If, then, we accept these statements of Christ's, we realize that sanctity is at our fingertips.

With a more accurate measuring rod we can go back once again and estimate in a little more detail the success of the four lives we mentioned at the beginning. To what extent did the millionaire playboy praise, reverence, and serve God? Did he reach an eternity of happiness with God? More exactly, to what extent did he share in the divine nature? The blind captain, though his life was to be one of dependence and darkness, could God also say of him: "Hail, full of grace"? The fullness, perhaps, of sanctifying grace in his soul? The corporal dead at twenty-three? There are canonized saints of eighteen. And my own life? To what extent do I share in the divine nature? Do I intelligently use the sacraments, prayer, and the means of increasing in sanctifying grace that God has so lavishly put at my disposal? How successful am I according to God's plan? Would He say to me: "Hail, full of grace"? How successful am I at this given moment? It may be that the life of grace is dead within me, through weakness or confusion. If it is dead, humbly, trustingly, hopefully, I will go to the source of life, Christ, and with His help I will begin to live again.

Now, in order to live our supernatural life well, God gave us a gift which at first sight may not seem to be breathtakingly valuable because we are so used to it. That is the gift of faith. Faith, technically, may be defined as an intellectual assent to truths which God has revealed and which we accept on His authority. "I am your loving Father." Faith answers, "This I accept as a truth." God says: "There is the resurrection of the body, and life everlasting, and the forgiveness of sins." And faith answers: "I accept these consoling truths; I hold them to be facts." However faith may also be described as a light for our intellect so that we can look out on this world and the next and see things as God sees them. All of us know how useful a light can be. Take a little pencil flashlight. If we have to go down to the basement, we won't pitch headlong down the steps, mangle ourselves on the mangle, or hang ourselves on the clothesline.

We can see what we are doing. Or, take the headlights on the car. When we are on a country road, no stars, no moon, and we press down the button for the brights, they open a pathway for three quarters of a mile down the road. We can see where we are going. Or take the great searchlights developed during the war which can send a probing finger of light into the highest heavens and point to a little speck of a plane. We, too, can see up into the very heavens. Faith is the light for our minds which enables us to see. We can see what we are doing. We can see where we are going. We can see into eternity.

But we might be inclined to take this tremendous gift for granted and think that we don't see things too much differently from the way the man down the street or the man in the office sees them without the gift of faith. "He likes his wife and children—so do I. He earns his living—so do I. We don't beat our wives. We are considerate. We are honest. We don't see things too differently." But I ask you, is that true? Suppose you were to bring your friend into your parish church; as you go in, you genuflect. The man asks you what you are doing. You answer that you are adoring Christ. "Where is He?" he would probably ask. The Blessed Sacrament is exposed, and you point up to the monstrance and say: "There!" He peers up and says: "You mean that gold thing? I see something in it that looks like a piece of bread!" And you answer: "Yes, it looks like bread, but Christ is really and truly present there." Does this make a difference in human living, in our daily lives? Christ's real presence or Christ's real absence? Does it make a difference to Christ to have His presence affirmed or denied?

Again, on Saturday night you might stop off for confession. As you go in your friend would ask you what you're doing. You tell him that you're going to Father McGillicuddy to confession. Then he would probably say: "What can he do for you? He's only a man. I could never understand going to confession to a man. I go straight to God." And yet you go in, and you come out conscious that you are in the state of grace, that your sins have been forgiven, and you have

an internal peace and serenity which the other envies
—but he cannot see things quite your way. Is there
a small difference between forgiveness as close as
the nearest confessional and an anxious, guilt-ridden
conscience?

Take a funeral or a wake. For some this is the
end. Dead end. But for us this is the beginning—the
beginning of eternal life. The "dead end" crowd may
direct that their ashes be sprinkled on a trout stream,
scattered over the ocean, spread on the runway of an
airfield. For us there is the consoling, reverent, requiem Mass for the dead. These rituals represent
totally different viewpoints. Dead end versus eternal
life. A vague, doubtful existence in the minds of men
or the beatific vision. There is also the matter of birth.
Some regard it as a casual thing. To others it is a
share in God's creative power by which a new life is
brought into the world, made in man's image and likeness and God's image and likeness. A life destined to
go on for all eternity. So, in regard to birth, and all its
circumstances; or death, and all its implications; or
even daily living, there are profound differences in
views. That difference is dramatically summed up by
recalling the blind captain who wrote: "If it were not
for my Catholic faith, I would commit suicide." Contrast this with Charlotte Perkins Gilman, who left a
note saying simply: "I have preferred chloroform to
cancer." Did the blind captain see more of reality, of
God's viewpoint, with his poor blind eyes, than this
talented woman with all her fine mind and natural
gifts? And what things did he see, I wonder, that she
did not see?

So, we thank God for the gift of faith, a gift we
should be eager to share with others, and say to Him:
"Lord, I see, but grant that I may see more clearly.
Lord, I believe, but help my unbelief." Our faith can
be there, but it may be faint and weak like a pencil
flashlight. Or it can be strong like the headlights of
the car. Or it can reach up to the very heavens and
see things steadily and clearly from God's viewpoint.
For example, one man will say Christ is present in the
Holy Eucharist, and then go to Communion once a
year. He sees, but dimly. Another will say, Christ is

present, and goes once a month. Good and commendable. Another, with the fullness of insight and vision says: "My God!" and goes whenever it is physically possible. "Lord, I believe. Help Thou my unbelief. Lord, I see, but grant that I may see more clearly."

I think we will discover, too, that when we are feeling low and despondent, we have forgotten to look at the situation or ourselves under the light of faith. To me, the most tremendous and instinctive act of faith that I have heard of in modern times was the heroic courage and calm awareness of eternity shown by Shirley O'Neill as described in the May 18, 1959 issue of *Time*. Surely this girl lived by faith, and to recall her faith deepens ours.

"It was a sunny afternoon in San Francisco. Shirley O'Neill and Albert Kogler, 18-year-old freshmen at San Francisco State College, went for a swim . . . near the Golden Gate Bridge.

"They were treading water about 50 yds. offshore when Al Kogler cried out. 'I turned around,' Shirley said later, 'and saw this big grey thing flap up into the air. I don't know if it was a fin or a tail. I knew it was some kind of fish. There was thrashing in the water. He screamed again. He said, "It's a shark! Get out of here." '

"Looking down on the ocean from the Presidio, . . . Master Sergeant Leo P. Day saw what happened next. 'I could see the boy in the foaming red water, shouting and signaling someone to "go back, go back." Then I saw the girl, swimming toward him, completely ignoring his warning. It was the greatest exhibition of courage I have ever seen.'

"Shirley reached Albert and seized his hand, 'but when I pulled, I could see that his arm was just hanging by a thread.' She slipped her arm around him and began to swim for the beach. . .After they were on the sand, Shirley, a Roman Catholic, scooped up some sea water and let it run over the head of her friend (who had never been baptized and belonged to no specific faith). 'I baptize thee in the name of the Father, the Son and the Holy Ghost,' said Shirley, making the sign of the Cross, and whispered to Albert, 'Is that all right?'

"O.K.," he gasped.

"She told him to repeat after her the act of contrition: 'O, my God, I am heartily sorry for having offended thee. I detest all my sins. . . most of all because they offend thee, my God, who art all good and deserving of all my love.'

"Just before Albert Kogler lapsed into unconsciousness, he whispered: 'I love God, and I love my mother and I love my father. Oh God, help me.' "

He died with the faith that she lived by and remembered, even in time of crisis, to share with him.

A final gift that God gave us to help us to live this supernatural life well is the gift of hope. And how desperately we need hope. We do not have to live too long before we recognize that we are weak. If we do not recognize this, then we are lacking in self-knowledge or we haven't lived long enough. Where do we get the strength to keep the Commandments and fulfill the day's duties? It is admirable to be pure and chaste, but where is the strength when the temptations are so intense and persistent—daily and hourly? It is fine to be honest, but where do we get the strength when it is so easy to make a "fast buck?" It is wonderful to live a patient, charitable, self-sacrificing family life, but where is the strength when, at times, personalities can be so difficult and thorny? If we look only to ourselves, we do not find the strength or the resources. We are weak and tend to quit so easily. That is why God gave us the gift of hope.

By the virtue of hope, I do not mean the thin gruel of Coue's doctrine, fashionable during the '20's. "Day by day in every way I am getting better and better." Even this is better than discouragement and has some psychological value. By the theological virtue of hope, however, I mean the firm confidence and trust that God will give us eternal life, and that He will give us the means to attain it. It assures us that after our brief struggle—with perhaps a little weeping, a little labor, a little cooperation on our part—He has in mind for us perfect and everlasting happiness. Divine omnipotence is found behind this sincerely declared purpose. God has the resources to accomplish His loving plan in us. Behind it is divine wisdom, so that

He knows how to do it, even though we may be tricky and selfish. With His infinite love and patience He will pursue us even though we may be somewhat slow to respond. Our spiritual success, then, is a well-founded hope.

From this practice of the theological virtue of hope comes eternal life, and in this life an accompanying gift of the Holy Spirit—joy. This is a joy which endures even though suffering may come. It survives in the face of disappointment, misunderstanding, pain, or failure. Oddly enough, or perhaps not so oddly, with hope and joy strong in us our natural resources are tapped and our talents begin to function at their best. Discouragement is the devil's master tool and it wrecks life—spiritual, physical, emotional, and intellectual life. Hope and joy make life grow and flourish.

So there is the gift of hope. It is the work-horse virtue needed for daily living. If we would like it summed up in a poem, I think it is done well in these few verses by Father Francis Le Buffe:

WE TWO

I cannot do it alone.
The waves run fast and high,
And the fogs close chill around,
And the light goes out in the sky,
But I know that we two shall win,

Jesus and I.

I cannot row it myself,
My boat on the raging sea,
But beside me sits another
Who pulls or steers with me.
And I know that we two shall come safe into port,

His child and He.

Coward and wayward and weak,
I change with the changing sky.
One day eager and brave,
The next not caring to try.
But He never gives in and we two shall win,

Jesus and I.

Strong and tender and true,
Crucified once for me.
I know He will never change
What'er I may do or be.
We shall finish our course and reach home at last,

His child and He.

This is the gift of hope. We may be weak, but we
have reinforcements from outside time and space to
support our weakness. There is divine omnipotence
at our command. We may get confused, but we have
divine wisdom (faith) to enlighten our darkness. Victory can and will be won if it is done, as we say in
the Mass, "per ipsum et cum ipso et in ipso" or
"through Him and with Him and in Him." Try to do
it alone and we will only bloody our heads and break
our hearts.

Now let's look back over what I said originally. I
mentioned that if we looked at ourselves carefully
under the X ray of reason and of faith, we might find
there a dignity, beauty, and greatness which would
force us to say: "I didn't know I had it in me." We
saw that we were made in God's image and likeness,
and we saw the essential equality of all men. But
much beyond that, we saw that through sanctifying
grace or supernatural life we share in the divine
nature. It gives us an internal beauty and attractiveness so that God Himself has to love us. Men in grace
stand out from the crowd, they are men of distinction.
In addition grace dignifies the least actions which we
perform so the daily routine contains sanctity and
produces saints like St. Joseph. It is also the basis of
our love and charity for one another. As St. Paul says:
"For all you who have been baptized into Christ,
have put on Christ. There is . . . neither slave nor
freeman . . . you are all one in Christ Jesus" (Gala-
tions 3:27-28). And as Christ Himself reminds us:
"When you did it to one of the least of my brethren
here, you did it to me." To live this supernatural life
well, God has given us the gift of faith so we can look
out and see things as He sees them; we can keep in
touch with reality. To get out of touch with God's
viewpoint is unreality and can lead to insanity. So,

Lord, grant that I may see things as you see them. Preserve my sanity.

He also has given us the gift of hope. We may be weak, but we have reinforcements from outside time and space. We do not have to do it alone. These are God's truths. With them in mind we can now evaluate more accurately the lives of the millionaire playboy, the blind captain, the corporal dead at twenty-three, and our own lives. To what extent do they share in the divine nature? Are these lives of faith, hope, and charity? Isn't this really the measure of successful living according to God's plan?

The little outline given below helps again for your fifteen minutes of meditation. The prayers suitable for either morning or evening, and which will keep you in the spirit of the retreat, will be found in the last chapter. If possible try to make daily Mass and Holy Communion during your retreat.

Do it yourself!

Points for your prayerful thinking (15 minutes)

PREPARATORY PRAYER
See page 18.

I didn't know I had it in me

1 When God made me He put a lot of Himself into me—made in His image and likeness. Intellect—free will—built for eternity. The essential equality of all men.

2 But more. A share in His own divine life through sanctifying grace or supernatural life. Life of plant, animal, man, son of God. Super life.

3 Human adoption cannot change a child's nature. But through baptism I am made a new creature, born again, made a sharer in the divine nature—a son of God. Read last Gospel at Mass. Value of life—the workman, not so much the work done. Importance of the sacraments—a matter of life and death. Holy Communion—nourishment. Penance—restores life, etc.

4 Two faculties that we have that we may live as sons of God: faith and hope. Faith: a light for the intellect. Do we see things differently because of our faith? Genuflection—a piece of bread or Christ present? A

41

retreat—lost weekend, or the most important job of the year?

Hope: divine omnipotence at our command to do the job at hand. I, coward, wayward, and weak—He, strong, tender, true. He never gives in and we two shall win. Mental and physical life weaken, but this life can grow and increase until dying gasp.

Conclude by saying one Our Father, a Hail Mary, and Glory Be to the Father.

◆◆◆◆◆◆◆◆◆◆◆

St. Ignatius, a former soldier and officer responsible for the lives and welfare of his men in combat, knew well the value of tactics. He did not want his men to become soldiers of a lost battalion, chewed up as so much cannon fodder. He wanted them to make the most of their resources; and, "for God's greater glory," to choose their field of operation, to control the impulses of their fervor by reason, and to systematize their work.

"Man is created to praise, reverence, and serve God, our Lord, and by this means to save his soul." This is the mission of every man and every man needs a principle to guide him in his free, deliberate choices. St. Ignatius suggests, "Whatever is for the greater glory of God."

This next chapter shows you how to achieve maximum personal security in the battle of life while making a truly significant contribution to the cause "for the greater glory of God." While it points to the deadly enemy of all souls in this conflict—sin—it does more. It positively shows us how to live a life of hard-headed holiness.

My mission

In our outfit overseas we had a colonel who was quite a character. He was tall and gray and gaunt, and he made warfare his profession. He was personally fearless and a good soldier, but he was also very much concerned with army rules and regulations. He knew the "book" and lived by it, yet, he was also convinced of the power of an idea. He figured that if a man got an idea, he might do something about it. Since this was his general attitude, he naturally picked up a nickname. In the comic strips at the time, Dick Tracy was running up against such characters as Pruneface, Flattop, BO Plenty, The Face, and all those weird and interesting people he meets. So, since the colonel knew the book and all the Army rules and regulations thoroughly, and lived by them, he picked up a nickname. It was not a very original one, but he was more or less affectionately referred to as The Book.

Now The Book insisted that every man in the outfit know the purpose or the mission of the outfit. His was an artillery headquarters group, so, he would go around to each man and say: "Soldier, what is the mission of a field artillery group?" At first no one knew the answer; but after a while the word got around that he wanted: "Sir, the mission of a field artillery group is to direct the activities of two or more battalions so as to bring effective fire upon the enemy." "Good," he would grunt and then push his questioning a step further. He'd say to each man: "Soldier, what is your particular mission in this outfit?" I remember the first time he went up to the cook, a fine, big Italian, built like a mack truck, and said to him: "Soldier, what is your mission?" The cook answered: "I ain't got no mission, Sir. I just do the cookin'." "No!" the colonel shot back, "That *is* your mission! An army marches on its stomach. If you don't get the food out, this outfit is ineffective— 'Kaput.' Understand?" "Yes, Sir, 'Kaput.' "

So when the colonel went up to the wire corporal, the man was prepared. He saluted smartly and answered: "Sir, my mission is to get the communications in and keep them in." "Good," said the colonel, and then he pushed his questioning still further. "Soldier, what is the first thing you should do when you come into an area? Look for the wine in the cellar?" "No, Sir." "Look for a comfortable place to sleep?" "No, Sir." Each man was supposed to say: "The first thing I do—I get the communications in and keep them in," or "I get the food." Each one, his job first! The Book wound up by saying: "Men, if we don't do this, we might just as well be back in Louisiana digging ditches."

Now he did have a point. Here was a mission to be accomplished, a job to be done. Here was the way to do it. "Let's get it done." Perhaps we might ask ourselves questions along the same lines. The questions would begin "What is my mission in life?" The answer would be, "My mission in life is to reach an eternity of happiness with God." Then what is the first thing I should seek for? Wealth? Pleasure? Social success? Popularity? "No, sir!" What should come first? If we have any doubts, our Lord spells it out for us: "But seek first the kingdom of God and his justice, and all these things shall be given you besides" (Matthew 6:33). And if I do not accomplish my mission in life, do not reach an eternity of happiness with God, it would be better if I had not been born. We can see that this is true. Our Lord insisted that it was so with that haunting, soul-searing question which has changed the lives of so many men: "For what does it profit a man if he gain the whole world, but suffer the loss of his own soul?" Or, from another angle, "what will a man give in exchange for his soul?"

The problem that faces us is this. We live in a very interesting world. Obviously it is meant for men and women to inhabit and to possess, to use and to enjoy. It is meant for men and women to live in and work in and love in. Angels, pure spirits as they are, would have no use for a Cadillac, or a fifth of Scotch, or a beautiful home. We do. This is a man's and woman's world to be used by us. So we have to ask ourselves: "How will I use the things that are in this life, and what things will I use?" Is there a principle to guide me in their use? St. Ignatius, another soldier, but a saint, gives us a clear, hard-headed principle. It sounds familiar (a little like The Book): "I will use the things in this life if they help me to accomplish my mission—to reach an eternity of happiness with God. I will refrain from using them if they stand in the way. The more a thing will help me, the more I will use it. The less it helps me, the less I will use it." We can see that this is obvious common sense. It is an immediate conclusion from the first great truth. My mission in life is to reach an eternity of happiness with God. And since I must necessarily get there or face eternal ruin, then I must use the things that will get me there. If I am smart, I will concentrate on the things that will help me the most. The things that are less helpful for me will be put in proper perspective and given their relative value. First things first!

So notice then, money is good. Enjoy it. But don't make a god out of it. Success, popularity, recognition, fame are all good. Get them if you can, but don't make gods out of them. Pleasure is good but don't make a god out of it. When I say: "Don't make a god out of money," I'm not necessarily thinking of millions of dollars. Thirty pieces of silver helped make a traitor out of Judas. In this connection, I recall a man in the Army who said: "When I was young I was poor, and I determined to get money. I did. I became a number-one salesman. Very successful. But this is the way I sold my product. I had three women who traveled with me and whom I called my 'business associates.' I would size up a prospective client, and after a while I would turn one of my 'associates' over to him. When he was compromised in the way that he wanted to be, well, it wasn't too difficult to get the contract. So I have money." He added thoughtfully and a little bitterly: "The only people I despise more than myself are the men who wanted and accepted this type of salesmanship. However," he said, brightening up, "I'm through with all that now. When I get out of the Army, just one more big killing. Then I'll quit." Obviously, he had made a god out of money.

I recall, too, that in the kidnapping and murder of Bobby Greenlease, one of the women involved said in her testimony: "Anything but poverty." And she meant it literally. Or take the last depression when the stock market toppled. A wave of heart attacks swept the country. Only many of the heart failures were induced by an overdose of sleeping tablets, by jumping out of hotel windows, or by piping carbon monoxide into the car from the exhaust. Money loomed so large in the lives of some people that when it was gone life had lost its meaning. So many notes ended pathetically, "I find that I can no longer face the future or my family."

Let us see how this Ignatian principle might come into practical daily living. See if you can picture yourself in a situation similar to this. A young man, a Catholic, was going around with a Catholic girl who was separated from her husband. Her first marriage was one of those hasty, unfortunate, war marriages. He asked if there was any way they could be married according to God's law. Her first marriage was investigated; but even though it was a young, foolish, hasty marriage, it was still valid. There was nothing that could be done. "Well, all right then," he said, "I'll give her up. I love her and I know that she loves me. I think that we could be happy together, but I love her enough not to want to endanger her soul's salvation. I'll be lonesome, but I've been lonesome before and I can get along by observing God's laws." Not an easy decision to make! Some would regard it as foolish. To some, human love comes above everything—including the salvation of one's soul.

Here is another instance of this principle in action. A Catholic girl, married to a Catholic, and mother of two children, was just twenty-three years old when her husband deserted her. Her father kept urging her to marry again, telling her that she was young and had a long life ahead of her. Her answer might have sounded a bit melodramatic, but, nevertheless, she really did say it. "Yes, I have a long life ahead of me, but I also have a long eternity ahead of me. With God's help, I'll be able to manage somehow." Not an easy decision to make. I will use the things in this world, including marriage, if they help me to accomplish my mission. I'll refrain from using them if they stand in the way.

St. Thomas More was placed in a similar situation, and I think we all feel a kind of sympathy and understanding for this personable, witty, married saint. He had four children whom he loved dearly: Margaret, Elizabeth, Cecily, and John. He was a talented and versatile writer whose reputation was established in his own day with legal, political, and religious treatises and has been secured until the present by the literary tradition he began with his *Utopia*. He was a lawyer, a judge, and eventually became chancellor of England. He was asked by Henry VIII, a close friend of his, to sign a statement which would acknowledge Henry as the head of the Church and prepare the way for his marriage to Anne Boleyn. Henry wished the approval of Thomas More above all others. But Thomas saw in this a denial of his faith and of his personal integrity, so he refused to sign. The issue was not as clear-cut then to men in the midst of the controversy as it is to us with the historical perspective of four hundred years. But Thomas More saw the issue clearly and declared that he would not sign such a statement. He was jailed and sentenced to death. During his trial and while he was in jail awaiting execution, his lawyer friends wrote to him and came to him urging him to sign, arguing that many good and eminent men had signed. Thomas answered that what others did was a matter for their own consciences. As for himself, he could not in conscience do it. ". . . in things touching conscience, every true and good subject is more bound to have respect to his said conscience and to his soul than to any other thing in all the world beside." A restatement of "For what does it profit a man, if he gain the whole world, but suffer the loss of his own soul?" Unable to ignore this basic truth, More was told that if he would sign he would still have the favor of the king. To this More said, "I am the King's good servant but God's first." In courageous words that send a thrill of strength coursing through our weak hearts and wills he added: "I never intend . . . to pin my soul at another man's back, not even the best man that I know this day living: for I know not whither he may hap to carry it."

His position was made still more difficult when his wife and his favorite daughter, Margaret, came to him urging him to sign, reminding him tearfully of themselves and his love for them, his lovely home, his family, and friends. More, deeply moved, said: "My dearly beloved daughter, nothing has touched me so as to see you labor to persuade me." And to his wife: "How long, then, Mistress Alice, do you think I may enjoy a happy life at Chelsea?" "A full twenty years," she said. "You are not old yet." "My good wife," he gently replied, "you are not very skillful at a bargain. Would you have me for twenty years, give up eternity?" More would regard himself as a very poor lawyer indeed to exchange the friendship of the King of Kings for the doubtful favor of his vacillating sovereign. ". . . what will a man give in exchange for his soul?"

If we recall the words which Shakespeare put into the mouth of Wolsey, who had chosen to serve the king first, we see how truly wise Thomas More was even in this life. Wolsey, in his old age, bitterly observed: "Had I but serv'd my God with half the zeal I serv'd my king, he would not in mine age have left me naked to mine enemies."

We can see how Thomas More made his decision by using the principle which St. Ignatius enunciated so clearly. If in every major decision we invoked and followed this principle: I'll use things if they help me to accomplish my mission—to reach an eternity of happiness with God, I'll refrain from using them if they are effectively blocking me, we would be securely on the way to eternal happiness and successful living according to God's plan. If, like More, we also used the obvious corollary: The more a thing helps me to reach an eternity of happiness with God the more I will use it, we, like More would be on the way to high sanctity.

As a matter of fact, we should, and generally do, use these as guiding principles in other areas of living as well as in that of the business of saving our souls. Suppose a salesman found it was very useful to meet the prospect on the golf course. The deal is wrapped up on the nineteenth hole; the boss is very happy about it. But suppose the golfing continued and no sales came in. Eventually the boss would call the man in and say: "Look, golf is good, fine, dandy. I like the game myself. But don't let it interfere with business, eh?" Or take the man who is handy with a do-it-yourself kit. He has all the directions on how to make a fine kitchen cabinet. Just as he gets the wood all sawed according to specifications and is ready to nail it together, he grabs the electric saw and continues cutting it up into a bunch of little pieces. He explains this action to a puzzled friend: "You see, I started out to make a cabinet; but once I get this little saw in my hands, I just can't quit. BZZ, BZZ, BZZ. I like to saw." His friend would look at him closely to see if he was serious and if he was, would probably say: "There's a little man in a white coat who would be interested in you."

We could vary the circumstances and the words. "Once I get a bottle in my hand, I just won't stop. I like to drink, come what may." Or, "I like to hear the rustle of those dollar bills. Anything for a buck, just so it comes in." Or, "Just give me sex, sex, sex! That's life!" But instead of the little man in a white coat, there might be the vision of a man with horns and a pointed tail in a red suit, looking very interested and pleased.

The minimum requirement for everyone is that if anything is effectively blocking him from an eternity of happiness with God, it must go, whether it be pleasurable or painful. With this principle in view, let us take another glance at the lives of the millionaire playboy, the blind captain, the corporal dead at twenty-three. How did the millionaire playboy use his wealth, his luxurious living, and his many gifts? How did the blind captain use the suffering God's providence sent into his life? The corporal dead at twenty-three? How did he use a short life? Evidently he used it well. I saw his wife after the war. She said simply: "I count it a very great privilege to have spent two years with him. He was a wonderful man."

Let us take a look at our own lives and some of the things that enter our daily living. Do I have time for God? What about Mass, Holy Communion, confession? If these will help me, I will use them frequently. Do I have time for morning and evening prayers? What about Catholic education for the children? It might involve sacrifices; but if it will help them to accomplish their mission, will I reasonably try to get it for them? What principle will I use on deciding between a fashionable, somewhat agnostic university, and one a little less glamorous, but Christian? How do I use liquor? Is it helping me to accomplish my mission? What about dangerous associations? What is my attitude toward money and economic status? If it is a question of a new car, a new house, and artificial birth control, what would my decision be? If I am a student, do I take time to study and prepare myself for the work which God will give me to do? Generally, when we make this inventory, we all find that we are a little unreasonable in one area or another. This is not at all surprising because we have a built-in bias toward the pleasurable and an instinctive aversion to the painful. But with God's grace and patience with ourselves, we can gradually cultivate those things which will help us to an eternity of happiness with God and eliminate those which bring with them disorder and unhappiness. Good habits can become almost instinctive, just as others can creep in and establish themselves in our lives almost imperceptibly; like the wrong attitudes or false judgments which we rationalize into a way of life. Lord, that I may see them for what they are! Lord, grant that I may know myself!

A killer

Now there is really only one thing that can keep us from accomplishing our mission. It is not our temperament, our environment, friends, family, or the powers of evil. There is only one thing and that is mortal sin: a knowing and willing violation of God's law in a serious matter. So it is good for us to take a steady look at mortal sin and to recognize it for what it is—the number one enemy of our eternal happiness. Now the purpose of this is not to go back over the past and pick away anxiously at our consciences. There is no future in the past. When God in His goodness and mercy forgives a sin, it is wiped out for good and forever. It is annihilated. So that is not the purpose. We want merely to look at sin and see it for what it is. An added reason for doing so is that we live in an atmosphere and a time in which sin is pretty much taken for granted and rationalized away.

This atmosphere of sin is part of our daily reading —the newspaper. I don't say that such things have no place in the paper. I am merely pointing out the content of our daily reading. The headline will probably be a murder. That's a sin. The next column will expose graft in political circles. That's stealing. The next story will be about a bank robbery. That's stealing. The next story will be about the breaking up of an abortion ring. That's murder. Another column might be a juicy bit of Hollywood or local scandal. That's adultery. The next one will be—you name it. And so it goes, for two or three pages, about men and women violating the laws of God. So we get rather used to it; just about shockproof. I can only think of three sins that meet with general public disapproval. One is a type of murder. I do not mean a good, clean-cut murder: "Husband Slays Wife's Lover," but rather the dismemberment murders when hacked-off limbs are packed away in oil drums. That still shocks the general public. Then rape is generally disapproved of because there is an element of force and duress in it. Kidnapping is the third crime that arouses indignation because people don't like to see children taken forcibly from their parents. But nearly all the others are pretty well rationalized away by many. Concerning the sins of young people we are told, "You are only young once." For the old, it is: "Isn't an old man entitled to a last fling and a few peccadillos?" In saying this we are not judging individuals and their consciences, but it does look as though some people who are violating many of the laws of God and man seem to get along very nicely. They shoot a good game of golf, they smile, they have a nice house, healthy children. They're not struck by lightening. They seem to be doing quite well. For all these reasons maybe sin isn't so bad after all?

God, our Father, tells us what He thinks of sin and what it really is. A story might help us to understand His view. There was a king who wished to impress upon his son the horrors of war so that when his son succeeded him he would keep the nation out of war if that was at all possible. For this purpose the king had three pictures painted. The first picture showed a modern village which was bombed, charred, and blackened, a heap of rubble, a scene of desolation. Standing alone in the midst of the ruins was a mother, with her child in her arms, weeping and staring empty-eyed at the place that was once her happy home. The king's son, studying the picture carefully, turned to his father and said: "What is that?" The father answered, "That is war!" The boy had not lived in wartime, but he could see it in its effects and he concluded gravely: "Then what a terrible thing war must be!" The second picture the father showed him was a battlefield with the dead and the wounded, the blood and the mud, the lonesomeness and the suffering. After studying the picture, the boy again asked: "What is that?" "That's war," the father answered; and again the boy remarked: "Then what a terrible thing war must be." The last picture the king showed to him was the Four Horsemen of the Apocalypse—War itself, Grinning Death, Gaunt Famine, and Red Pestilence—riding roughshod over a country: the aftermath of war. The people were pictured shrinking and shrieking in horror at the onslaught. And when the boy said: "What is that?" the father answered grimly: "That is what war really is." And the boy answered, "Then what a terrible thing war must be!"

Now our heavenly Father shows us three pictures of sin. These are real, not imaginary. The first picture he shows us is that of the angels. The angels, like ourselves, were created to praise, reverence, and serve God. Thus they would reach their eternity of happiness with Him. Unlike ourselves, they did not have a body to weigh them down. They were pure spirits with fine intellects and strong wills, creatures of light and exceedingly great beauty. We do not know what their problem or temptation was. Theologians speculate and say that possibly these pure spirits were given a knowledge of God's plan for the redemption of mankind: that God would become man, and as man would be their Lord and Master, and Him they would adore. This seemed beneath angelic dignity to some of them, or else they did not agree with God's plan of a crucified, suffering Redeemer, and they rebelled. We do not know exactly what it was, but only that it was a sin of pride. They said, "I will not serve." That was a case of a weak, created intelligence preferring its judgments before the infinite wisdom of the Creator. It was a clash of wills—a sin of disobedience. Wherever this sin entered in, it struck an angel down. From angels of beauty and light, they were instantly transformed into ugly, twisted beings. They plunged into hell, smouldering in their pride for all eternity. Lucifer, who was called the light bearer because of the brilliance of his shining, is now the leader of the fallen angels whose name is Legion, for they are many. We might apply here our Lord's own words to describe this rebellion and the ruin it brought on those involved: "I was watching Satan fall as lightning from heaven" (Luke 10:18). And St. Peter reminds us of this terrible tragedy. "For God did not spare the angels when they sinned, but dragged them down by infernal ropes to Tartarus, and delivered them to be tortured and kept in custody for judgment" (2 Peter 2:4).

As we study this ruin and disaster we see that it is

53

filled with mystery. Our minds cannot grasp it. Eternal hell for one sin! But we do know that God cannot do a disproportionate thing and that He is all merciful. In the rebellion of mortal sin there must be something that strikes at divinity and subverts the basic order of the universe. A creature attempting to be God and insisting that his will, not God's, be done. We might reflect, too, that in pure spirits there are not the extenuating circumstances that are found in the weakness and confusion of fallen human nature. So as we study this grim reality, these damaged angels, we humbly ask God, our Father: "What is this? What is it that has caused such ruin?" And He answers, "This is mortal sin." And we say: "Then what a terrible thing mortal sin must be, as You saw it in the angels and as, perhaps, You have seen it in me."

The second picture that our Father shows us comes home to us a little better because it is the picture of a man and woman like ourselves. Like ourselves, they were created by God and were placed in this world to praise, reverence, and serve Him and thus reach their eternity of happiness. Also, like ourselves, they were given the things of this world to use. Unlike us, their bodies did not rebel against their minds, and in God's original plan they were not destined for physical death. They had gifts of mind and body that we do not possess. As we watch their situation unfold, it seems familiar. It seems as though we have been in like situations ourselves.

We are told in Scripture, in the book of Genesis: "And the Lord God took man, and put him into the paradise of pleasure, to dress it, and to keep it. And he commanded him saying: Of every tree of paradise thou shalt eat: but of the tree of knowledge of good and evil, thou shalt not eat." All these things are yours to use and enjoy, but this you shall not do. Now, we do not have to think of this in terms of eating an apple or a piece of fruit. The command was one of basic importance that fitted in with man's relationship to God. To impress upon men that it was serious, God told them: "For in what day soever thou shalt eat of it, thou shalt die the death." The issue is clear.

And the serpent said to the woman: "Why hath God commanded you, that you should not eat of every tree of paradise?" Notice the exaggeration and how the doubt is skillfully sown in the mind. And the woman answered him: "Of the fruit of the trees that are in paradise we do eat: but of the fruit of the tree which is in the midst of paradise, God hath commanded us . . . that we should not touch it, lest perhaps we die." The serpent said soothingly, persuasively: "No, you shall not die the death. For God doth know that in what day soever you shall eat thereof, your eyes shall be opened: and you shall be as Gods." To be like God! This was the appeal that made the angels fall from heaven and it is an appeal that finds a responsive cord in the heart of everyone. Instinctively we might be tempted to say: "No, I don't want to be like God. I am too weak and confused to play the part of God." Yet isn't it quite easy for us to turn to God and say: "O God, not Thy will, but mine be done?" Naturally we regret that our desires cause conflict between us and God. We prefer to have His friendship, but if the issue is raised, then regretfully we say: "*My* will be done," because when we want something badly enough, we really want it.

"And the woman saw that the tree was good to eat, and fair to the eyes, and delightful to behold: and she took of the fruit thereof, and did eat, and gave to her husband who did eat." Then God came to them and they hid themselves, because they were naked. God said to them: "And who hath told thee that thou wast naked, but that thou hast eaten of the tree whereof I commanded thee that thou shouldst not eat?" Humanly, oh so humanly, each puts the blame somewhere else. Adam replied: "The woman, whom thou gavest me to be my companion, gave me of the tree, and I did eat." And Eve said: "The serpent deceived me, and I did eat." The punishment of all involved is immediate. God said to the serpent: "Because thou hast done this thing, thou art cursed . . . I will put enmities between thee and the woman . . . she shall crush thy head, and thou shalt lie in wait for her heel." To the woman: "I will multiply thy sorrows . . . In sorrow shalt thou bring forth children, and thou shalt be

under thy husband's power, and he shall have dominion over thee." To Adam: "Because thou . . .
hast eaten of the tree, whereof I commanded thee that
thou shouldst not eat, cursed is the earth in thy
work; with labour and toil shalt thou eat thereof all
the days of thy life. Thorns and thistles shall it bring
forth to thee; . . . In the sweat of thy face shalt thou
eat bread till thou return to the earth, out of which
thou wast taken: for dust thou art, and into dust thou
shalt return." And God drove them from the garden
of paradise and placed a cherub with a flaming sword
to guard against their return.

Through our first parents we, too, feel the weight
of this sin. Every time we hear a church bell toll for
a funeral or we attend a wake, we are sharing in and
seeing the far-reaching effects of this first sin. Physical
death is now an inevitable part of human life for all of
us. It is a punishment for this first sin. Every time we
feel the rebellion of our bodies and our emotions
against our minds, we are aware of the disorder and
mutiny this first sin has brought to mankind. Original
integrity was shattered in our first parents and lost to
us. As we look back through the ages, we see the torch
of passion kindled because of this sin: Abel lying dead
at the hand of his brother Cain; the lust of Sodom and
Gomorrah; the sins of Greece and Rome; the pride
and hate and brutality that have turned our world into
a great battlefield. As we contemplate this wreckage
all about us, we say to God, our Father: "What is it
that causes such havoc?" He answers, "That is mortal
sin." And we say to Him: "Then what a terrible thing
mortal sin must be as You saw it in the angels, as You
saw it in Adam and Eve, and as You, perhaps, have
seen it in me."

The final picture our Father shows us is not taken
from Scripture. He merely bids us look around
our world of the sixties and realistically see what it is
that brings unhappiness into the lives of men and
women right now. This is independent of whether
there is an afterlife or not. What is it that brings unhappiness to people? Just suppose that three major
sins were eliminated from the world in which we live.
First, murder. By that I not only mean the occasional

56

killing in which a family is deprived of a loved one, with its accompanying heartbreak and hardship, but especially the mass murders which have gone on in our day and still go on. Whole nations are wiped out! Human beings are experimented on as guinea pigs, shot, worked to death in concentration camps, starved, gassed in a carnage that has made our world one big cemetery of mass burials. The threat of repetition keeps every man subject to military service and puts him in uniform. It reaches out to the personal lives of everyone and to our life savings. All must keep constantly armed and alert to ward off nuclear annihilation. If only the fear of murder were removed, what a wonderfully peaceful, secure world we would live in.

If, in addition to murder, adultery could be eliminated what a difference it would make. I am not thinking of the occasional mistake which a good person may make, but rather of legalized adultery by which men and women, having pledged themselves "till death do us part," go on to a second, third, or fourth marriage, leaving behind the broken lives of children as a natural and inevitable consequence. Broken lives come from broken homes. This situation is so common that outside of safeguarding our atomic secrets, juvenile delinquency has become the chief concern of the F.B.I. If only divorce were removed and there was fidelity in marriage, what a peaceful, emotionally secure world we would live in. Children would be able to say: "I have a mother and a father, one of each. I'm not asked to choose sides. They love each other, and they love me."

If, in addition to murder and adultery, major dishonesty was eliminated, much of human suffering would be eased. I am not referring here to a holdup or a bank robbery, but rather to the social conditions in which whole segments of people or colonies are kept in destitution without the basic necessities of life. Think of the slums that are kept alive for the sake of profit, and people who have been kept in subjection through the centuries for profit. If only major dishonesty were removed, many people who think they have nothing to lose by death except their unhappy lives, would find their lives worth living and communism would lose its first appeal. So, as we look at the world about us, the world of the sixties, which we know so well, we say to God, our Father: "What is it that causes such unhappiness to so many people?" Our Father answers, "That is mortal sin." We say to Him: "Then what a terrible thing mortal sin must be as You saw it in the angels, as You saw it in Adam and Eve, as I can see it in the world about me, and, perhaps, as You have seen it in me."

Experimentally, for we have all sinned, can we think of even once that sin has made us happy? Even once? Of course, sin can and does give us pleasure, but that is not happiness. Pleasure is passing, a superficial sensation. It can be had from a cigarette, an ice cream cone, a drink, sex, but it isn't happiness. That is the promise sin always holds out to us, "Come to me and I will make you happy." Yet it never does. You know, most of us do not mind making an occasional mistake—to err is human—but none of us likes to be a professional fool. If we buy the Brooklyn Bridge once, we can charge it off to experience. If we buy it twice, we might explain that we are a little slow to learn. After the third or fourth time, though, people begin to whisper and shake their heads. If we buy a gold brick—O.K., it makes a good doorstop. If we buy two of them they might serve as bookends or an interesting conversation piece. But a closet full of them! That's something different. That's stupid—as stupid as sin! The big hoax is that sin is sophisticated and exciting. The big lie is "the lilies and languors of virtue," and "the roses and raptures of sin." If sin is supposed to be so rapturous, why aren't those who have made sin a way of life more enraptured? Look at the poor unfortunates who have dedicated themselves to it. No roses here. There are the D.T's and the nightmares of dope. There is softening of the brain and hardening of the liver. There are hard, tough women, all femininity gone. There is despair. If the devotees of "roses and raptures" are so happy, why so many suicides? Even in the sixties our experience tells us that the wages of sin is still death.

Still, the essence of sin is not that it is stupid and makes men immediately unhappy, but rather that it is ingratitude to the most loving of fathers. When we recall all that God, our Father, has done for us and the long litany of blessings which deserve at least a "Thank you," when we think of His loving plans for our future happiness, then sin shows up in all its black ingratitude. If we want a picture of the ingratitude of sin it is given to us in the Old Testament in the heartbreaking story of David and his son Absalom. Absalom as we recall was the well-beloved son of King David. In return for his father's love, Absalom organized a revolt against him. He drove his father from his kingdom, took over his palace, his possessions, and all that he had. Finally a counter-revolution swept back against Absalom, and as he fled the city his long hair and helmet got entangled in the branches of an overhanging oak tree. Joab, David's captain, finding him thus, thrust three spears through Absalom's ungrateful heart. Humanly speaking, we might say, what a son deserved who had treated so good a father so basely. It is only a picture, but a rather vivid one of the ingratitude of sin to the most loving of fathers and the punishment it might well deserve. And yet King David, being informed of his son's death: "went up to the high chamber over the gate, and wept. And as he went he spoke in this manner: My son Absalom, Absalom my son! Would to God that I might die for thee, Absalom my son, my son Absalom!" (2 Kings 18:33). Sin is ingratitude to the most loving of Fathers and to Christ our Savior, who, in the revelation of His Sacred Heart said: "It is the ingratitude of men which hurts Me more than all the sufferings I underwent during My Passion."

Another view of sin is more personal. Recall that we are living temples of the Holy Spirit and within us the Blessed Trinity dwells, making us more precious in God's sight than St. Peter's in Rome or any soaring cathedral, however beautiful and hallowed. Sin desecrates that living temple of God. We have seen pictures of a bombed cathedral, the roof broken through, the insides charred and blackened, altar broken, crucifix shattered—these are the pictures of the wreckage mortal sin makes of a living temple of God. Sanctifying grace, a share in the divine nature, makes us so compellingly attractive and beautiful that God has to love us. Sin disfigures this beauty. It is like throwing acid in the face of a beautiful woman. "Ugly as sin" is not an idle phrase. If left unchecked, mortal sin could be accurately described as the beginning of hell.

As we consider these facts we wonder why, when we have sinned, God has been so good and merciful to us? Why have we been spared? He did not spare the angels. Their punishment was immediate and eternal. The punishment of our first parents after they sinned was severe and prolonged. How about me? Here I am alive. I can still save my soul and reach an eternity of happiness with God. Why has God been so patient and good to me? Why?

St. Ignatius suggests that whenever we meditate on sin or these grim subjects, we should always end up at the foot of the cross close to Christ. So, as we gaze trustingly at Christ crucified, we ask: "Lord, why is it that You have come from eternal life to temporal death? What is the meaning of these wounds in Your hands and Your feet, Your side?" As we study Him lovingly, perhaps here we will get the answer to why we have been spared. "But he was wounded for our iniquities: he was bruised for our sins. The chastisement of our peace *was* upon him: and by his bruises we are healed" (Isaias 53:5).

Knowing that we have been saved, that we have been spared through Him, we might ask ourselves three thoughtful questions. "What have I done for our Lord in the past?" If we answer honestly, it may be good, or poor, or medium. The second question, "What am I doing for Him now?" There, happily, we can all answer: "My poor best." Because those who are willing to follow along in this retreat in the midst of busy and demanding work show a deep concern for God and the things of God. So, the good will which Christ hopes for and can work with is here now. But the next question is the most important. "What will I do for Him in the future?" The answer to that question is individual and unique for each one, because we are different. God deals with each one differently, never violating the unique person whom He created. He never tried to make St. Peter over into St. John, or the other way around. So as we give our individual answers we do not have to be afraid. We can trust completely, for He loves us and knows us more intimately than we know ourselves. He will not ask me to violate my personality. He will only ask me to bring it to its full attractiveness. "What will I do for Him in the future?" That is the question!

For one, the answer may be in this general area. "Lord, some things have crept into my life. I scarcely recognized them for what they are. It is going to be a little difficult to set things right, but with your grace and strength I will work at it patiently." There may be public opinion to face. People may notice the change and have comments to make. "What in the world has come over you? Have you got religion?" I may even lose some "friends." Then, there is my own weakness. "It's hard, Lord, to admit that I have been wrong and stubborn all these years, but with your grace, it will be done." Or, "Lord, I have taken on some wrong attitudes and I have been fooling myself—rationalizing. Help me to think honestly and straight."

For another, it might be: "I find myself in a very difficult situation. I'm tempted to quit, throw it all over and get out. I'm discouraged. But with Your help, Lord, I'll carry on, trusting in You to make things work out, somehow."

For another it might be that God is asking for the dedication of your life in some special way—the religious life, the priesthood, Catholic action — some particular use of talents that might make demands and involve sacrifices that are difficult for weak human nature. "Lord, with Your help I offer myself. And knowing my weakness, You know how much You'll have to help."

To give a really good and generous answer to the question, "What shall I do for Him in the future?" it might be useful to recall a story that came out of World War II. There was a French captain who abandoned his men in the face of enemy fire. He was court-martialed and sentenced to death. In reviewing his case the court found grounds for clemency. He had been a good officer. He had been on the line for a long time. It seemed more like nerves breaking than deliberate cowardice and abandonment of duty. Just before the execution was to take place, a general came to the captain and told him that he was pardoned and handed him back his sidearms. The general then said: "Now, what will you do?" The captain drew himself up to attention and said quietly, gratefully: "Sir, I'll die for you." If our Lord were to ask us: "Now, what will you do for Me?" knowing that we have been spared, our answer might be, not: "Lord, I'll die for You"; but, something more realistic and perhaps more difficult: "Lord, I'll live for You."

If we could say: "Lord, I'll live for you," even though we might not have the courage to say it wholeheartedly and with complete sincerity, it would be a wonderful beginning. To encourage us to give it meaning, we might recall what Christ said to St. Margaret Mary when He revealed the love of His Sacred Heart for men: "Sinners shall find in My Heart the source and the infinite ocean of mercy. Tepid souls shall grow fervent. Fervent souls shall quickly mount to high perfection." He added: "It is the ingratitude of men which hurts Me more than all the sufferings I underwent during My Passion. If they give Me a return [of love], then all that I have done for them would appear but little to My love."

At this point, we might sum up by letting St. Ignatius's great principle and foundation speak for itself.

FIRST PRINCIPLE
AND FOUNDATION
OF THE SPIRITUAL EXERCISES
OF ST. IGNATIUS

1 Man is created to praise, reverence, and serve God, our Lord, and by this means to save his soul.

2 All the other things on the face of the earth are created for man that they may help him attain the end for which he is created, that is, to save his soul.

3 From this it follows that man is to use these created things only in so far as they help him to his end. He must not use them in so far as they hinder him from his end—namely, the salvation of his soul.

4 To achieve this, we must make ourselves detached from all created things. Therefore, we should not desire health rather than sickness, riches rather than poverty, honor rather than disgrace, a long life rather than a short life, and so in everything else. But we should desire and choose only what is better for us, for the end for which we are created, that is to save our souls. Every thought, word, or act should be all for the greater glory of God—A.M.D.G.

Do it yourself!

Points for your prayerful thinking (15 minutes)

PREPARATORY PRAYER
See page 18.

My mission

1 Soldier, what is the mission of a field artillery group? Soldier, what is your mission?
If we fail in this, we might just as well be back in the USA.

2 What is *my* mission? To save my soul. Seek wealth first? Fame? Pleasure? No!
Businessman: Golf is o.k., but don't let it interfere with business.
Transfer this attitude to the business of saving our souls, and it becomes hard-headed holiness.
If I fail to save my soul, it would be better if I had not been born.

3 Conclusion: I will use the things in this life if they help me to accomplish my mission. If they stand in the way, I won't use them. The more they help me the more I'll use them.

4 Mortal sin is the only thing that can stop me. I must learn to hate it no matter how attractively it may be presented. Sin is stupid. "Ugly as sin!"
Three pictures of war: a bombed village, a battlefield, war's aftermath.
The king's son: "What a terrible thing war must be!"
Three pictures of sin: angels, Adam and Eve, the world because of murder, adultery, dishonesty.
God's children: "What a terrible thing sin must be, Lord, as you saw it in the angels, in Adam and Eve, in the world, and perhaps in me."

5 Mortal sin—kills supernatural life—ingratitude to greatest of benefactors, most loving fathers—Absalom and David—ruined temples of the Holy Ghost. Why have I been spared?

French captain: "Sir, I'll die for you." We: "Lord, I'll live for You."

Conclude by saying one Our Father, a Hail Mary, and Glory Be to the Father.

P.S. If you find it a little hard to meditate for fifteen minutes turn to the last chapter for different ways to make a mental prayer. Either of these methods could be used on the "Principle and Foundation" of St. Ignatius given in this chapter and would get you into the swing of meditation. Keep on "doing it yourself."

◆◆◆◆◆◆◆◆◆◆◆

The next chapter, like an Aristotelian tragedy, elicits the emotions of pity and fear. The pity comes as we consider the possibility of men and women wrecking their lives and going down to eternal ruin. The fear comes from the realization that "there, except for the grace of God, go I." This leaves us contrite, humble, and purified. We are cleansed from our pride.

Then consolingly, comfortingly, it leads us with complete confidence and trust to the sheltering arms of God, our Father, and to the all-merciful heart of Christ. "Within Thy wounds hide me. Never permit me to be separated from Thee. From the wicked foe defend me." I think you'll like the next chapter because "God's mercy is above all His works."

◆◆◆◆◆◆◆◆◆◆◆◆◆

In case
of emergency

Fear is a normal part of living and we take it for granted. By fear I do not mean the fear of panic which in the parlance of cowboy movies would be described, "He jumped on his horse and galloped off in all directions." This is futile. I mean the fear of caution. The type of fear that parents try to instill in their children. For example, if you lived near a busy street with heavy traffic, reasonably you would show a child the cars whizzing by and forbid him to play in the street. "You'll get killed!" You'd warn him not to cross the street until the lights turned green or to wait until an older person could see him safely across. You wouldn't figure that he would grow up with a psychic trauma because he had a healthy respect for speeding autos. Rather, you would figure that he might grow up if he followed this corny bit of advice: "To avoid that rundown feeling, don't get in front of speeding automobiles."

This same fear of caution is what they try to teach in the armed forces. They train for courage and endurance, but they also teach security. We were shown how boobie traps were rigged, the different types which might be used, and then warned: "Don't go wandering around needlessly in combat zones. If you're careful you'll come back home with a head on your shoulders instead of underneath your arm." Any soldier will remember the signs along the road: "Warning! Mines cleared to the shoulders." Despite such warnings, I remember one day when we were on a beach in Normandy. A dud shell was lying off to one side. One of the new men went over there curiously, picked it up, and shook it. Why, no one will ever know. It blew off his head and that of the man next to him. The only comment I heard was a caustic, "What did he think it was, an alarm clock?" That man had no fear of caution—and no head.

If we have the right kind of fear at the right time, it can save our physical lives. It can also save our emotional and mental lives, too. If we find that we are overtaxing ourselves, working to the point of mental exhaustion, if the nerves are getting ragged, we fear the consequences and prudently tell ourselves to stop. The fear of caution can also save our spiritual lives, if we have it. It is worth developing.

Now fear is not meant to be the primary motive in serving God, but it always remains somewhat in the picture. St. Ignatius suggests that it is a good emergency motive. He points out that gratitude to God, which should be one of our major motives for serving Him, fades out at times. It can grow a little dim. We can lose our sense of responsibility. God has given us a work to do, but on occasion we just don't care. Ordinarily we would like to do a good job for Him, but even love grows cold. At times God can seem a little unreal or a little unloving, and in such moments of stress St. Ignatius suggests that we fall back on fear as an emergency motive. Saints have mentioned that at times when all else was gone, the only thing that steadied them was fear of hell. So if it was of use to them, we also might find it of some assistance to us.

Another idea behind this very brief consideration of hell is to use on ourselves the same technique that the Commies use to brainwash a victim. I think they fall back on Pavlov's experiments with dogs, a method of inducing a conditioned reflex. You ring a bell, give the dog some meat; ring a bell, give the dog some meat; ring a bell, give the dog some meat; ring a bell, *don't* give the dog any meat. Still, in response to the bell, the dog's whole digestive system swings into action. He drools, barks, and so on—he has set up a reflex arc connecting the ringing bell with food. If we could set up in ourselves something like a conditioned reflex to mortal sin, it would be useful. If when a mortal sin is proposed to us a warning signal would ring out, B-O-N-G, in the back of our heads; we would have a nice, built-in safety device. We would be alerted and put on guard. These are some of the ideas behind this brief consideration of hell.

One retreat master I know says that if hell were vividly, consciously present to us at every moment, we'd never commit sin. Say it were as vividly present to us as a gun stuck in our ribs. He gave as an example: "Boy and girl drive out to the forest preserve. Boy turns off ignition, turns off headlights, turns off conscience, and things begin getting quite cozy and intimate. But just at that point, the door is violently jerked open, a gun is stuck in his ribs, and the intruder rasps out: 'This is a stick-up.' I find it very hard to hear the man saying: 'Go away, I'm overcome by passion.' No, his hands go up and he hands over his wallet. Fear takes over and overcomes, at that given moment, his passion." The instinct for self-preservation is more basic than sex. Fear of hell can also be more compelling than fleeting satisfaction. We wouldn't want to have fear pressing vividly on our consciousness, like a gun stuck in our ribs. But at least, if we do happen to make a mistake and part from God's grace, this fear of hell should quickly bring us back to repentence and to a loving union with God again. That's the idea behind this meditation.

Our Lord does point out that it is possible, since we are free agents, to end up as eternal failures. He gives us some idea of what that "failure" consists in Mark 9:42. He tells us, "If thy hand is an occasion of sin to thee, cut it off! It is better for thee to enter into life maimed, than, having two hands, to go into hell, into the unquenchable fire, 'Where their worm dies not, and the fire is not quenched.' And if thy foot is an occasion of sin to thee, cut it off! It is better for thee to enter into life everlasting lame, than, having two feet, to be cast into the hell of unquenchable fire, 'Where their worm dies not, and the fire is not quenched.' And if thy eye is an occasion of sin to thee, pluck it out! It is better for thee to enter into the kingdom of God with one eye, than, having two eyes, to be cast into hell-fire, 'Where their worm dies not, and the fire is not quenched.' For everyone shall be salted with fire." Now we know that we are forbidden to mutilate ourselves, to cut off an arm, to pluck out an eye; but our Lord is pointing out that the pain and sufferings involved in such a loss would be slight and worth the sacrifice compared to the pains of hell "where the fire is not quenched."

Now our Lord mentions fire, as it is mentioned many times in other parts of the New Testament in connection with hell. Theologians ask if this means fire as known to us on earth. They state that it is an agent, a punishing agent, external to man, other than the loss of God, and since this term is used so often, it is either fire as we know it on earth, or something very much like it. However this fire can reach a disembodied spirit. While we know how friendly a fire is when it is in a fireplace—we enjoy the play of the flames, its warmth—we also know what a terrible thing fire is when it is out of control. Recall the horror of a school fire, or the fires in night clubs and hotels where men and women have jumped out of fifth-story windows, piled up in panic at exits, and trampled one another to escape the flames. I vividly recall pictures that appeared in a daily paper of a gasoline truck that had rammed into a streetcar near a viaduct. The papers didn't dare print half the pictures of the people who were trapped in agony within the fiery furnace of the streetcar. Flaming horror! Terrifying! We know that a flame thrower will bring a man out of concealment because he prefers certain death by bullets to searing by flames. But I think the most dreadful thing about hell will be that it is everlasting. In this life when pain reaches a certain degree of intensity, we mercifully go unconscious. In hell, it would be vivid consciousness and awareness in the midst of suffering forever. There is no merciful black-out there.

Our Lord speaks of the worm of conscience—remorse and regret. "Where their worm dies not." We know how the memory of lost opportunities can stay with us and haunt us. I know of a man who had an opportunity to get into the Coca Cola business when it was first expanding. It only required a small investment, but for some reason he didn't do it. In conversation with him it always seemed to pop up. Somebody would be talking about a mix for a drink and he'd burst into the conversation with: "You know, I had a chance to get into the Coca Cola business." I think every time he saw the sign "Drink Coca Cola" he began to feel bad all over again. This is a simple regret over a lost business opportunity. What would be the remorse of an eternal failure? A man would go back over his life: his first communion, the blessings of a good family, Catholic education, perhaps; then sin, and repeated sin; then carelessness, indifference, callousness, hardness of heart; mercy offered a thousand times over and mercy a thousand times refused; finally time running out and dying in that state, to lament for all eternity: "Why didn't I? Why didn't I? It would have been so easy. It wouldn't have been difficult! Why didn't I?" playing over and over again the broken record of his life, "Eternal Failure!"

Is it possible for a man to refuse the mercy which God so generously offers? Reluctantly we must admit that it does seem possible, because there are a few consequences of sin that don't always appear on the surface. They are mentioned in the catechism, but we tend to forget them. Sin long-lived in, with no attempt to come out of it, affects us psychologically in two ways. It blinds the mind and it hardens the heart. The great truths of the faith seem empty and unreal, they lose their impact. A man just gives them notional assent. Even if they do run through the mind the will seems to be paralyzed and finds it very difficult to change. Our Lord said: "seeing they do not see, and hearing they do not hear, neither do they understand." The state of sin can almost become comfortable. People can almost get used to coexisting with guilt. Almost. Thank God for that "almost!" For when God no longer speaks to us or is no longer heard at all, that is a sad day.

In his "Rules for the Discernment of Spirits," St. Ignatius shrewdly observes how and when God speaks to us in contrast to the techniques the devil uses. As an observant psychologist, he noticed that: "In these persons who go from mortal sin to mortal sin, the enemy proposes to them apparent pleasures, making them imagine sensual delights and pleasure in order to hold them more and more and make them grow in their vices and sins. In these persons the good spirit uses the opposite method, pricking them and biting their consciences, through the process of reason."

This all goes into reverse when a person is trying to come out of sin. "In persons who are trying intensely to cleanse their sins and to rise from good to better in the service of God, our Lord, then it is the role of the evil spirit to bite, sadden, and put up obstacles, disquieting with false reasons, that one may not go on. It is proper to the good spirit to give courage, strength, consolations, inspirations, and quiet easing and putting away all obstacles, that one may go on in well doing." With this insight into something which we may have experienced, we can say that forewarned is forearmed in the battle with temptation!

But that the mind can be blinded and the heart hardened by sin was vividly dramatized for me by a sergeant I met overseas. He was tough. He was a leader. He was a Catholic. He called me "Father." He had not been to the sacraments in years and the men in his outfit knew it. When we had been alerted for overseas shipment, about two-thirds of the careless Catholics realistically and humbly shaped up and left the burden of their sins at the merciful feet of Christ. On the trip over—a man tends to become a believer when he faces the sea and the submarines in the cold, gray North Atlantic—another group of tough sinners came to confession. Enemy artillery brought in almost all of the remainder, with the exception of the sergeant. I finally appealed to him personally. "How about it? We all need God's mercy and time may be running out." He was obviously struggling with himself. He wanted mercy and needed it so badly. But, he kind of drew himself up and gritted out: "Do you think I'm going to crawl just because I'm afraid?" The best I could manage was: "A man on his knees before God saying, 'O God, be merciful to me a sinner,' is not crawling!" But his answer was a flat, sad, despairing, "No!"

For purposes of drama it would be very impressive if I said that shortly after this he was terribly wounded or that a sniper's bullet cut him down. But, as a matter of fact, he got through the war very nicely— nary a scratch. Possibly he is saying now, and I sincerely hope not: "Do you think I'm going to crawl when I'm not afraid?" As I recall the incident, I realize that even a tough sergeant cannot live long in sin without blinding his intellect and somehow justifying his condition. If you would translate his statement into basic English, it would be: "I am a sinner. I am not sorry. I will not ask forgiveness or mercy." But that is honesty and sin long dwelt in blinds the mind to truth. Instead he made impenitance into a virtue. He put a halo of bravery around it and declared himself courageous. "I'm not a coward. I don't crawl." Thus does sin harden the heart and darken the mind. Our Lord observed this in the people around Him and said: "with their ears they have been hard of hearing, and their eyes they have closed; lest at any time they see with their eyes, and hear with their ears, and understand with their mind, and be converted, and I heal them" (Matthew 13:15). Christ understood human nature and its struggle with pride, so He simply points to His Sacred Heart. To St. Margaret Mary and to us He says: "Behold this heart that has loved men so much. Sinners shall find in My Heart the source and infinite ocean of mercy." He doesn't argue with us; He simply says, "I love you." And so there is a prayer which is always and immediately answered. It is very brief, just eight words, "O God, be merciful to me, a sinner." This is not crawling. Try it! "O God,. . . . .

Continuing His description of hell, our Lord in Luke 16:19, tells a story. I think it is doubly effective because the situation is underplayed a little and there are human touches in it that make it seem so very real to us. He tells this story: "There was a certain rich man who used to clothe himself in purple and fine linen, and who feasted every day in splendid fashion. And there was a certain poor man, named Lazarus, who lay at his gate, covered with sores, and longing to be filled with the crumbs that fell from the rich man's table; even the dogs would come and lick his sores. And it came to pass that the poor man died and was borne away by the angels into Abraham's bosom; but the rich man also died and was buried in hell. And lifting up his eyes, being in torments, he saw Abraham afar off and Lazarus in his bosom. And he cried out and said, 'Father Abraham, have pity on me, and send Lazarus to dip the tip of his finger in water and cool my tongue, for I am tormented in this flame.' But Abraham said to him, 'Son, remember that thou in thy lifetime hast received good things, and Lazarus in like manner evil things; but now here he is comforted whereas thou art tormented. And besides all that, between us and you a great gulf is fixed, so that they who wish to pass over from this side to you cannot, and they cannot cross from your side to us.' And he said, 'Then, father, I beseech thee to send him to my father's house, for I have five brothers, that he may testify to them, lest they too come into this place of torments.' And Abraham said to him, 'They have Moses and the Prophets, let them harken to them.' But he answered, 'No, father Abraham, but if someone from the dead goes to them, they will repent.' But he said to him, 'If they do not harken to Moses and the Prophets, they will not believe even if someone rises from the dead.' " They'll say: "I think I saw a ghost: I must be imagining things." Or they might say: "Really, there can't be such a place. A good God couldn't do that." Or, "Do you think I'm going to crawl just because I am afraid?" The mind can be blinded and the heart can be hardened so that "even if someone rises from the dead" to tell them there *is* a hell, "they will not believe."

Also in connection with hell, our Lord speaks of darkness—eternal darkness. We know how we love the light, the sun, the bright days, and we know how overcast skies and long sleepless nights depress us. In jail, solitary confinement in the dark will break down the most hardened and stubborn criminal. In hell, there is eternal darkness and eternal lonesomeness. Our Lord speaks of "weeping and gnashing of teeth." These are some of the things that can be said of hell. One author described hell simply, "Hell is not to love anymore." Not to love God or the Blessed Virgin or our Divine Savior, not to love ourselves, anybody, anything; eternal hate which is the total perversion of a human being and a human heart—all-pervading hate. If we reflect on what Augustine remarked: "Our hearts were made for Thee, O God, and they will never be at rest until they rest in Thee," then there is eternal restlessness, eternal frustration. There is eternal knocking at a door that will not be opened, extending one's arms for an embrace and the answer coming: "I know you not. Depart from Me." These are the saddest words ever to be spoken in time or eternity by Christ to the ones for whom He died.

This is the essence of hell, to be without God for all eternity. He is infinite wisdom, beauty, goodness, and love. To be united with Him, to possess Him is the purpose of life. In hell, He is lost for all eternity. In this life we say: "My God and my all"; but if God is absent, we can fill in the emptiness with "things" and distract ourselves. However, when the soul is separated from the body and there are no distractions, we are vividly aware that God is all and that all is lost for all eternity. These are a few of the things that can be said about hell. I'm not going into it further.

One of the reasons for this brief treatment is that you can spend more time on it yourself if you wish. I know that when I make my own retreat, I go very lightly in this area. But the man I often make it with likes these meditations on hell, and as we finish one, he'll say: "Let's get another one. Let's get the Italian authors; they'll be really vivid. So vivid, you'll hear the screams and the yells and everything." My answer is, "Hell? No! It's not for me." I asked him what he gets out of it. I get petrified. "First of all," he said, "it makes me quite satisfied with the present state of things. This life at its worst is relatively comfortable. Even this type of weather we are having, (it was hot and humid) isn't as hot as hell. I find the thought of hell settles my discontent." Then he added: "It gives me zeal to work for others. Pasteur, seeing the torment in which people died from rabies, spent his life seeking a cure for the disease, and thought it worthwhile. If I could save one person, or be instrumental in keeping even one from hell, my life would be worthwhile." Then he made this interesting observation: "Look, there are different types of souls. There are different appeals. Some work under pressure, some don't. Some do better if there is a big stick in the picture, others don't need it. I often think about a couple of my nephews. One of them we call 'Old Iron Sides.' He is a little fellow and he is all bubbly and smiley. If you frown at him or shake your finger at him, he thinks you are playing a game and he smiles back, shaking his finger at you. But if you give him a whack on the rubber pants, then he moves along very nicely. He does much better with motivation from the rear. The other nephew is a sensitive little fellow. If you frown or show displeasure with him, that is enough to get him moving." My priest friend concluded, "I'm pretty much like 'Old Iron Sides.' With the kind of temperament I have, I do a little better with a big stick in the picture." So, depending on which you find more useful, spend a little more time or a little less time in this area. The fact that we don't overemphasize the "big stick" doesn't mean that hell doesn't exist; but for our purposes, it may not be too useful in getting closer to God, which is our purpose in all things.

Hell is a mystery. There is no question about that. And it does present a difficulty, often proposed, for which we need some kind of answer. You will hear people wonder: "If God is the all-good, merciful, loving Father which you claim He is, how could He possibly do this to His child, no matter what His child would do?" The implication is that if He would do it, He is not an all-merciful and loving Father. I believe that is putting the question the wrong way. It's a loaded question, like asking: "Have you stopped beating your wife?" If you say "No," then the answer comes: "Well, stop it." If you say "Yes," then the next question is: "Why did you beat her in the first place." Hell is not so much God rejecting man, as man with his freedom rearing back and saying to

God: "I don't want You." For example, the sun is shining and it is warm and bright. Anyone who wishes to can go out and enjoy its health-giving rays. However, since we are free agents we can also choose to live in a cave. If we hide ourselves away in that fashion, we will grow sick and anemic, even though the sun is still there, warm and bright. So, also, God is infinite love, mercy, forgiveness, always and forever. He does not change. He keeps on saying, "Please come to me." But we can say, "No." He can, over a period of time, urge, beg us to reconsider; but if we insist He says: "I respect your freedom, I will not violate it. I reluctantly accept your decision. I will not force you to love Me, for that would not be love." So it is not the good, merciful God rejecting man; it is man rejecting God and putting himself outside the range of God's mercy and love. That is why I think the nuns who taught me had a very wise emphasis. In their trusting way, they were sure that you had to work pretty hard at going to hell, otherwise God in His infinite mercy and goodness was going to save you. "Since He died for us," one nun reasoned, "He does not want His blood to have been shed in vain."

Human weakness and God's mercy

The second part of this meditation is much more important because it is a consideration of God's mercy. "His mercy is above all His works." As we study this attribute of God, we are getting a little closer to understanding God. "God is love," St. John reassures us. That love for us, in this life, is shown chiefly by His patience with us, His forebearance, and His infinite mercy. I can safely say that though Christ mentioned hell a number of times, the emphasis on mercy in both Old and New Testaments far outweighs the emphasis on justice and punishment. His mercy is written large there on many, many pages. If we miss that we are missing the message that God has given to us: man's thoughtless sinfulness and God's infinite mercy.

An added reason for spending some time on mercy is that there are a lot of good people who go through life under a little cloud of anxiety. They are forever going back over the past, weighing and reconsidering. They spend hours probing and picking away at their consciences, trying to reconstruct past acts and judge their guilt. This activity robs them of peace of mind. It is unproductive, futile, and totally negative. They are like the man in "Little Abner," with the thunder-cloud over his head. Wherever he goes buildings fall down, lightning strikes, clouds burst, people drop into sewers, and so on. Joy in living is gone. So these people who are doing their poor best to serve God keep forever anxious. Has God really forgiven me? Was I truly sorry? Now this can be, and often is, a slight anxiety neurosis, a compulsive doubt, or both which shows up in the area of religion. But regardless of the nature and origin of the anxiety, dwelling on God's fatherly mercy is helpful and a powerful antidote to anxiety. God reassuringly asks us: "Can a woman forget her infant, so as not to have pity on the son of her womb? And if she should forget, yet will not I forget thee. Behold, I have graven thee in my hands" (Isaias 49:15-16).

Then, there is the other type of person who does not actually worry about the past but feels that past sins, though forgiven, stand between him and a close friendship with God. How can I draw close to God? Look at what I have done in the past! I have broken every commandment in the book—many times. The record is too bad. It's too late. "Too late have I known Thee." Both of these attitudes, the anxiety and the crippling, corroding sense of guilt, do God's mercy an injustice! So, just as we listened to Christ talk about hell, let us listen to Him talk about mercy.

Our Lord was talking to a group of people on the street corner one day, while the Pharisees, with their hostile eyes, stood on the outskirts of the crowd criti-cizing. "Now the publicans and sinners were drawing near to him to listen to him. And the Pharisees and the Scribes murmured, saying, 'This man welcomes sinners and eats with them.'" (Luke 15, 1-2). They probably figured: "He can't be God; He's nice to these sinners." Our Lord, knowing their thoughts, corrected them and perhaps us. He told them a story which is the world's best short story. From a technical viewpoint it is a masterpiece; there isn't a word out of place. As far as content goes, it emphasizes a truth which men most need to hear over and over again. Our Lord said to them, and He says to us: "A certain man had two sons. And the younger of them said to his father, 'Father, give me the share of the property that falls to me.' And he divided his means between them. And not many days later, the younger son gathered up all his wealth, and took his journey into a far country; and there he squandered his fortune in loose living. And after he had spent all, there came a grievous famine over that country, and he began himself to suffer want. And he went and joined one of the citizens of that country, who sent him to his farm to feed swine. And he longed to fill himself with the pods that the swine were eating, but no one offered to give them to him.

"But when he came to himself, he said, 'How many hired men in my father's house have bread in abundance, while I am perishing here with hunger! I will get up and go to my father, and will say to him, Father, I have sinned against heaven and before thee. I am no longer worthy to be called thy son; make me as one of thy hired men.' And he arose and went to his father.

"But while he was yet a long way off, his father saw him and was moved with compassion, and ran and fell upon his neck and kissed him. And the son said to him, 'Father, I have sinned against heaven and before thee. I am no longer worthy to be called thy son.' But the father said to his servants, 'Fetch quickly the best robe and put it on him, and give him a ring for his finger and sandals for his feet; and bring out the fattened calf and kill it, and let us eat and make merry; because this my son was dead, and has come to life again; he was lost, and is found.' And they began to make merry.

"Now his elder son was in the field; and as he came and drew near to the house, he heard music and dancing. And calling one of the servants he inquired what this meant. And he said to him, 'Thy brother has come, and thy father has killed the fattened calf, because he has got him back safe.' But he was angered and would not go in.

"His father, therefore, came out and began to entreat him. But he answered and said to his father, 'Behold, these many years I have been serving thee, and have never transgressed one of thy commands; and yet thou hast never given me a kid that I might make merry with my friends. But when this thy son comes, who has devoured his means with harlots, thou hast killed for him the fattened calf.'

"But he said to him, 'Son, thou art always with me, and all that is mine is thine; but we were bound to make merry and rejoice, for this thy brother was dead, and has come to life; he was lost, and is found' " (Luke 15:11 ff.).

Now, that is our Lord's story about how God, our Father, and He Himself feel when we are away from Him. We know that unhappiness and misery, perhaps only too well, but we may forget God's attitude, both while we are away and as we turn to come back home. We may protest: "Not a son, but a servant"; but always the answer is: "Bring hither the finest robe, a ring for his finger, shoes for his feet, be glad, rejoice!" We are always restored to the fullness of sonship, sharing again in the divine nature. It might be interesting just to kind of overwhelm ourselves by considering a few facts: When we commit a mortal sin, we lose our sanctifying grace! Now we might think that we are totally bankrupt, that we will have to start all over again from scratch. Even this would be a great mercy. But instead, when we come back, we're given the sanctifying grace we had before, with an additional amount because we've made a new act of sorrow and received the sacrament of penance with the increase of sanctifying grace that accompanies it. So we are back in business with a bonus. His mercy is above all His works!

But the human mind is tricky and we might say: "Surely, God would forgive the Prodigal, but not me. When I sin, I sin a little differently. There's malice in my sins. I know what I'm doing, so mercy doesn't quite extend to me. Then when I'm sorry, it's a mixed emotion. As many little children mistakenly say: 'O

My God, I am *partly* sorry for having offended Thee.'
That's the way I am." This type of mind can argue
that the story of the Prodigal Son is just a story and
question what Christ would do if He were faced with
a sinner. What if the sin were personal and embarras-
sing and shameful? Wouldn't there be a certain cool-
ness, contempt, aloofness, at least, on Christ's part?
We have the opportunity of seeing our Lord put to
this test. "And at daybreak he came again into the
temple, and all the people came to him; and sitting
down he began to teach them. Now the Scribes and
Pharisees brought a woman caught in adultery, and
setting her in the midst, said to him, 'Master, this
woman has just now been caught in adultery. And in
the Law Moses commanded us to stone such persons.
What, therefore, dost thou say?' Now they were saying this to test him, in order that they might be able
to accuse him. But Jesus, stooping down, began to
write with his finger on the ground." Commentators
say that either He was jotting down the sins of some
of these men so eager to condemn, or He was showing
His lack of interest, the way we scribble or play with
paper when someone is carrying on an uninteresting
conversation. "But when they continued asking him,
he raised himself and said to them, 'Let him who is
without sin among you be the first to cast a stone at
her.' And again stooping down, he began to write on
the ground. But hearing this, they went away, one by
one, beginning with the eldest. And Jesus remained
alone, with the woman standing in the midst.

"And Jesus, raising himself, said to her, 'Woman,
where are they? Has no one condemned thee?' She
said, 'No one, Lord.' Then Jesus said, 'Neither will I
condemn thee. Go thy way, and from now on sin no
more' " (John 8:2 ff.). In the whole incident can you
notice any coldness or contempt? You might say:
"There is the immaculate Son of God, and there is a
woman fresh from her sin. Wouldn't He shrink?" Instead there is protection, understanding, forgiveness—
all freely offered, and the gentle reminder: "Go thy
way, and from now on sin no more." Our Lord told a
story of forgiveness and mercy, and when He was
faced with the actual situations in His own lifetime

on earth, or is faced with them today in the 1960's, His reaction is always the same. This, I think, should wipe out the misconception that God does not forgive sins. Some people say, "I'll never forgive myself." The answer to this is: "If God does, why won't you? He has better judgment."

Now let us correct that other false notion that our sins, though forgiven, stand as an obstacle between us and God. The following incidents in our Lord's life should destroy that misconception, I think. There was a man whom we could describe as having received the finest Catholic education. He had three years of intense training, and was taken aside for special instruction by Christ Himself. Miracles were worked to confirm his faith. As we watch this man we are drawn to him. He is that mixture of love and courage and strength blended with weakness which goes to make up most of us. We see him in the garden defending our Lord with a sword, even though he is outnumbered ten to one. Our Lord pointed out that He did not need this type of defense when "Simon Peter therefore, having a sword, drew it and struck the servant of the high priest and cut off his right ear" (John 18:10). But Jesus said to Peter: "Put back thy sword into its place . . . dost thou suppose that I cannot entreat my Father, and he will even now furnish me with more than twelve legions of angels?" (Matthew 26:52-53)

Observing this, we admire Peter for his well-intentioned courage and loyalty. However, a short time later a change has come over Peter. His courage is gone and his heart is heavy with fear. He feels all alone. Christ is on trial within. The cause seems lost. A brief time before he had fought off the soldiers but now, ironically, he will deny Christ under the questioning of a servant girl. "Now the servants and attendants were standing at a coal fire and warming themselves, for it was cold. And Peter also was with them, standing and warming himself" (John 18:18). "And while Peter was below in the courtyard, there came one of the maidservants of the high priest; and seeing Peter warming himself, she looked closely at him and said, 'Thou also wast with Jesus of Nazareth.'

But he denied it, saying, 'I neither know nor understand what thou art saying.' And he went outside into the vestibule; . . . And the maidservant, seeing him again, began to say to the bystanders, 'This is one of them.' But again he denied it. And after a little while the bystanders again said to Peter, 'Surely thou art one of them, for thou art also a Galilean.' But he began to curse and to swear: 'I do not know this man you are talking about' " (Mark 14:66 ff.). This was the man he had lived with for three years. This was the man he had defended a few hours before. Humanly speaking, we might say that Peter had lost all right to Christ's friendship. Certainly there would be no close association after this. Here was a critical situation. A friend should stand strong—at the very least acknowledge acquaintanceship.

Although Peter failed—not once, but three times— in this test of friendship, our Lord never rebuked him. Instead He gave him a glance full of loving forgiveness the next time they met, when Christ was being led through the courtyard, alone and friendless, on His way to the cross. He referred to the triple denial only once, implicitly, some days later after His resurrection. The friends met once more on a seashore, and appropriately enough there was a fire, but this scene was one of joy. "When, therefore, they had landed, they saw a fire ready, and a fish laid upon it, and bread. Jesus said to them, 'Bring here some of the fishes that you caught just now.' " When they had finished breakfast Jesus said to Simon Peter (significantly three times): " 'Simon, son of John, dost thou love Me?' Peter was grieved because he said to him for the third time, 'Dost thou love me?' And he said to him, 'Lord, thou knowest all things, thou knowest that I love thee' " (John 21:9 ff.). It was then that our Lord confirmed him as head of His Church, His first vicar on earth. "Feed my lambs, feed my sheep." The man who denied Him three times He made His first vicar on earth! Our Lord was teaching us that forgiven past sins do not stand between us and close association with Him.

If we have any further doubts, recall Mary Magdalene who, according to one strong tradition, was a woman of sin. Yet she was the one who stood shoulder to shoulder with Christ's immaculate mother under the foot of the cross. We always associate the two Mary's, Mary Immaculate and Mary Magdalene. And it was to Mary Magdalene that our Lord appeared first on Easter Sunday morning, after having visited His own mother. Many of the saints are "retreads"; men and women who failed and learned to love humbly, penitently, gratefully. Peter, himself. Doubting Thomas. St. Paul, persecutor of the early church, a vessel of election who said: "It is now no longer I that live, but Christ lives in me." St. Augustine. Go down the list sometime to convince yourself that forgiven sin is not an obstacle. "His mercy is above all His works."

And notice, too, how God can draw good out of evil, virtue out of vice. From sin we can become humble or discouraged. This discouragement is self-centered. "I have failed. I'm no good. I can't do it. I quit." Humility is God-centered. "I have failed. I am weak. I am very dependent upon God, so I will stay close to Him. I must, or I will fail again. 'With His strength I shall win. We two!' " From sin we can draw abiding sorrow for sin or a corrosive sense of guilt. The latter, again, is self-centered. "How could I do such a thing? I'm terribly disappointed in myself. I will never forget and forgive myself." This is egocentric. Abiding sorrow for sin is gentle, peace-giving, and God-centered. "O God, be merciful to me, a sinner. I cast myself entirely on Your mercy, and though I have sinned Your mercy is above all Your works. Confidently I entrust myself, with all my sins, imperfection, and weakness to Your loving kindness."

But man, so vividly aware of his sinfulness, is slow to be convinced of God's mercy. So, if you don't mind another convincer, here is one taken from a Cleveland newspaper. A murder took place in Cleveland on New Year's day. Harold Beach, twenty-three, made advances toward eight-year-old Sheila Ann Turley. When the young girl resisted him, he stabbed her with a small kitchen knife, seven times in the back and the head. The attacker fled; the girl crawled to the porch of a nearby house and clawed at the window. No one was home. Sheila fell exhausted on the porch and died. The killer was captured and sentenced to death. The story of what happened in the death chamber was told by Harold Beaufait, a staff writer for the Cleveland *News*.

"Death is a time for prayers. I realized that with sickening force last night, when I saw Harold Beach electrocuted for the murder of eight-year-old Sheila Ann Turley. The small electrocution chamber in Ohio's crumbling penitentiary was as full of prayers as a funeral parlor is crowded with flowers. Walking upright and calm, the last dozen steps to the chair, Beach was as bolstered by prayer, as a scarecrow is held up by its rigid props. Beach died clinging desperately to the last syllable of a 'Hail Mary.' I had the impression that every one present in that close, severe room, its walls lined with the photographs of the two hundred and sixty-two persons who had preceded Beach to the chair, would have collapsed without their individual appeals to God. Beach's hands were folded in front of him. They held a large wooden cross. With the priest at his side, he walked slowly toward the awkward, waiting chair, repeating the Lord's prayer 'Our Father, who art in heaven . . . forgive us our trespasses.' Beach completed the Lord's prayer as he seated himself in the chair. The priest reached over and took the wooden cross: 'Hail Mary, blessed art thou among women, pray for us sinners, now, and at the hour of our death,' Beach said the words clearly. Next was the act of contrition: 'O my God, I am sorry, I confess my sins.' Beach was breathless and nearly shouting. A deputy pressed a button. Beach jerked. The prayers of the living continued. Beach's hands clenched on the arms of the chair. From his left hand dangled a rosary."

This is not the whole story however. Beach was a Catholic when he died; he did not grow up in the faith. Another murderer had influenced him to become a Catholic. Robert Daniels had been condemned to death for triple murder, and while awaiting execution he became a Catholic. He went to the electric chair saying over and over: "Most Sacred Heart of Jesus, I place my trust in Thee." Before he died, he told Harold Beach about Christ and the infinite mercy of His Sacred Heart. A triple murderer teaching a single murderer to say with love and trust and confidence, "Most Sacred Heart of Jesus, I place my trust in Thee." And we think possibly that God's forgiveness does not reach out to our sins—as though finite sin could exhaust infinite mercy.

Now God's mercy is there and we should dwell on it often and long. But we don't want to abuse God's mercy for ourselves because it cost Him so dearly. He took the scourging, the crowning with thorns, and the crucifixion, while he leaves us the Our Fathers and the Hail Marys to say. However we might abuse God's mercy for other people, God is always looking for any reason to give a man a last grace and a last help; and we can be the instruments of that saving grace.

This was brought home to me in the Jesuit novitiate. You have a lot of K.P. to do there—you wash the windows, sweep the floors, do your own housekeeping. On one occasion I had charge, a tremendous responsibility, of the little spoons (teaspoons). You collect five hundred little spoons; wash five hundred little spoons; and put five hundred little spoons back in their places. The novice master calls you over every once in a while to ask if you are happy and to see how you are doing. Well, these teaspoons were on my mind. I told him I was doing fine and was happy, but the little spoons were getting me down. I was kidding a little. "There's no future in them," I said. "Well," he answered, "I see it is a job you don't like. Did it ever occur to you that you could offer that up for the dying? Insurance companies estimate that every time I raise and lower my hand somewhere in the world someone is dying—about one a second." He added: "God is looking for a chance to give them a last grace. Your little sacrifice could win that grace for them."

I thought that was a pretty good idea, so as I went around putting each spoon down I said to myself: "There is another one dead, there is another one dead, there is another one dead." At least I had a motive for doing a monotonous job. I wondered, too, if there was any truth to this statement of his.

Later, as a priest, I had an opportunity to see God's mercy at work in extraordinary ways on many occasions. This one incident convinced me that God would accept even little spoons to save souls. I was chaplain in a hospital for a couple of months. A young girl was brought in who had taken an overdose of sleeping tablets. The background of her life was a little sordid; she had run away from home, was pregnant out of marriage, and had sought an answer to her problems with the sleeping pills. The doctor said to me: "Father, I am pumping enough stuff into her to make her jump out of bed, but I don't think she's going to come around." After about twenty minutes her eyes fluttered open. I leaned down and said, "I am a Catholic priest." She gasped pleadingly, "Anoint me." I gave her quick absolution, anointed her, and in about five minutes she shuddered, went black, and died. These brief moments of consciousness were very important.

The next day her mother came to claim her body. She told me: "My girl was a good girl. She ran away from home, but I know she was good." And I was happy to be able to tell her that her daughter had received the last sacraments and had died peacefully. The mother added: "I've always been praying for her, but yesterday [the day her daughter died] I offered some special prayers for her. I was worried about her." You may not be able to prove this scientifically to a doubter, but to me this mother's prayers obtained the grace that this girl needed for a happy death. God is willing and eager to reach out another grace to anybody and everybody on request, personal or otherwise. So, devotion to the dying is a very apostolic work. Your prayers, sacrifices, and your little spoons can save souls.

At Mass we can remember those who are to die this day, and when we have an unpleasant task to perform we can offer it up for those who are dying while we are doing it. It is good to remember, too, that it is not only the unpleasant things and duties that are meritorious, but also the pleasant things. True, sacrifice and the cross are the test for love, but pleasant things are also meritorious. We can even offer a coke for the dying. Christianity doesn't essentially mean a religion of pain, a cult of the difficult. It is human living, pleasing and acceptable in God's sight. Like St. Theresa, we may say on occasion: "I'll take these delicious grapes for the greater glory of God!"

One final point, the only prayer of petition which I know is always answered is a simple, eight-word prayer. It is: "O God, be merciful to me a sinner." We have our Lord's word for it. He said of the publican who first said it, " . . . this man went back to his home justified."

Blessed Claude de la Colombiere, S.J., St. Margaret Mary's confessor and a great apostle of the Sacred Heart, expressed this confidence in God's mercy most eloquently: "My God, I am so convinced that You keep watch over those who hope in You, and that we can want for nothing when we look for all from You, that I am resolved in the future to live free from every care, and to turn over all my anxieties to You. 'In peace, in the selfsame, I will sleep and I will rest; for Thou, O Lord, singularly hast settled me in hope.' Men may deprive me of possessions and of honor; sickness may strip me of strength and the means of serving You; I may even lose Your grace by sin; but I shall never lose my hope. I shall keep it till the last moment of my life; and at that moment all the demons in hell shall strive to tear it from me in vain. 'In peace, in the selfsame, I will sleep and I will rest.' Others may look for happiness from their wealth or their talents; others may rest on the innocence of their life, or the severity of their penance, or the amount of their alms, or the fervor of their prayers. 'Thou, O Lord, singularly hast settled me in hope.' As for me, Lord, all my confidence is my confidence itself. This confidence has never deceived anyone. No one, no one has hoped in the Lord and has been confounded.

"I am sure, therefore, that I shall be eternally happy, since I firmly hope to be, and because it is from You, O God, that I hope for it. 'In Thee, O Lord, have I hoped; let me never be confounded.' I know alas! I know only too well, that I am weak and unstable. I know what temptation can do against the strongest virtue. I have seen the stars of heaven fall, and the pillars of the firmament; but that cannot frighten me. So long as I continue to hope, I shall be sheltered from all misfortune; and I am sure of hoping always, since I hope also for this unwavering hopefulness.

"Finally, I am sure that I cannot hope too much in You, and that I cannot receive less than I have hoped for from You. So I hope that You will hold me safe on the steepest slopes, that You will sustain me against the most furious assaults, and that You will make my weakness triumph over my most fearful enemy. I hope that You will love me always, and that I too shall love You without ceasing. To carry my hope once and for all as far as it can go, I hope from You to possess You, O my Creator, in time and in eternity. Amen."

The prayers for morning or evening, depending on how you are pacing yourself, are found in the last chapter. Keep up the good work of the retreat. If possible get to Mass and Holy Communion tomorrow and don't forget the little meditation which follows.

Do it yourself!

Points for your prayerful thinking (15 minutes)

PREPARATORY PRAYER
See page 18.

In case of emergency

1 Hell is a study in failure.
  One who has failed to accomplish his mission in life. Fear of hell is a motive to draw on in times of emergency. Zeal to save others from this. Everlasting fire—where the worm dieth not—lost opportunities—weeping and gnashing of teeth. My God and my all, lost for all eternity. "Depart from me you cursed."

2 His mercy is above all His works:

Prodigal son	Woman taken in adultery	Peter's denial	Judas's mistake	Good thief

87

3 But we do not take advantage of this mercy (except for the dying and for others).
   He took the scourging and the crucifixion and left us the Our Fathers and Hail Marys to say.

4 I shall never lose my hope and my confidence.
   "Most Sacred Heart of Jesus I place my trust in Thee."

Conclude by saying one Our Father, a Hail Mary, and Glory Be to the Father.

◆◆◆◆◆◆◆◆◆◆◆◆

The next chapter is a practical instruction on the sacrament of penance—how to use the confessional more effectively. At a time of retreat it is useful to go over our routine religious practices, to enrich them. Now the sacrament of penance can be received following a brief formula that has a tendency to seem trite to the penitent. But with a little attention the routine: "Bless me, father," can bring so much relief, security, and grace that it well deserves the title the sacrament of peace.

I remember when I was student counselor at Loyola University we provided a confessional, for the convenience of the students, with a door opening on the main corridor. It was a kind of "drive-in" confessional, and it seemed to be very well patronized. But one student, after attending classes in the building for four years, said to me in surprise: "Is that a confessional? I always thought it was a fire-escape door." I couldn't resist the obvious temptation to say: "You're right. That's exactly what it is—a fire-escape door." But as you will see, it should also be a doorway to peace.

Bless me, Father,
for I have sinned

It was about five o'clock in the evening and I was sitting at the bar in the officer's club—drinking a coke, believe it or not. That isn't why I remember the incident so vividly, but it did provide the occasion for a question and a little religious discussion. A question generally begins with: "Padre, I always admired the Catholic Church, but . . ." That "but" is then followed by an objection, a barbed criticism, or a sincere inquiry.

So there I was, drinking a coke, and a colonel at the end of the bar asked: "Would you care for a beer, Padre? Have one on me." "No thanks," I said, "I'm saying Mass in a couple of hours and that means no alcohol right now." "You do have rules, don't you?" he observed matter-of-factly. "Yes, we do, and I think you'll agree that you need some rules if there's going to be order and discipline." "Right, Padre, right," nodded the colonel. "But let me ask you a question. I've always admired the Catholic Church— now don't be offended—people confess their sins to you, don't they? But do you really think you can forgive sins? I never could understand that."

Everybody at the bar looked at me. "Before I answer, Colonel, may I ask you a few questions— a typical Irish trick?" "Fire away," he said, and I began. "Do you believe and hold that the Bible, the four Gospels, are the written word of God?" "Why, yes," he said, "in fact I read it a bit. I always have. I don't go to church much, but now and then I do read the Bible. It's a good book; my folks always had one in the house."

"Good," I said. "Now, from your reading do you believe and hold that Christ is God become man?"

"Well—uh—well—He is the Son of God." "Let me put it a little more clearly and definitely, Colonel. Is He God become man? Yes or No? Can you say to Christ, 'My Lord and My God' as Thomas did?" "Yes," he admitted, slowly, thoughtfully, "I guess I'd say that. I'm a Christian." "Well, then, what do you make out of this? Christ, who you say is God, said to His apostles—it's right there in the Gospel of St. John, in your King James version too—'As the Father has sent me, I also send you.' Then He breathed on them and said: 'Receive the Holy Spirit; whose sins you shall forgive, they are forgiven them; and whose sins you shall retain, they are retained.' What do you make out of that? Could these men, mere men, remember, forgive sins after Christ said to them: 'Whose sins you shall forgive, they are for-given them'?" There was a long pause. "Y-e-s, I guess you would have to say that." He could see where it was leading and he didn't like the possibilities, but he was fair-minded. "Yes, they could. I guess you would have to say that."

"Then it isn't absurd, it isn't unthinkable that a mere man could forgive sins in the name of God?" I urged. "It has happened at least once in history, hasn't it? And Christ set it up?" "Yes, but . . ." "Well, I won't go into the fact now that I am a legitimately ordained Catholic priest and that power has been given to me through ordination. But, I can forgive sins in the name of God."

A couple of Catholics at the bar relaxed and breathed a sigh of relief. But the colonel still didn't look too convinced. There may have been a thought lurking in his mind that went something like: "I'm a colonel, and I can't forgive sins, so how can a mere captain forgive sins?" But at that point one of the other officers at the bar said: "Well, that's fine for you Catholics, but what do we Protestants do? Just go through life with a big bag of sins on our shoul-ders?" and he hunched over like a burglar carrying off a heavy bag full of loot. Everyone laughed. "Well, if you're smart," I said, "you'll join the Catholic Church and enjoy the peace that confession brings. But, if you can't see your way to that, come around to my room some time and I'll show you how to make an act of perfect contrition for your sins. That will take care of you in your present condition. And, by the way," I added, for general consumption, since I felt they were listening, "our Lord knew what He was doing when He instituted that sacrament. It's good psychology. Any psychiatrist will tell you that it is good for mental health to ventilate guilt feelings once in a while. It eases the burden."

Allowing a mere man to forgive sins in His name is not such an extraordinary thing for God to do. As we watch His dealings with men, we observe that He is always giving men a vote of confidence by entrusting some of His powers to them and giving them a work to do. He created the universe and set the planets spinning. Man, made in His image and likeness, imitates Him by sending Explorers and Sputniks into orbit, making a miniature, man-made universe. God is the author of life. To men and women He gives a share in His creative power so that they can cooperate in bringing new life into this world. That is the dignity of parenthood. It is also to men that He entrusts the administration of His sacraments that bring spiritual life into this world. "Go into the whole world and preach the gospel to every creature"; "baptizing them in the name of the Father, and of the Son, and of the Holy Spirit"; "This is my body. This is my blood. Do this in remembrance of me"; "As the Father has sent me, I also send you"; ". . . whose sins you shall forgive, they are forgiven them; and whose sins you shall retain, they are retained"; in each case God is using mere men, with all their limitations and shortcomings, to do a work for Him. He has established the law of mutual dependence on one another in every area of life—physical, intellectual, spiritual—so it is not too surprising that He has entrusted to men the power to forgive sins in His name.

At a time of retreat it is useful to look over some of our routine religious duties in order to give them deeper meaning and make them more fruitful. Since confession is one of those duties, we might spend a little time on it. It might be helpful, too, for those who are not familiar with the Catholic practice of confession. Notice that when Christ communicated the power to forgive sins, it was a twofold power: to forgive the sins or to retain the sins. Now if that power is to be exercised intelligently, the priest cannot go down the street and say arbitrarily: "All of you people on the sunny side of the street—your sins are forgiven—except you with the mustache. And all of you on the shady side of the street, your sins are retained." That would be silly. The only way the priest can know if you have sinned and if you need and want forgiveness is for you to tell him what you've done. You are the only one who knows what sins you have committed. I am the only one who knows mine. We have to tell on ourselves. So the first part of confession is the examination of conscience. The penitent looks over his actions and determines what sins he has committed and to what extent he is guilty and declares himself to be sorry.

The sacrament of penance is meant to be a very simple sacrament because it is designed for the use of people from seven to seventy, with degrees of intelligence ranging from the low-grade moron to the genius. Anything which is to be used by such a varied group of people can't be complicated. It has to be something almost as simple as walking, or all these different people won't be able to do it.

What are the sins, then, that we must look for and confess? Only mortal sins must be confessed, according to the exact name and number of times the sin has been committed. This reminds me of the missionary priest who was driving that point home in one of his sermons. "You have to tell mortal sins according to name and number. Remember, name and number, name and number." In the confessional that same night when he heard: "My name is John P. Smith, 9494 Albion," he couldn't quite decide whether he had been misunderstood or was being gently ribbed for beating the obvious to death. The point is that the names and numbers of the mortal sins must be given, not your own name and mailing address. This should be easy. You can't commit a mortal sin without knowing it. It is impossible because three things are required. There must be serious matter; sufficient reflection—so that I know it is serious—and full consent of the will. I must be acting as a conscious, free agent in a serious matter, or else I am not guilty before God of mortal sin.

You can't commit a mortal sin when you are half asleep. You have to perform a complete, human act. So to those who say: "I don't know whether I committed a mortal sin, or not," the answer is: "Then you didn't." There has to be certain knowledge. Our psychology professor said that mortal sin, for a person who is trying to be good, is like having a lion lurking in your room. You don't say, "Maybe there is a lion lurking in this room." The lion is there or he isn't. If a lion is present you would be quite aware of him lashing his tail, padding up and down, growling, making his presence felt. It's very difficult to hide a lion in the living room. It is also difficult to be unaware that you have committed a mortal sin.

Here is a helpful rule of thumb—not a complete catalog of sins—in answer to the question: "What are the more common areas of sin where serious matter is involved?" The big ones are contained in the Ten Commandments and, for Catholics, in the laws of the Church. Just to indicate how simple the examination of conscience can be, let's take a brief glance at both lists. For Catholics, there is the obligation of attending Mass on Sundays and holydays of obligation. This means that I could have gone to Mass without considerable inconvenience, and I chose not to go. If there is considerable inconvenience I am not obligated. Each one is ordinarily the best judge of that, because considerable inconvenience is a relative matter. For example an older person, say seventy years old, living eight blocks from the church might find it considerably inconvenient to get to church on a snowy Sunday. A teen-ager, very likely, would not find it that inconvenient. The seventy-year-old would not be obliged to go, the teen-ager would. Each decides for himself, and when in doubt he should consult a priest.

Sinning by eating meat on Friday means that I could have abstained from meat without considerable inconvenience to myself or others, and I chose to eat meat. An example of considerable inconvenience in a social situation would be where the hostess, forgetting the Friday obligation, would be quite embarrassed because she had prepared meat. This would occasion considerable inconvenience to her, so we are at liberty to eat meat if we so desire. No sin. Now, for those who are anxious and want to take along their chemistry set to test whether the soup listed as "vegetable" might have a trace of meat in it, they might recall that the law of Friday abstinence can be violated venially. Suppose, even deliberately and for no reason at all, I took a bite out of a hot dog. That would be venial. I bring out this point merely to allay the anxiety of those who scrupulously worry about mortal sin in this matter, the "soup scrups." In regard to the law of Friday abstinence in general, it is useful to recall that Christ died for us on Friday. We abstain from meat on that day. There isn't much proportion between being crucified and abstaining from meat, but it does show a little good will and appreciation on our part and keeps the spirit of penance and discipline in our lives.

To move into the area of purity, the sixth and ninth commandments are called the difficult commandments simply because everyone finds them difficult. But the sins here are pretty clean-cut and definite. For single people there would be fornication —sexual relations between unmarried persons; adultery—if a married person is involved; passionate kisses, embraces, impure touches, self-abuse, or masturbation. There is obscene entertainment and reading. For married people there would be adultery—involving someone other than the married partners —and some form of birth control. Then there are areas of perversion, homosexuality, etc. These are best treated individually under the direction of an understanding and skilled confessor. This covers the main external acts in regard to sex. There are other mortal sins, but these are the obvious ones. It could be safely said that an adult could hardly commit any of these sins without being aware of it. The chief doubts, questions, and confusions arise in regard to impure thoughts, desires, and to what constitutes passionate kissing. So, for the sake of clarity, we can take those up in a later chapter which will offer some practical suggestions on handling temptations relative to the sixth and ninth commandments.

Continuing with our rule of thumb, we come to the violations of justice. Serious injustice is involved in stealing considerable amounts of money, or participating in business transactions which are obviously unjust and involve large amounts of money, or the wanton destruction of property. Further problems in the area of justice should be taken up individually with a confessor. Then there is perjury in a law court, calling upon God to witness to the truth of what you are saying under oath and then telling a lie. In the area of violence, there is abortion and the serious abuse of the person of another without sufficient cause. There is also serious matter involved in the area of charity if we reveal the serious sins of another without sufficient cause or knowingly and falsely attribute serious sins to another person. Lastly, there is drunkenness, a serious sin in which the higher faculties of intellect and will are suspended.

Having a few too many, in itself, would be a venial sin. For example, one man in describing his New Year's Eve experience said: "I'd been drinking pretty heavily, but thank God I was getting home safely. However," he added sadly, "I was just rounding the last turn home when somebody stepped on my knuckles." He knew where home was and one way of getting there. He was not theologically drunk, that is there was no mortal sin. Admittedly he wasn't putting his best foot forward. If excessive drinking were the cause of other sins, such as extreme and violent quarrels, adultery, heavy petting, endangering the lives of others, serious neglect of the duties of a state of life, and if one knew that these serious sins invariably followed excessive drinking, it could be serious matter. Intemperate drinking, which is a proximate occasion of sin, must be avoided. I think it can be said without exaggeration that along with a nagging, biting tongue, excessive drinking is the most consistent and persistent source of unhappiness, unrest, and embarrassment in family living. The sharp, intemperate tongue and the excessive drinker, both, keep everybody edgy and put a question mark over every social gathering; yet neither of them would be classified as mortally sinful in itself.

Now in regard to venial sins, we don't have to tabulate them at all, if we don't want to. Venial sins do not even have to be confessed. But if we choose, we can confess them in a general way, such as: "It is three weeks since my last confession. I have a habit of using God's name irreverently; I have a habit of telling little lies; I have a habit of being irritable and impatient"; or specifically, such as: "I told three lies, got angry twice, was a little intemperate in drinking three times." We may choose certain venial sins to confess and deliberately omit others. In fact some confessors recommend that instead of a long bill of lading, we might pick out one or two areas to concentrate on, thereby working toward improvement in a restricted area. In this way we are more likely to improve than if we try to cover the whole water front with a vague statement, "I'll be good."

We can see that undue preoccupation with the recital of faults is a limited and negative attitude toward confession. It is good to recall that penance is a sacrament and that confession is only a part of that sacrament of penance. Every time we receive this sacrament of penance, there is an increase of sanctifying grace and added actual graces are given to take care of day to day needs. So the examination of conscience and listing of sins should be a rather simple thing—mortal according to name and number; venial, not at all, in a general way, or specifically. For a more complete examination of conscience that might be useful, turn to the back of the book. What I am giving here is a "rule of thumb."

Some people say worriedly: "My confessions are pretty much the same year after year, month after month. They aren't even interesting." This is rather to be expected and should not be a cause for worry because, after gross sins are eliminated and fully deliberate venial sins diminished (as they often are when one is happy and settled in a way of life), the sins that will crop up are temperamental faults and occupational sins. People dealing constantly with small children, the sick, and the senile will very likely be irritable, edgy, impatient. Those in authority will be tempted to become somewhat impatient, dogmatic, arbitrary in their decisions. Those who are subject to authority will be tempted to unfair criticism of those in authority and to undue complaining and resentment. Probably none of us measures up to the law of charity and we all fail especially in the area of speech. "If anyone does not offend in word, he is a perfect man" (James 3:2).

In addition to these samples of occupational hazards, there are faults which generally accompany a given temperament which otherwise has many good qualities. Temperament-wise, for example, those who are gentle and sensitive and understanding may be inclined to be oversensitive, to have their feelings too easily hurt, to be a little suspicious, to be too eager to please, and subject to moods. Those who are efficient and hard-working may tend to be inconsiderate, angry, self-opinionated, or over-demanding. Probably these temperament faults will never totally disappear, but a watchful eye keeps them from becoming a weed patch. However that is why many good people's confessions become stereotyped—their sins are mostly occupational and temperamental faults. Confessing them keeps us humble and should not leave us discouraged. The advantage of confessing them is that over the years, with God's grace and love, they gradually diminish, or at least the sacramental graces, along with God's purifying love and our own vigilance, keep them from taking over and distorting an otherwise nice personality.

But confessing sins isn't the end of the affair. There is also the very important matter of sorrow for sin. Now if I am "sorry" for sin I mean that I regret the sinful act. I wish I hadn't done it, and with God's help I will try to avoid it in the future. I regret the act. Why? Because God might punish me for it; He might withhold a reward; but "especially because I have offended God who is so good and worthy of all my love." These three motives are summed up in the act of contrition when we say: "O my God, I am heartily sorry for having offended Thee. I detest all my sins (1) because I dread the loss of heaven, (2) the pains of hell, (3) but most of all because I have offended Thee, my God, who art all good and deserving of all my love." These, then, would be the chief motives for my regret, for my sorrow. Notice, too, that we do not have to say that the sin didn't give us pleasure. Surely sin gives us pleasure and some kind of satisfaction. It has to give us something if it is going to rob us blind. Sin has to offer some satisfaction or else we would not commit it. But we realize that it was a forbidden pleasure, and so we regret having taken it, and with God's help, we will try not to do it again. "I firmly resolve with the help of Thy grace to confess my sins, to do penance, and to amend my life. Amen."

In regard to feeling sorry, if the feeling is there we can be grateful. If it is absent we do not have to worry. Sorrow is an act of the will. My mind tells me that what I did was morally wrong; my will turns away from it and rejects it. "I'm sorry." There may be little or no feeling or emotion but the sorrow is still genuine. Often this unemotional type of sorrow and determination can be more sincere than a passing, superficial feeling of sorrow and a passing pang of regret. It is also good to reflect that the act of perfect contrition or sorrow is not an impossible thing. It means that the emphasis in our contrition is "I have offended God who is all good and deserving of all my love." A simple way to come to this disposition is to take a loving look at the crucifix or at the Sacred Heart of Jesus. As we study Christ on the cross, His outstretched arms and lance-pierced heart, we reflect that this is God who died for ME. With St. Paul we can say: "He loved me—even me—and delivered Himself up for me." How He must love me, unworthy though I am. How grateful I should be. Then, using His love for me and my gratitude to Him as stepping stones, we ascend to the consideration: "Why should I want to offend one who is so good, so wonderful, so deserving of all my love?"

Well, I don't want to offend one who is so good. I am sorry. I am sorry for all my sins, big and little. This could give our contrition the flavor of perfect contrition.

It is consoling to recall that if we have sinned mortally, our act of perfect contrition immediately restores us to sanctifying grace. True, we still have the obligation to go to confession and to mention the sin, and this confession must be made before we receive Holy Communion; but, in the meantime, we are back in the state of grace. We are in God's friendship and are functioning supernaturally. Time is not lost. There are other advantages to acquiring the habit of a quick act of perfect contrition after mortal sin. It gives us security. We can get into an airplane without breaking into a cold sweat. We can relax on the highway. But, in addition, when we have sinned we are coasting down a hill. An act of contrition stops the descent with the roadblock of sorrow. We level off and ascend back to the open highway of supernatural life. When we do this, temptation loses some of its force. The Holy Spirit again dwells within us. If we continue in sin, without contrition, the attitude can be one of discouragement. We are empty. "I've done it again. Who cares? So what?" In this mood sin may even be repeated. In sheer disgust with ourselves or to prove that we really are no good, we sometimes sin again. This is forgetting that sin offends God. We don't belt a little brother or a wife and then hit him or her again just to prove we are brutal. It hurts them too much, and it only makes us hate ourselves for our thoughtlessness. God doesn't hate us. So for God's sake, if not for our own, we shouldn't hate ourselves. We should be patient with ourselves and humbly, hopefully, begin again.

According to the rules an insincere confession is not a valid one, but we should be very slow to accuse ourselves of insincerity. We can't make a bad confession unless we intend to make a bad one and are conscious of this fact as we are confessing. It can happen that a person goes to confession with his will turned away from sin; he regrets it and promises to do better with God's help. Maybe a half-hour later, under the stress of strong temptation and because of acquired habit, he slips again. Does that mean he was insincere when he went to confession? No! It could mean that he is weak and that the habit is strong. It could mean that he is not too prudent in regard to occasions of sin, but it does not invalidate the confession already made. Insincerity in the act of confessing means that we are not sorry for the sin and have no intention of trying to avoid it or that we are knowingly and deliberately concealing a serious sin. The ordinary person does not go to confession to make a bad one. He goes in order to get help; he goes to get absolution and forgiveness; he goes to begin again. Delivering oneself with these dispositions assures the required minimum sincerity. In this whole area of sins of weakness, we should be patient with ourselves, for God is patient. With His help we can begin again and again and gradually acquire habits of virtue.

A few other hints on confession. We should never be afraid to go to confession no matter what sins we have committed or how frequently we fail. Penance is a very human sacrament and it is meant to take care of human weakness. It takes care of the sins you and I commit and the way in which we commit them. Naturally, we are not going to look too good when we go to confession since we are going to report our failures and sins, not our virtues. The confessor knows us at our worst because we are telling him about our sins. But he also knows us at our best because we are sorry and trying to do better. The priest ordinarily, then, has only sincere admiration for the person on the other side of the screen for he knows that it takes humility and sorrow to bring a person to confession. It might be helpful to recall, if you are edgy, that the priest himself is required by canon law to go to confession once a week. The pope goes very frequently. We are all in the same box.

Obviously you can't shock the priest with your sins. If you think he will be unduly shocked and horrified, you are implying that he hasn't read his theology books. Every sin that has ever been committed by human beings has been spelled out in the moral theology books; you won't be telling him anything new. Men have been sinning since Adam and Eve's time and there is nothing new under the sun. Don't go figuring: "I'll bet this will make him gasp" or, "Wait until he gets a load of this; it'll rock him back on his heels!" He's probably heard it before and certainly has read about it. He is there to give absolution. You have not offended the priest by your sins; they are not his commandments that you have broken. So the priest doesn't take it too personally.

There is also a tendency when we go to confession to knock out a few flies before we get down to the real ball game. This may be a good way to warm up, but we shouldn't slide over the big ones. Loud and strong there comes out: "I missed my prayers three times; I was a little impatient five times." Then fast and low: "I burned-down-an-orphanage-with-all-the-orphans-in-it." Then loudly, "I also told a lie." The priest, not catching the fast one, has to ask: "What was that one in the middle? I didn't quite hear you." Then we have to repeat louder and clearer, "I burned down an orphanage with all the orphans in it." When you come to the big ones, then, don't boom them out as though you were boasting about them, but at least make them audible. If you don't know how to confess a sin, or feel embarrassed because you are not sure of some technical terms, simply say to the priest: "Father, would you please help me?" or, "I'm going to find this difficult." With a couple of questions he can quickly get to the heart of the matter and you will leave with the peaceful consciousness of a well-made confession.

Never leave the Church because some priest bawls you out. (That can happen, and people have left the Church for such a reason.) Be charitable. Reflect that maybe his gout is bothering him, or that he has been in the confessional too long, or that he may have heard the same thing over two thousand times and you just happen to come along and get the full benefit of the blast. Some people's reaction to a mild blasting is: "I'm never coming back to confession again. I'm quitting the Church." If you happen to get a bawling out—and it doesn't happen too often—take it in stride, maturely. Say to yourself: "Either I deserved it or I didn't. If I did, well, O.K. It's humiliating, but I'll offer it up as part of my penance." If you think you didn't deserve it, forget it. Don't be like the little boy who, scolded by his parents, tearfully takes his pencil box and his space helmet and goes off into the wide, cruel world alone. If he stays away too long he just gets lost, hungry, cold, and very unhappy. If Father is that shook up let him leave the Church, not you.

Since we are all penitents, priest and people alike, it is good to recall one of the rights of a penitent. Suppose a penance is imposed which you figure, knowing yourself and your circumstances, will be extremely difficult to fulfill. Just suppose you were given the stations of the cross for the next seven days, or daily communion for a week, and you think you might not be able to fulfill it. You may have some kind of mental block. Reasonably, you might say to the priest: "Father, would you please give me some other penance?" If he insists you might respectfully say: "Well, then, I think I had better go to someone else." With that you could take your business next door and receive maybe five Our Fathers and Hail Marys. The point here is that if we accept the absolution we have to accept the penance. If we do not accept the absolution, we do not have to accept the penance.

It is very commendable to say the penance right after confession. It deepens our sorrow and we might otherwise forget to say or do it. But the obligation is to say it within a reasonable time. The penance imposed in connection with confession has a special efficacy to remove the temporal punishment due to our sins. We should not be too chagrined, then, at the penance which might take a little time. It is better than purgatory.

To sum up, then, these are the simple elements of a good confession: (1) examination of conscience: mortal sins, name and number; (2) sorrow for sin; (3) confession of the sins; and (4) performing of the penance.

There is a final question, "How often should I go to confession?" The Church commands confession once a year, during the Easter season, if we have committed serious sin. Another law of the Church is that if mortal sin has been committed confession is necessary before receiving Holy Communion. Otherwise, how often we go is left up to us. Prudently, if we have committed mortal sin, we should make our act of perfect contrition and get to confession as soon as possible. This is common sense. Otherwise, once a month is laudable. If we go every two weeks we are in a position to gain all the indulgences which the Church grants under the usual condition of confession and communion. It is interesting to note that for the clergy and religious, canon law says once a week. When we consider the fact that every time we receive the sacrament we receive an increase of sanctifying grace and an outpouring of actual grace for our immediate needs, we can recall and apply the principle: "If a thing helps me to accomplish my mission, I will use it. The more it helps me, the more I will use it." Some people simply say, "I take a bath once a week whether I need it or not."

We have gone into some suggested, practical attitudes toward confession. The sacrament of penance is essentially a sacrament of peace and reconciliation. Our Lord went through the agony of His Passion to win us forgiveness, and we should accept this mercy gratefully. It is meant to be a sacrament of peace, not something which we worry about for hours in advance, tremble through in a cold sweat, and fret about until the next confession. "My peace I give you. Fear not," our Lord said. We should accept the peace of mind and soul which He alone can give and not be afraid.

There is a very practical consideration which should recommend confession to us when, at times, we find it hard to go to a "man" and tell our sins. It is the emotional and mental health aspect of the sacrament of penance. Wise men down through the ages have urged the value of self-knowledge. Over the temple of Delphi was engraved the dictum of Thales, "Know thyself." St. Augustine, a master psychologist, added a prayer for further knowledge: "O Lord, that I may know Thee and that I may know myself." The sacrament of penance, used intelligently, helps us to arrive at a useful amount of this twofold knowledge without making us unduly introspective. We observe tendencies in ourselves and check them before they get out of hand. We are aware, through our regular confession, of areas of weakness and can seek means to strengthen ourselves. If there are recurring problems in our lives, the confessional provides a sympathetic, objective, prudent counselor. If there is a corrosive sense of guilt or self-hate, it can be dispelled under kindly direction and the comforting words of absolution. If we seek regular spiritual guidance to draw closer to God, a regular confessor is very important and recommended by all spiritual directors. The sacrament of penance meets the emotional, psychological, and spiritual needs of the guilty. The absolution removes our guilt before God and the humble verbal acknowledgment that we were wrong helps to dissipate guilt feelings. The sacrament of penance, if properly used, could be described as the sacrament of mental health. If it is not a sacrament of peace, the disturbing element comes from us, not from Christ.

In our age, which is so psychologically oriented, we have had to re-create a kind of secular counterpart of the confessional—the psychiatric couch. Psychologists appreciate the role of a verbal confession. Ventilation can be very good. Psychiatrist and priest can often be mutually helpful. But the couch alone can never be a substitute for the confessional where the consoling words of absolution wipe out objective guilt. After absolution we are no longer guilty before God. We are no longer sinners. "If your sins be as scarlet, they shall be made as white as snow: and if they be red as crimson, they shall be white as wool" (Isaias 1:18). "Whose sins you shall forgive they are forgiven them."

What peace has come to people through the years as they learn to follow the simple procedure for confession. "Bless me, Father, for I have sinned. It has been ———— weeks since my last confession. I accuse myself of the following sins: (Mortal sins, by name and number; and venial sins.) I am sorry for these and all the sins of my past life." Then the consoling, healing words of absolution as the sinner renews his act of contrition: "May our Lord, Jesus Christ, absolve you, and I by His authority absolve you from every bond of excommunication and of interdict in as far as I can and you require it. Therefore I absolve you from your sins in the name of the Father and of the Son and of the Holy Spirit. Amen.

"May the passion of our Lord, Jesus Christ, the merits of the Blessed Virgin Mary and of all the saints, whatever good you may have done, whatever evil you may have suffered, be to you unto the remission of your sins, the increase of grace, and the joy of life everlasting. Amen. Go in peace, and God bless you."

Do it yourself!

Points for your prayerful thinking (15 minutes)

PREPARATORY PRAYER
See page 18.

Bless me, Father, for I have sinned

1 Do you really think you can forgive sins? Yes!
2 How do I use this sacrament? Intelligently? Frequently? Peacefully?
3 At this point in the retreat it would be good to go to confession, if possible.
4 A complete examination of conscience is found in the last chapter, page 268. A help to self knowledge.
5 "Whose sins you shall forgive, they are forgiven." The sacrament of penance was instituted by Christ as a sacrament of peace and forgiveness. Keep it such. The sacrament of mental health.

Conclude by saying one Our Father, a Hail Mary, and Glory Be to the Father.

◆◆◆◆◆◆◆◆◆◆◆

The next chapter has something for everyone. Take your pick. However, knowing human nature a bit (having a share of it myself) I suspect that the single will also read the sections on marriage and the engaged—to get a preview of things to come—and the married will check over the part on the engaged and the single to see if it squares with their experience. So here's to a brief but I hope balanced outlook on love, courtship, and marriage.

However, if you wish to omit these instructions on the various states of life, you can continue with the main theme of the retreat by skipping to page 158 and the chapter called "A More Excellent Way."

◆◆◆◆◆◆◆◆◆◆◆◆◆

They're married

Whenever I have occasion to talk on marriage-and the family, I recall the story of a young, newly-ordained priest who gave a sermon on marriage. He was sure of himself. He had all the answers and was positive and detailed about how husbands should treat their wives, and how wives should care for their husbands. He knew exactly how children should be raised and how a home should be run. "Follow these rules," he concluded triumphantly, "and you will be happy." Two old Irish ladies who had suffered patiently through the sermon met on the steps of the church after Mass. One said to the other, "He's a fine young priest." "He is," the other agreed, "and it was a fine sermon he gave on the holy sacrament of matrimony." "It was indeed," the other nodded. Then feelingly and fervently, "And I wish to God I knew as little about marriage as he does."

But a priest talking in this area, however young or old, has many things in common with all human beings. He was not born with a Roman collar. He had a mother and father and he lived in a home. So he is a human being like the rest of us. Then he has the added advantage of knowing intimately the family life of thousands of people, and in his studies he has searched through the accumulated wisdom of the ages on the subject of marriage. In matters of faith and morals he is safeguarded by the teaching authority of the Church. So, despite many inadequacies on the part of this observer, a few "observations" on marriage and the family are in order.

It is useful during a retreat to take a fresh glance at this familiar subject. The first point can be given with authority. It is the law of God in regard to birth control. So here goes. But, since this is negative, a matter of "thou shalt not," I will be very brief.

"When is the Church going to change her laws in regard to birth control?" This is a question you and I have often been asked. Since the question contains a few false suppositions, I find myself answering in this fashion: "Don't you know that the Church has no law in regard to birth control?" The Church instituted the law: "Don't eat meat on Friday," and she can and does change or modify it. The Church made up the law: "Go to Mass on Sunday," and she can dispense from this law for a good reason. The Church did not make up the law about birth control. That is God's law—the natural law—and it is binding on all men, Catholic, Protestant, and Jew alike. The Church cannot dispense from it any more than she can dispense from the law "Thou shalt not commit adultery."

Artificial birth control is morally wrong because it is an unnatural act. For the sake of clarity and to bring out the fact that it is unnatural, the subject may be approached this way. I ask, will you agree that sex can be misused? Alcohol can be misused: this is called intemperance. Food can be misused: this is called gluttony. Anything can be misused, including sex, and that misuse, that abuse, is morally wrong —sin.

Would you agree that sex could be misused in the following way: If there is sex activity with the wrong species? This is unnatural. It is morally wrong; it is a sin; it is called bestiality. If there is sex activity with the right species but the wrong sex, that is unnatural. It is morally wrong; it is a sin; it is called homosexuality. If there is sex activity with oneself, alone, this is unnatural because sex is supposed to be outgoing. It is morally wrong; it is a sin; it is called masturbation or self-abuse. If there is sex activity with the right species, the right sex, but the wrong person, this is morally wrong; it is a sin. If a married person is involved, it is called adultery. Among the single it is called fornication. If there is sex activity with the right species, the right sex, the right person (the marriage partner), but in the wrong way—frustrating the natural act and its natural functioning—this is unnatural. It violates nature; it is morally wrong; it is a sin. The various methods and practices of frustrating the natural act and its natural functioning are commonly called artificial birth control. The Church cannot change the facts and cannot give permission to commit sin.

This subject has been exhausted in books and articles. In this area it would seem that argument is rather ineffective. People seem to come to this subject with their wills made up and their minds closed. Unquestionably there are many problems that arise which deserve sympathetic understanding and infinite patience. God's commandments can be very burdensome at times. However, though the Church realizes that heroic virtue may be required on occasion, she cannot change the law. It is not hers to change. Sometimes, behind the hostility to this law, there is a general attitude of: "Really, God has no business interfering and meddling in my private life." This is putting it bluntly, but it is implied in such fairly common slogans as "Business is business; religion belongs in Church." Remember the member of the euthanasia society in England quoted in Chapter Two? He rather logically and calmly said it is "nonsense" to hold that death "should be 'left to God.' Do we leave birth to God?"

So, instead of dwelling on the negative side of things—preventing birth—we might accentuate the positive and consider the dignity of parenthood. It is a share in God's creative power. Through the cooperation of a man and a woman God brings a new life into the world—a life which will go on for all eternity.

To appreciate the greatness and dignity of parenthood, we might reflect on some of man's great natural achievements. Some would say that to put an Explorer into orbit would be a satisfying and great accomplishment. Some would say that to find a cure for cancer and thus to prolong life would justify a lifetime of laborious research and deserve the gratitude of mankind. Some would hold that the production of a great painting, writing a great book, composing an opera, would be worth a lifetime of effort. If a man spent his whole life on the left bank of the Seine, living in poverty in a garret, and at the end produced a masterpiece of art, the heritage of future generations, most people would say the sacrifice was worthwhile. Yet, what are these compared to bringing a new life into the world, not just prolonging it? What are these compared to producing a human being, made in God's image and likeness, and in our own image and likeness, a heritage of future generations built for eternity and for an eternity of happiness?

They tell the story that as Michelangelo finished his statue of David, a breathtakingly beautiful work of art, he was so enthralled with his own handiwork that dramatically, longingly, and lovingly, he struck it with his sculptor's hammer and cried: "Live." He could not give it life, great artist that he was. Parenthood involves a much greater accomplishment. To bring a new life into the world and guide it to mature adulthood is a work of art and truly creative. That it involves some pain, labor, sacrifice, is taken for granted. Are these sacrifices, these labors, really worthwhile? Which is greater, to produce a statue of a man or to produce a man? This little flight of fancy may help to bring out the dignity of parenthood, the inherent greatness that goes with being a mother or a father.

The land of dream-children is populous. In this land of dream-children, there are some who might have been born had not their dream-parents been summoned by duty, or God's purpose, to give up the dignity of parenthood. Such dream-children, one likes to fancy, are happy. It was according to God's plan that they should remain among the unborn. They are content to have it so. But there is another group, far more numerous, who are sad and play listlessly. They stretch out their arms to life with longing, but their longings are not fulfilled, and they call in vain to their dream-parents. They are not wanted—and that hurts. So they have written a letter to their dream-parents, explaining their case and pleading for life. It is a simple letter and runs as follows:

Dear Mother and Father,

Yesterday we heard you discussing whether you ought to have children, and as we are the children in question we should like to tell you how we feel about this matter. Only too often, we think, our side of the question is left out in these discussions. We know that if you make us real children we will be a great care and responsibility to you—even quite an expense. We babies come rather high in this modern age. But, dear dream-parents, in your experience of life, you know that everything worthwhile costs dearly; and you will be giving us the greatest of all gifts, life. Perhaps you have grown used to the marvel of your existence, and do not realize how sweet it is to be alive—to be somebody. But we are crying to you from our nothingness. We know. We are pleading with you for life which you alone can give us—life with all its tears and laughter, joy and woe, hope and fear, but at its conclusion an eternity of happiness with God. The thing after all that is most like God is life. Do you wonder then that if you are to draw us from our nothingness and cooperate with God in creating us, some sacrifice will be asked of you?

We realize, of course, that we won't be of much practical use during our baby days. Our helplessness will demand your constant care; we will absorb your life and fill your waking hours. For our sake you may have to give up some bridge parties, dances, movies, even some of your pretty clothes or perhaps a new radio. But there is a majority opinion among us babies that we are worth these sacrifices. We provide more satisfying, heart-warming happiness than all these things. . . . We know too that our presence in the house will increase the love you have for each other. Look about you and see if this is not true. Bring us into your home and we promise to unite your hearts and lives in that lasting union of love which only a baby can create. . . .

But perhaps this unselfish thought occurs to you and makes you pause. "Will it be really worthwhile or even fair to bring a child into the world when we cannot offer it every advantage in upbringing . . . ? Isn't that an injustice?" We dream-children are unanimous in our answer and we protest, "No!" . . . After all, smart clothes, the best education, and comforts do not give life its real value. Only give us life and we will gladly take all the hardships that go with it.

Lovingly and longingly yours,

Your Dream-children

If we recognize that something is tremendously worthwhile we are willing to put effort into it. If we don't realize its worth, naturally there are complaints about the sacrifices and labor involved. When a proud father hands out the cigars and glows: "It's a boy!" "It's a girl!" God, our Father looks down approvingly at another father, recognizing someone made in His image and likeness. He likes this resemblance to Himself. All paternity comes from God. St. Paul speaks of it glowingly: "I bend my knees to the Father of our Lord Jesus Christ, from whom all fatherhood in heaven and on earth receives its name, that he may grant you from his glorious riches to be strengthened with power through his Spirit unto the progress of the inner man" (Ephesians 3:14-16). A human father and God the Father understand each other and should be very close. God the Father's calm steadiness and protective love should be the model for human fathers. And to mothers, our Lord Himself speaks words that are consoling and which also reveal complete understanding: "A woman about to give birth has sorrow, because her hour has come. But when she has brought forth the child, she no longer remembers the anguish for her joy that a man is born into the world" (John 16:21).

The heartbreak of parenthood is that perhaps, even after our best efforts, the life entrusted to us may turn out quite contrary to hopes and expectations. This can be a source of anxiety and worry. It can be heartbreaking. A man and woman have done their poor best to be good parents, but a son or daughter may not measure up to God's laws. This must be the hardest part of parenthood. Surely parents can turn to God the Father and say trustingly, confidently: "Heavenly Father, thank you for the gift of parenthood and please take care of my mistakes. Please watch over the life you entrusted to me." As a saintly bishop said consolingly to St. Monica, who spent so many years praying for her wayward son, Augustine: "It is not possible that the son of these tears should be lost."

Difference between men and women

Man complements woman — woman compliments man.

I recall one Sunday when I had been assigned to help out at a nearby church and was to preach at all the Masses. I looked at the suggested diocesan subject for the day and paled. I was to preach on the topic, "Wives be subject to your husbands." Now I am a peace-loving man and I like to keep my friends. So, coward that I was, I went looking for another priest to "sub" for me. "Would you please take my place this Sunday?" I asked my next-door neighbor. "I'm a little pressed for time this week. I don't have enough time to prepare." "What do you have to preach on?" he asked cautiously. When I told him, "Wives be subject to your husbands," he looked hurt that I had tried to trap him. His only answer was a meaningful, "I'll pray for you," and he turned back to his book. I tried another pal of mine. Surely he would help me out. After all, hadn't we been through the novitiate together? Anything for a friend. But when I told him the topic he patted me encouragingly on the shoulder and said: "It couldn't happen to a nicer guy. I know you will do well. Count me—out." In desperation I went to a priest who taught psychology and explained the problem. He refused to take it but he did offer some help. "The topic isn't that bad. In fact it is a natural and desirable relationship which, deep down, the woman wants. So sit down," said he, "and I will give you a 'father and son' talk on the difference between men and women." I used what he said for my sermon and I pass it on for your thinking now.

Books have been written on this subject, but I will plunge bravely ahead and try to explain the fundamentals in the man-woman relationship. Believe it or not, just a few paragraphs will contain the secret and the key to this age-old mystery. Seriously, see if it isn't basically true. If it is true, and if this truth is grasped, then detailed instructions on how husbands can make wives happy and wives keep husbands at home and content will not be necessary. Once the basic needs of the other are understood they can lovingly be met.

In the man-woman relationship, woman is by nature inadequate. An indication of this inadequacy is that any man could beat her up. I don't say that he will, but he could. When a man fights a man, the outcome is uncertain. When a man fights a woman, he wins, unless, perhaps, the woman has taken lessons in judo. So essentially she is inadequate. Secondly, if she is bearing a child she cannot earn her own living. She needs someone to support her and take care of her. When a man is an expectant father he can earn his own living very nicely. This is another reason for her basic inadequacy. From this inadequacy which is natural to a woman, it follows that she is by nature lonely. A man can also be lonely, but a woman is more so. A woman then is inadequate and lonely by her nature.

A man is by nature discouraged. Why? Because with a rather clear, legal mind he knows that he doesn't measure up to the standards, either self-imposed standards of achievement, or standards imposed by his religion and by morality. He has ideals and he does not measure up to them. Generally he is quite conscious of this, though he may be slow to admit it verbally and may even overcompensate for it by bragging. He is discouraged. Secondly, he lives in a competitive society and the minute he does not achieve it shows up in his pay check, his work, and his position in a firm; or, in the case of a student, in his school grades. The minute he begins to fade there is someone to take over, and no matter how qualified he may be, there is always someone else who is better. This is another constant source of competition. So he is discouraged. It is a kind of permanent state for a man.

Observe how all of this is understood and practiced, at least subconsciously, by both men and women. Every woman knows instinctively that an excellent technique for getting a man interested is to bloat up his ego. If this is done merely as a technique, it can be a little shallow. If it is done with the recognition that she is dealing with a discouraged person, it can be very sincere and charitable and meets a basic need. I overheard one girl advise: "If a fellow has a great big body and no brains, tell him he's a dreamboat. If he has brains and no body, tell him he's a genius. If he has neither, tell him he's cute. It will work!" And it does!

However, men are not quite the idiots that this would seem to imply. A man knows that he is not a "dreamboat." He is quite aware that he is not a genius. Above all, he knows he is not cute. So the man accepts "You're cute" to mean "I like you. I love you," or "I like you despite your faults. I see your good qualities." His discouragement is lessened by this admiration and acceptance and he responds. If he accepts this love permanently, he finds a warm place in a somewhat competitive, hostile universe. When he comes home he knows that here he is wanted, accepted, as he is. Here is warmth and love. His discouragement is lightened and he can return to the arena strengthened. The children run up and are obviously glad to see him. His wife gives him a hug and a kiss, and the dog barks a welcome and wags his tail.

In return as the man says to the woman, "I love you," she finds a companion for her loneliness and a protector for her inadequacy. Most men will take care of their wives who are bearing children and will be grateful and protective of the lives entrusted to them. If a burglar enters the house or someone seeks to do her violence, a man will try to protect his wife. Thus each meets the others basic need. The woman has found a protector for her inadequacy and the companion for her loneliness. The man has found a warm place in a competitive universe and his discouragement is lightened.

Notice, then, how deadly nagging is on the part of the woman. Why does it always fail? She is simply discouraging the discouraged. It is fatal. Still, well-intentioned and desiring to improve the one she loves, there is hardly a woman in the world who can resist the temptation to say, as she sees her husband or son dead drunk in the gutter: "You know, you're drinking too much." I do not always know how to improve a man, but I do know that nagging never did and never will. Somewhere in the area of sincere encouragement, admiration, and love the solution will be found. True, Socrates became a philosopher under the nagging tongue of his wife, Xantippe; but jail looked like a welcome haven of peace to him, and the cup of deadly hemlock which ended his life may have had certain redeeming features in his eyes. Compared to Xantippe, it was an encouraging draught.

Men, on the other hand, can also fail to meet the basic need of women. They do not communicate. "He doesn't talk to me" is the complaint of many women in regard to otherwise admirable husbands. This is really a cry of loneliness. On the other hand at times very successful men complain, "I don't find quite the love and affection from my wife and family that I reasonably expect." Under questioning they will answer: "Surely, I love them dearly. I've worked myself to death for them, often overtime and on weekends. I hardly knew what a vacation was for years. I gave them the best of everything. We have a beautiful home, a car, and good clothes. They have gone to the 'best' schools. I always figured that I would give them the best and I think I did. And, yet . . . " Though he was well-intentioned in his expression of love, he forgot that a Cadillac is not a companion for a wife's loneliness and a mink coat is not an adequate protector except against the weather. Finally, no accumulation of the best things fill her inadequacy. She needs a companion, a man; her husband should fill this need. The man expressed his love by giving of what he had. He forgot to give of himself. Obviously a man has to work and make a contribution in his chosen field of work—business or professional—which takes him away from the family and outside the home. On the part of the wife and family, there ought to be an appreciative understanding of this. But the man might also keep a tender eye on the difficulties and problems that can arise in the home life—lack of companionship for wife and children. Prudential judgments need to be made and the man must achieve a happy balance of giving both of himself and of what he has to meet the basic needs of wife and family. It is not unflattering that they might prefer him to what he has to give and provide.

I have said that woman is by nature inadequate and lonely and man by nature, discouraged. However, men do not have a monopoly on discouragement. Everyone who is trying to be good has ideals and is tempted to discouragement. I would be inclined to say that it is the most common temptation of good people. So the following story, like some movies, is for family consumption.

It seems that the devil, old Beelzebub himself, decided that he was going out of business, or at least that he would take a long leave of absence. Perhaps he figured that the world was going his way well enough and that he could afford to relax. At any rate, he put up for sale all his patented slogans and half-truths which had confused men so successfully during the centuries. A lot of motivational research had gone into them and they centered mostly on the concupiscence of the eyes (money), the concupiscence of the flesh (disordered sex), and the pride of life (self-will). He also put up for sale the traps and nets by which he snared men like helpless rabbits. "You're only young once." "I'm not a hypocrite. I don't go to church." "Business is business. A buck is a buck."

"Pamper yourself." "No one, I mean no one, is going to tell me what to do." "Love 'em and leave 'em." "All men are equal but some men are more equal." "I think I'm pretty good but I don't go in much for religion." All of these were tagged with very fancy prices. But off to one side placed unobtrusively in the corner there was a rusty and drab looking little tool that looked something like a burglar's jimmy for opening windows in a man's home. Seeing it, a prospective buyer asked what it was used for and what its price was. The devil shrugged off the question with: "Oh, you wouldn't want that worthless old thing. Just some rusty junk. Besides," he added casually, blowing a few smoke rings to cloud the issue, "it comes very high." He named a staggering sum, on account of sentimental reasons and proceeded to walk away, his long, pointed tail arched haughtily.

"Now look here, Beelzebub, sir," the man said, appealing to his diabolical pride, "you're the father of lies. I respect you for it. There must be something special about this or you would not have said it is worthless." "Well, now that you appeal to my pride," Beelzebub said, his red eyes flashing, "it is my most effective tool. It is my master tool. Once I get this into a man's life I have free entrance and can come and go as I please. His life is my house." "Well, what is it?" asked the man. Nicholas Q. Beelzebub laughed diabolically at his own cleverness and said: "The best part about it is that no one knows that it is mine— all mine. It's discouragement!"

Now that we have inside information it can be said without qualification that discouragement never comes from God. He does not go around tearing the heart out of a man. It either comes from our lower self or from old Beelzebub directly. This is true whether the discouragement is over business, studies, domestic affairs, occasions of sin, habits of sin, advancement in the spiritual life (the temptation to quit or give up), giving in always comes from the devil. Despair and hate, which are the essence of the devil, both flow from his diabolical pride. He tries to make us in his image and likeness. If he cannot lead us to hate he will settle for making us less loving and somewhat hostile. If he cannot lead us to pride he tries to lessen our humility. If he cannot lead us to despair he will settle for discouragement. If this is true, an antidote is needed. Devotion to the Sacred Heart of Jesus is one antidote to discouragement. It removes the insecurities we have about ourselves. Pointing simply to His heart flaming with love, Christ said: "Behold this Heart that has loved men so much." With such love in our lives we can never remain too long in lonesomeness or discouragement, whether we are "inadequate women" or "essentially discouraged men," because He takes us as He finds us and from there we go forward together—"Sinners shall find in My Heart the source and the infinite ocean of mercy. Tepid souls shall grow fervent. Fervent souls shall quickly mount to high perfection."

Things-people, idea-people, people-people

Another aspect of family living that deserves a look-see is the variety of temperaments and personalities that show up under the roof of a single family. Unity there is, but there is also variety, which makes for something very beautiful. God, in His infinite creativeness, is always surprising us with a new person who is unique. After God makes a person He breaks the mold and there will never again be another quite like him. At times it seems incredible that such different persons can come from the same parents. But there they are! And, there should be, I think, a tremendous respect and appreciation for these differences—the uniqueness of a person. To violate a person or crush a personality is tragedy. God respects the different persons He creates and we should too. Joseph A. Breig, I think, gives us this outlook so useful for family living.

In his book, *A Halo for Father*, (published by the Bruce Publishing Company) he reflects on the different types of people in the world and especially in his immediate family. He classifies them as predominantly "idea-people," "things-people," and "people-people." He then makes some interesting applications to family living.

He says that he is mostly an "idea-people." As a

writer for a large Catholic newspaper, he lives pretty much in the world of ideas and words. He is not too aware of the material things about him and can sit comfortably in the midst of the debris of manuscripts, clippings, ashes on the floor, and old issues of the daily newspapers without a twinge. He is somewhat like G. K. Chesterton whose great weight had given his bed the contours of a sway-backed horse. A friend, seeing him lying there but absorbed in writing some poetry, said: "You must be very uncomfortable." Chesterton said in surprise: "Now that you mention it, I must be." Obviously idea-people are not overly concerned about things. There are many such idea-people. Perhaps there is one in your family who regularly disappears into his "little brown study" even in the midst of conversation with visitors in the home, and can scarcely be reached. Some children at times can be so absorbed in reading or their dream world that a shouted command to "Go to the store. Do you hear me!" hardly reaches their consciousness.

"My sister," says Breig, "is definitely a 'things-people.'" She likes to clean and dust and bake and sew and set things in order. When she sweeps into his room, both literally and figuratively, the dust runs in terror at her approach. She probably regards her brother as a one-man slum, and cannot understand how anyone could possibly live in such confusion, not realizing that underneath the apparent chaos is a substructure of order. "In fact," Breig remarks, "after she has set everything in order, for weeks I am searching for things which she has so carefully put away." Obviously he and his sister will never see eye to eye on the relative values of ideas and things. There will always be a Lucy and a Charlie Brown and a Schroeder.

"My father," he observes, "is a 'people-people' or 'people-person.' He likes people singly and in quantity. He is always shaking hands with people. On the streetcar or in a room his booming, friendly voice includes everyone in his conversation. When he comes home if there isn't company, four or five extra people around, he asks: 'Where is everybody?'" Breig himself, shrinks a little from this hubbub and would like time to write and think. But for Papa life is just one big convention. "Hurrah for people," says Papa. "Hurrah for things," says his sister. "Hurrah for ideas," says Breig himself.

The moral he draws from this is that we are all different, and in family living we should learn both to respect and appreciate the emphasis in living which others have, being patient with one another. "Bear one another's burdens, and so you will fulfill the law of Christ" (Galatians 6:2). Breig concludes that if "things-people, idea-people, and people-people" are all God's people, then things, and ideas, and people are all nicely taken care of. And taking the larger family of man, wouldn't this be a wonderful world if scientists, philosophers, writers, poets, artists, tradesmen, businessmen, manufacturers, politicians, the clergy, mothers, fathers, and educators were all God's people! How wonderful this world would wag on, and how well all its varied activities would be managed.

After God made each of us, he broke the mold. There will never be another one quite like you. He has given each one of us a work to do that He has given to no other, and each one of us is necessary and as important in our place as the Blessed Virgin in her glorious place or Michael the archangel in his. This is true of every person God created. So, while we thank God for our common denominator, "Vive la différence" in ourselves and others. Wouldn't it be dreadfully dull if everyone was just like ourselves, made in our exact image and likeness, and thought, judged, acted, and reacted exactly as we do?

Vocations

One of the obvious ways for God to show His approval of a family would be to call one or more of the children to His service. A religious or priestly vocation would seem to indicate that a child had been trained not only to mature adulthood, but to mature Christianity; he or she had been gifted with a living faith, a spirit of sacrifice, and a generous loving heart willing to give all to God. Parents certainly should not be insulted if God, for His own good reasons, should call one of their children to serve Him. On the contrary, it almost seems that Christ Himself is saying "well done" to the parents who have raised such a child. "And going up a mountain, he called to him men of his own choosing, and they came to him" (Mark 3:13).

Christ has put Himself pretty much at the mercy of parents as to whether His kingdom is to be spread or not, since He did not choose to stay on earth visibly and do the work Himself. Nor did He send a band of angels although they might be more efficient. He chose men to do His work. If they do not do it, it will be left undone for all eternity. His kingdom will not be spread. Obviously, too, these men and women who will do the specialized work in His vineyard must come from a family. Where else? One who would oppose or discourage such a vocation has a responsibility that is a little frightening.

Does God need men? He told us He did, and He explained His needs. "And Jesus was going about all the towns and villages, teaching in their synagogues, and preaching the gospel of the kingdom, and curing every kind of disease and infirmity. But seeing the crowds, he was moved with compassion for them, because they were bewildered and dejected, like sheep without a shepherd. Then he said to his disciples, 'The harvest indeed is great, but the laborers are few. Pray therefore the Lord of the harvest to send forth laborers into his harvest'" (Matthew 9:35-38).

This view of the world seen through the eyes of Christ has a pathos and an appeal that goes straight to our hearts, and there is an instinctive tendency to offer ourselves to be of help. Our Lord spoke of the crowds, "bewildered and dejected," and yet the world of His time was sparsely populated compared to the teaming millions who inhabit our "exploding" world of today. And people are still "bewildered and dejected." His appeal then, "Pray therefore the Lord of the harvest to send forth laborers . . ." takes on an added eloquence and urgency in our day and prepares us for the time when God might call one from our own family to a priestly or religious vocation.

Consider that here in America where there is religious freedom, and where the number of vocations is relatively large, the need for laborers is reaching the crisis stage. There was in 1960 a Catholic population of over forty million. This is an increase of more than thirteen million Catholics or more than forty-seven per cent in the last decade. To care for this number, there are approximately 229,000 priests, brothers, and sisters, an increase of less than sixteen per cent for the same period.

The Catholic population has grown twice as fast as the number of priests in the last decade. Ten years ago there was one priest for each 646 laymen. Today there is only one priest for each 759 laymen. So if the confessional line seems longer, it is because there are a hundred and thirteen more people in it than were there ten years ago. Be patient, then, and "Pray therefore the Lord of the harvest send laborers into his harvest." You will get better service.

Even more distressing are the figures that reflect the growth of the sisterhoods in the U.S.A. where the Catholic population has grown four times as fast as the number of sisters in the last decade. Ten years ago there were a few more than 147,000 sisters. Today they number less than 165,000. This is an increase of not quite 18,000 or less than twelve per cent.

Only the brothers have kept pace with the growing Catholic population with an increase of almost forty-two per cent in the last decade. The total number of brothers in 1950 was a little over 7,000. Today, with the addition of about 3,000 brothers, they number over 10,000. Unfortunately, though, the brothers make up less than five per cent of the total of priests and religious.

Notice that these figures refer only to our immediate domestic needs and do not take into account the mission responsibilities of the Church in America.

As you are praying for "laborers" you might seriously consider whether Christ's invitation "Come follow me" might be directed toward one of your children. Certainly, if He is to find laborers, He would seek them in families such as yours where they have been taught to believe in something besides the "buck," and other material comforts. Such children are young and generous and idealistic; they are not beatniks (who are in a state of acquired, calculated confusion) and so they can respond to a noble cause, the salvation of souls, and aspire to the closest intimacy with Christ. Being realists they know that Christ can make good on His promise: "And everyone who has left house, or brothers, or sisters, . . . or wife, or children, or lands, for my name's sake, shall receive a hundredfold, and shall possess life everlasting" (Matthew 19:29).

It has been my experience that not too often do parents oppose their mature son's decision to become a priest. It is done occasionally when parents have strong, predetermined, detailed plans for their son's future. However, when it comes to approval of their daughter entering a convent, opposition from one or other parent is not uncommon.

The following is a story of parents' cooperation with a vocation in a father's own words.

"What gratification it is to be a Catholic. This was particularly true for me the night our daughter, just nineteen, asked me, her father, to go with her for a short walk. It was then that she surprised me with the electrifying news that she was seriously contemplating becoming a religious . . . and she wanted to know if I would go along willingly with her heart's greatest desire. I must frankly and sincerely confess that I was completely surprised at her request but not shocked or disappointed. My first consideration was, naturally, for her continued happiness and peace of mind. So my immediate answer was that if she was convinced that a vocation to religious life was really in her heart, her mother and I would do everything possible to assist whole-heartedly in working out her future plans. I also told her that if I were really a Catholic in the true sense of the word, I had no right to say no to her vocation because in doing that I was in effect saying to God: 'We have no further need for nuns or priests.'

"On the way back to the house I was happy in my acceptance of her plans, but, without doubt, there were also a few tears. The quiet acceptance of God's will in this matter has brought deep joy to us and to our entire family. We gave back to God our daughter —a soul He had sent to us for a while to love and protect, but still belonging to Him. And because He is God and can never be outdone in generosity, He has already rewarded us a thousandfold. . . .

"Each time we went to the novitiate it was a real thrill to see our daughter coming down the corridor to meet us, her face wreathed in smiles of welcome. . . . I am sorry to say that some parents were deliberately staying away from the novitiate because they did not approve of their daughters' decisions to enter the convent. This feeling of separation from family caused their novice daughters many sad moments at a time when one hundred per cent moral support from home was most needed.

"Occasionally I had an opportunity to spend a few moments in conversation with these disapproving parents. My suggestion to them was always to be more objective in their viewpoint—to think more about their daughter's great happiness, which anyone could readily see, and less about themselves and their own loneliness. We have never for a moment regretted the decision given to our daughter during that evening's walk a few years ago. We have not lost her love and affection, rather she is more strongly attached to the family, and more deeply interested in anything that concerns us than if she had married and had family problems of her own. We have no worries about her present or her future, surrounded as she is with a loving superior and community of devoted friends. For our part, as a result of our daughter's example and prayers, we feel that our faith and the faith of our family has been deepened."

It is not a great stretch of the imagination, having listened to this grateful father, to hear our Lord saying to parents who encourage and generously give their sons or daughters to God: "Anyone who gives up son or daughter for my name's sake shall be blessed one hundredfold and shall possess life everlasting." Generosity is met by generosity. God is never outdone!

Not all parents will have an opportunity to show God how generous they can be in cooperating in the religious vocation of a son or daughter. And the question of accepting a religious vocation does not arise in "young" families—even "early" vocations are not apt to present any problem for the romper set. But whatever the vocation potential of a family may be, all mothers and fathers have the privilege of consecrating their families to the Sacred Heart of Jesus and the Immaculate Heart of Mary. Such consecrations can help to guide a family and all its members to a generous and loving dedication to the will of God— wherever it may lead them.

The recitation of the act of consecration before a picture, plaque, or other representation of the Sacred Heart is a simple but impressive ceremony. It is suggested that it be done on some particular Sunday or feast day, by the head of the house, who consecrates his family as a whole to the Sacred Heart. Such a ceremony would be long remembered by children and certainly goes straight to the heart of Christ.

Following are the acts of consecration to the Immaculate Heart of Mary and the Sacred Heart of Jesus. To those so dedicated to His Sacred Heart, our Lord makes most generous promises. They are also added for your remembrance and consolation.

ACT OF CONSECRATION TO THE SACRED HEART OF JESUS

Sacred Heart of Jesus, who manifested to St. Margaret Mary the desire of reigning in Christian families, we today wish to proclaim Your most complete regal dominion over our own. We would live in the future with Your life, we would cause to flourish in our midst those virtues to which You have promised peace here below, we would banish far from us the spirit of the world which You have cursed; and You shall reign over our minds in the simplicity of our faith, and over our hearts by the whole-hearted love with which they shall burn for You, the flame of which we shall keep alive by the frequent reception of Your divine Eucharist.

Deign, Divine Heart, to preside over our assemblings, to bless our enterprises, both spiritual and temporal, to dispel our cares, to sanctify our joys, to alleviate our sufferings. If ever one or other of us should have the misfortune to afflict You, remind him, O Heart of Jesus, that You are good and merciful to the penitent sinner. And when the hour of separation strikes, when death shall come to cast mourning into our midst, we will all, both those who go and those who stay, be submissive to Your eternal decrees. We will console ourselves with the thought that a day will come when the entire family, reunited in heaven, can sing forever Your glories and Your mercies.

May the Immaculate Heart of Mary and the glorious patriarch, St. Joseph, present this consecration to You, and keep it in our minds all the days of our life. All glory to the heart of Jesus our king and our father!

ACT OF CONSECRATION TO THE IMMACULATE HEART OF MARY

The members of this family, with all we have and possess, come today to make our abode in your heart, O holy Mother of God. As you were constituted by our Heavenly Father true mother and heart of the family of Nazareth, so we all wish to have thee as the mother and heart of our home. To you, to your immaculate heart we dedicate and consecrate ourselves entirely. We take shelter in your heart in order to experience its powerful protection and your maternal goodness. O heart of Mary, defend us, our children, our property, and our work that we may serve to spread your maternal kingdom all over the world for the salvation of souls and the conversion of sinners. Bless us and help us, O sweetest heart of Mary, as you blessed and helped the home and family of your cousin, Elizabeth, and the home and family of the spouses at Cana. From this moment on, your sacred image, O heart of Mary, will reign in the place of honor of this home to be truly our queen and our mother. We beg you that the kingdom of the Heart of your son, Jesus, may come with your enthronement in this home. Since we are dedicated and consecrated to your immaculate heart, do keep us as your very own now and at the hour of our death.

THE PROMISES OF THE SACRED HEART

1. I will give them all the graces necessary in their state of life.
2. I will establish peace in their homes.
3. I will comfort them in all their afflictions.
4. I will be their secure refuge during life and above all in death.
5. I will bestow a large blessing upon all their undertakings.
6. Sinners shall find in My Heart the source and the infinite ocean of mercy.
7. Tepid souls shall grow fervent.
8. Fervent souls shall quickly mount to high perfection.
9. I will bless every place where a picture of My Heart shall be set up and honored.
10. I will give to priests the gift of touching the most hardened hearts.
11. Those who shall promote this devotion shall have their names written in My Heart never to be blotted out.
12. I promise you in the excessive mercy of My Heart that My all powerful love will grant to all those who communicate on the first Friday of nine consecutive months, the grace of final perseverence, they shall not die in My disgrace nor without receiving their sacraments; My divine Heart shall be their safe refuge in this last moment.

They're engaged—or on the way

Everybody loves a lover. So the engaged are dear to the hearts of everyone. It is good to see love and hope live again in them. Their plans for the future give new confidence to the disillusioned and a promise of a new generation to parents. In each newly engaged couple the prophecy of Joel is at least partly fulfilled: "Fear not, O land, be glad and rejoice . . . And it shall come to pass after this, that I will pour out my spirit upon all flesh: . . . your old men shall dream dreams, and your young men shall see visions . . . upon my . . . handmaids . . . I will pour forth my spirit . . . every one that shall call upon the name of the Lord shall be saved" (Joel 2:21 ff.).

There is a little problem, though, that faces every engaged couple. It is this: they know each other well enough, they feel enough at ease with each other, they love each other enough, they are physically attracted to each other enough to get married—but they aren't married yet. Everything is there, emotionally and psychologically. Perhaps even the apartment is leased, the furniture picked out, the wedding list made out, the honeymoon planned in detail—everything is there except the sacrament of matrimony which makes them man and wife. Obviously this is going to present some difficulties. There is the desire to communicate totally, mind and heart and body, but it must be controlled.

The intensity of the love they have for each other two months before the wedding day probably will not differ much from their love for one another as they say "I do." Even though the marriage ceremony may not make any psychological or emotional contribution, there is still a tremendous difference between an engaged couple and a married couple. If the bridegroom were killed in an accident on the way to the church, or if the bride, in sheer excitement, dropped dead on her way up the aisle, he or she would leave behind only a betrothed, both legally and before God. If the groom is killed on the way to the wedding breakfast he leaves behind a widow, both legally and before God. We see this same profound change in relationship, with its accompanying rights and obligations, take place in other areas of human living. A simple ceremony, a spoken word, a contract, can change a person's life essentially. Ten minutes or two months before the president-elect is inaugurated, his signature is of value only to an autograph hunter. Immediately after taking the oath of office the same signature can make a law of the land that affects the lives of millions. Before induction into military service the striking of a military officer would be no more than another fight, but after it would be quite a different matter and the same sock in the jaw could land a man in a federal penitentiary. A candidate for the priesthood has studied long years to prepare for ordination. He desires the priesthood, he is theologically and psychologically prepared, but he is not yet a priest. Before ordination his words, "This is my body, this is my blood," have no effect. Spoken after ordination Christ, God Himself, responds to the words of consecration and becomes really and truly present.

It is understandable that the engaged desire to express married love. That is why they are getting married. But those who reason: "We are engaged and love each other very much; we intend to get married; therefore, we have the privileges of married people," are obviously in error. The urge to communicate is there. To fulfill it is natural and an expression of love, but it is not morally permitted until man and woman become husband and wife.

Long engagements obviously intensify the physical problem. That is why young people thinking of marriage prudently pace themselves in this whole process of going steady, falling in love, getting engaged. If they do not, frustration and/or moral problems can very easily loom large in the picture. That's the way the mop flops.

Some people say that they can fall in love early, remain long engaged with marriage in the distant future, and handle all these problems with ease because they love each other so much and because they are different. Of course there is always an exception, but as one counselor said to a couple who protested strongly that they were different: "Why, if you are so different, have you already made the same mistake that thousands of other ordinary people make—falling in love and getting engaged with marriage in the long distant future?" To safeguard the couple who enter upon a long engagement there are these practical suggestions: frequent reception of Holy Communion for both is an effective safeguard during the difficult time of engagement. An occasional rosary, or even a decade of the rosary, said together brings our Blessed Mother into the picture with her strong protective help in this matter of pre-nuptial purity. Then, prudently, don't be long alone in an apartment, watch the "goodnights," and watch out for parked cars. Naturally, there is a strong desire to be alone together—three is a crowd—but this can be done in a public place where one is safeguarded by external surroundings. While personal, intimate conversation can be held in a public place, it's a little difficult to make "mad passionate love" in a booth at Walgreens.

This may sound a little like finger wagging and a bit negative, so instead, take a glance at the Church's splendid vision of human love that she holds up to those planning marriage.

The Catholic Church and love

The Catholic Church is incurably romantic. She takes love songs seriously and lovers at their word. Love songs, old and new, always sing of "forever and ever," "constancy and faithfulness," "not for just a day, not for just a year, but always," and to all this the Church nods enthusiastic assent. She takes it for granted that true love should be deathless and that it should speak the language of eternity. So, too, when lovers protest that their love will endure in penthouse or cottage, and though youth and beauty may fade, the Church says: "Why of course." She knows the transforming power of love and has enough trust in human nature and the sincerity of lovers to answer: "I believe you. I take you at your word." Even when lovers claim that nothing is too hard for them, that "they would climb the highest mountain or swim the deepest river" for the loved one the Church understands them, for sacrifice is natural to love. She realizes that they are claiming for human love some of the ardor of St. Paul's love: "For I am sure that neither death . . . nor things present, . . . nor height, nor depth, nor any other creature will be able to separate us from the love of God."

Love that does not talk this language is suspect both by the Church and by all right-thinking persons. Imagine, if you can, a true lover whispering these vows of love under a June moon. "Dearest, I will love you forever—or at least until your beauty begins to fade." "Darling, we shall go through life together—unless I meet someone else who will make me happier." Or again, "I am yours forever, my love —that is, if our temperaments do not prove incompatible." This is not the language of love; it is the language of comic valentines. Yet such love is not uncommon today. It may not be expressed so bluntly, but too often that is the shoddy content of "I love you." This is the love of men who love only half-heartedly and who fear the complete surrender which true love demands. They will give themselves, but with reservations. And it is precisely for this half-hearted, conditional love that divorce laws make provision. Even should a lover sincerely protest, "forever and always," the divorce laws are there to challenge his word and remind him cynically: "That is what you say now. But when the going gets hard, when there are little clashes of temperament, when poverty makes itself felt, or someone else attracts you, remember there is a way out." There is no need for a strong, self-sacrificing love when we have provided an easy, legal process. Just pay the fee, and "off with the old love and on with the new."

Naturally the Church will have none of this because it is a vote of lack of confidence in the human heart and the power of love; because it is rank defeatism, a standing invitation to surrender in a moment of weakness; because it is against God's law: "What God has joined together let no man put asunder." Love, in the eyes of the Church, should be made of sterner stuff, and anything short of "until death do us part" has the ring of counterfeit love and is rejected. Moreover, this is not mere theory. The Church has the courage of her convictions, and so, taking lovers at their word, she will join them only in a lasting union. The Church is, as you can plainly see, incurably romantic.

In the marriage rite the Church shows this same romanticism and lovingly provides a ceremony that delights all lovers. It is not just a business formality casually transacted over a counter, a drab, routine affair. The Church feels that beautiful things should have a beautiful setting, and so there are music and flowers and candles and prayers and a gleaming white altar and a priest in beautiful vestments. But above all there is the charming Wedding Guest, Christ in the Holy Eucharist. The same Christ who worked His first miracle at a wedding party is there to bless the union of the lovers.

Now, while the Church is romantic in her attitude toward love and lovers, she is also an incurable realist. She does not allow her children to rush headlong into marriage, perhaps swept off their feet by the passion of a moment. She bids lovers stop and consider, before they enter into a union which is to last forever. Even when the lovers are standing before the altar she speaks to them in an instruction that is wise with the wisdom of centuries, in words that are well worth pondering. She tells them frankly:

". . . you are about to enter into a union which is most sacred . . . established by God Himself. . . . This union then is most serious, because it will bind you together for life in a relationship so close and so intimate, that it will profoundly influence your whole future. That future, with its hopes and disappointments, its successes and its failures, its pleasures and its pains, its joys and its sorrows, is hidden from your eyes. You know that these elements are mingled in every life, and are to be expected in your own. And so, not knowing what is before you, you take each other for better or for worse, for richer or for poorer, in sickness and in health, until death."

This is realism! There is no promise of a lifetime of "moonlight and roses" and "June in January," cloudless days and calm sunlit waters. The Church does not say that marriage is a gift of happiness, but rather she insists that it is an opportunity for happiness which the lovers must make a reality. Happiness is theirs not for the taking but for the making. She sees the lights and the shadows, but despite the shadows which will fall across their lives she has unshaken trust in the power of love. She continues:

"It is a beautiful tribute to your undoubted faith in each other, that, recognizing their full import [of the words of the ceremony], you are nevertheless so willing and ready to pronounce them."

The lovers look into each other's eyes and find mutual love and trust. They listen with attentive reverence to a Church who understands the yearning of their hearts, and who has such confidence in them that she demands only the best and noblest.

"Henceforth you belong entirely to each other; you will be one in mind, one in heart, and one in affections. And whatever sacrifices you may hereafter be required to make to preserve this common life, always make them generously. Sacrifice is usually difficult and irksome. Only love can make it easy; and perfect love can make it a joy."

This romantic realism of the Church is an inheritance from Christ. He is the Great Lover, and His cross is proof of it. The Church naturally expects her children to follow in His footsteps and to remember that sacrifice is the test of love. To love such as this the Church unhesitatingly promises happiness, an approach to heaven on earth.

"And if true love and the unselfish spirit of perfect

sacrifice guide your every action, you can expect the greatest measure of earthly happiness that may be allotted to man in this vale of tears."

Only when a realistic Church has thus looked into the future with the lovers, only when the lovers are confident that their love is strong and able to endure, come what may, only then does the Church unite them in holy matrimony. In words that express human love at its noblest, in words that are the echo of a thousand love songs, the lovers pledge themselves forever and forever.

"I take you . . . to have and to hold, from this day forward, for better, for worse, for richer, for poorer, in sickness and in health, until death do us part."

This is love as the Church sees it, and the whole world must acknowledge the beauty of her vision. The world, as a matter of fact, does acknowledge that the Church speaks the language of true love and the world is even willing to use love's beautiful phrases —but it is unwilling to be taken at its word. "I'll sing your love song," the world says, "but don't take me too seriously." Chesterton has described this attitude perfectly in *The Defendent:*

"It is the nature of love to bind itself, and the institution of marriage merely paid the average man the compliment of taking him at his word. Modern sages offer to the lover, with an ill-flavoured grin, the largest liberties and the fullest irresponsibility; but they do not respect him as the old Church respected him; they do not write his oath upon the heavens, as the record of his highest moment."

The Church does write the lover's vow upon the heavens in words that the lover himself naturally chooses: "forever and forever." But she is not content with that. She gives him, through the grace of the sacrament, strength to keep it written there. When trials come and love is put to the test, there is power beyond space and time that strengthens human weakness. God Himself is there with His grace to keep that vow in the heavens until death, and after death to welcome the faithful lovers in an embrace of infinite love.

They're on the way
How to fall in and out of love

Four seems to be quite a busy number in these pages. From time to time we've been taking a look at four lives, and we mentioned the Four Horsemen of the Apocalypse. Now we're going to consider four elements in the attitude of anyone who says those magic words: "I love you," and related to them, four easy steps for falling out of love. "I don't love you!" The four elements "in" ought to be very attractive, but the four steps "out" may not be so appealing. "Who would ever want to fall out of love?" you might skeptically ask. Still, it is possible that the heart could rush ahead of the head and that the resulting love affair must be broken off. Or say the loved one turns out to be an obviously undesirable marriage partner. Then there's always the possibility of what the English so poetically refer to as "unrequited love" with its poignant "Dear John, I have met . . . know you will understand . . . Goodbye."

As we study the positive elements involved in falling in love we can see that the four easy steps for falling out of love (each of which will be agony) are necessary.

First there is the love of friendship which is ordinarily thought of in terms of common interests, common tastes, similar likings. More than that, a friend is one to whom we can go for sympathy, encouragement, helpful advice, and, above all, one who will share sorrow as well as joy. A friend is a kind of other self. There is deep understanding between friends and even disagreements are amicable. A true friendship should also be morally helpful to both parties. Love of friendship is characterized by a spirit of self-sacrifice and helpful interest in the other's welfare and happiness.

Countless books have been written on the nature of friendship, one of the truly consoling and heartwarming relationships that make life a meaningful joy. Such words as these have given only an extremely sketchy and inadequate picture of a "friend." And it is certainly an understatement when we say that this

135

love of friendship, which can exist between two men, two women, or a man and a woman, is a very important and lasting element in a happy marriage and can lead to marriage if other elements are present.

If true friendship does exist between a man and a woman there is the likelihood that the second element, which might be called general sex attraction, also comes into the picture. Men are interested in women and women are interested in men. Both like the differences. Men, for instance, are attracted by the grace, the emotional response, the beauty, and the tenderness of a woman. Women are attracted by the strength, courage, energy, and calm deliberation of a man. This interest and attraction is shown by a certain toning up process that occurs in the presence of the opposite sex. A group of men are chatting and another man joins the group, and it's "Hi, Bill." An attractive woman approaches the group and all the men are alerted. The same would hold true if the situation were reversed. A handsome man joins a group of women and there is a little flurry quite unlike that caused by the arrival of even the most vivacious woman. There is a natural element of mystery that surrounds the opposite sex. The responsiveness to the complementary qualities of the other sex is the second element in the man-woman relationship. It can be taken for granted but it does enter into the process of falling in love. One girl detected the difference between this general sex attraction and personal love for her when she shrewdly observed, "Every time I think that he is interested in me personally I find out that he just likes women in general." The opposite situation can also be true. Some women like men so obviously that any man they meet is inclined to take it personally.

This leads us to the third element of falling in love. It is called particular sex attraction. It has this in common with love of friendship. It is an attraction to a person—a definite person. It is not merely a general interest in the opposite sex or a physical attraction to the body. The most distinctive characteristic of personal sex attraction is its exclusiveness. A person thus attracted wants complete possession of the loved one.

A third party is resented—three is a crowd. In friendship the friend is good. In particular sex attraction the other person is wonderful!

The development of this attractive force is hard to describe, but it results in discovery of the "one and only." The object of a lover's attention may be just another nice person to his or her roommate, but the lover's interest in this person is so intense that all others are excluded. Absence is hard on this exclusive love. It creates a yearning for the other's presence. It is hard to do one's work and hard to think of other things. It is difficult to study or read. The mind is always coming back to dwell lovingly and longingly on the loved one. Letters are frequent and effusive. This kind of love is not content with mere presence but is impelled to express itself in terms of endearment, protestations of love, in kisses, and caresses. If this particular sex attraction is mutual, then it tends to have both parties totally absorbed in each other. It locks the hearts together and is a perfect psychological inducement to marriage. No two people can cultivate a companionship like this and assure themselves that they will not want to get married. It is of this element of love that many love songs sing: "I've got you under my skin," and a thousand others that will immediately come to mind. The very intensity of this love indicates that it cannot last at such a pitch. It is wonderful to have because it helps to insure fidelity in marriage. "You and you alone." But if it were still there after marriage, with the same intensity as it was present during courtship, the husband would find it difficult to go to work and earn a living. Particular sex attraction mellows and when it does, some erroneously feel that "love is gone."

It is easy to see where all this is leading, especially when we consider the fourth element—physical sex attraction. As the words indicate it is an attraction of body to body. One sex seeks the other as a means of stimulating and satisfying physical passion. It urges one, therefore, to such acts as will afford this satisfaction, chiefly to intimate and personal embraces and finally to sexual intercourse. When these four elements are together they add up very simply:

Love of friendship
General sex attraction
Particular sex attraction
+ Physical sex attraction

_____

MARRIAGE

It is not ordinarily possible to postpone marriage for any great length of time when these four elements are present in any intensity. The stress and strain is too much. The danger of violating chastity increases as this stage is prolonged without its logical culmination in marriage. That is why the following directions may be very useful.

Directions on how to fall out of love may sound like a cruel and heartless interruption at this point. To repeat, "Who would want to fall out of love?" The instinctive answer would be, "No one!" But what can a person do when the "Dear John" letter arrives? Commit suicide? Enlist in the Marines? Join the Foreign Legion? Get drunk? Run at once to hide one's broken heart in a nunnery or a seminary?

The fact is that all emotions can be controlled— even human love. Falling out of love has been done countless times, deliberately, successfully, and it is being done every day. A broken heart does mend and time always works its healing magic. Here are the recommendations of the experts. Pray for the grace of conviction that "it's over." Offer some little self-denial to obtain God's help and then follow these rules. They will tear your heart out but they work. One consolation is that usually "it only hurts for a little while." First, separate physically; second, separate mentally; third, have the conviction that your life is not ruined; fourth, lead a normal social life.

The reason for separating physically is pretty obvious. There is nothing like propinquity for keeping love alive. Keep an alligator around long enough and you will probably get attached to him and miss him when he's gone. This separation means no dates, no phone calls, no correspondence. This sounds like a death sentence if one has been deeply involved. It sounds very much like "You will be hanged by the neck until you are dead." And so the temptation is strong to see each other "just once more." The "once more" is as misguided a kindness as it is to cut off a dog's tail in small pieces so it won't hurt him so much.

Mental separation is equally important. There is not too much point to physical separation if the person remains constantly present in our thoughts, imagination, and dreams. But with a combination of conscious thought control, perseverance, and practice, the other person can be "washed right out" of the brain. The dance program, snapshots, and letters, kept lovingly for sentimental reasons, simply prolong the agony. One girl, as she deliberately and calmly tore up the packet of love letters, found herself somewhat liberated by this symbolic act. It is quite impractical to try to build up a gigantic hate for the once-loved one. Such a project can easily have the result, not desired but most logical and natural, of keeping the person only too vividly and painfully present to the mind all day long. And above all, be convinced that life is not ruined. Human beings have a tremendous capacity for love. If a love affair is dead, the human heart can and very likely should love again. Being bitter doesn't make things better. Exaggerations like "All men (or all women) are . . . no good," are the instinctive cries of the heartbroken. All women are not Delilahs and Santa Claus is still a jolly, lovable man. Try to rebuild a normal social life. This is perhaps the most important thing. The attitude "If you love you get hurt, so I'm through loving anything or anybody," is an expression of excruciating emptiness —emptiness that was made to be filled. So the heart should be opened to the possibility of new, life-filling friendships by leading a normal social life. Hiding away like a wounded animal is no solution. The first attempts at reconstructing social life may be a little mechanical. We have to go through the motions of smiling and appearing interested, and here a sense of humor can be a saving grace. The laugh at first may be a little hollow and mirthless. "Ha Ha," he laughed, showing his strong, white teeth, but this forced laughter can gradually mellow and eventually come from inside. We *can* love again.

How long can I kiss a boy (or girl)?

There is a question which keeps showing up in various disguises but which might be reduced to, "How long can I kiss a boy (or girl)?" For the single person, this problem is a matter of trying to distinguish between passion and affection and to what extent, on what occasions, and in what manner affection may be shown. That it is a recurring problem when one gets involved in the boy-girl relationship was brought out very refreshingly at one of the sessions of the Summer School of Catholic Action. The general discussion was on dating and one little dewy-eyed girl, about fifteen, charmingly and innocently unfolded her problem: "Father, it was my first date. We went to the early show. It was wonderful—I mean the movie. We kind of held hands in the popcorn box. Afterwards we stopped for a coke." Then, breathlessly, she continued: "Then he walked me home, and I want to know, do-you-think-he-should-have-kissed-me?" The priest thought, then smilingly said: "No, dear, I think he had done enough for you already."

Obviously there is going to be no mathematical answer to the question of "How long can I kiss a boy (girl)?" since there are four unknowns in the equation and you can't solve a math problem, much less one of human relationships, if there is more than one unknown per equation. The first unknown is that normal sex ranges from very hot to very cold. It is not just a point on a line, but a whole area. Abnormally cold would be: "Nothing, nothing at all bothers or excites me." Abnormally hot would be: "Everything, simply everything is stimulating." This is the first unknown. We all differ. But we would all like to know "Where do I fit in the normal area of sex?" This is a good question because self-knowledge is very useful.

The second unknown in the equation is that a person changes with the season (spring and "good ole summertime"), age (flaming youth), and climate (the tropics). Even though a person might have a pretty accurate estimate of himself on the temperature scale, changes do take place.

The third unknown quantity is the difference between men and women in their reactions to sexual stimulation. It is a difference which will not be fully understood or appreciated by a member of the opposite sex. Yet this difference has to be taken into account because in showing affection there is always that other person in the picture. Kissing is not done in the abstract or in a vacuum. There is always the kisser and the kissee. It is a matter of cooperation and has moral implications.

Every comparison limps and cannot be totally accurate, but the following one does give an emphasis which is generally true. A man's reaction to stimulation is somewhat like turning on the electric light switch—the light goes on. A woman's reaction is more like turning on an electric iron. A gradual heat permeates the iron. Eventually it becomes as hot as the electric light but the process has been more gradual. The difference has to be taken into account. Generally speaking, women stay on the affectionate plane longer than men. Men move more readily into the area of physical passion. So an action which might leave a woman serene could be quite stimulating to a man.

The fourth unknown is that kissing one person could be like kissing a doorknob. Kiss another and the reaction could be atomic.

But even though there is no possibility of a clear-cut answer with these four unknowns, there is a guiding principle that can be of considerable use. It might be formulated this way. If I like someone I may show affection. Affection is ordinarily adequately shown by passing kisses, a casual embrace, holding hands, arm about the other, the endearing terms, the tone of voice, and the eyes. These acts show affection and may be permitted. The second part of the principle is that single persons may not perform any action which, of its own nature, would cause sexual excitement. While the following acts would generally show affection, of their nature they would generally cause sexual excitement to one or the other party and therefore are not permitted to single people: long-held kisses, over-frequent kissing, unusual types of kissing, long-held, close embraces, intimate touches, and caresses. If these actions didn't cause sexual excitement to one or the other party, then how could such stimulation be achieved? To repeat: single people may not perform an action which, of its own nature, would cause sexual excitement.

Expression of affection should be a sincere reflection of the regard two people have for each other. Casual, indiscriminate displays of affection given to many and given on short acquaintance would be dishonest and insincere if nothing else. One can't honestly say he likes everyone that much. Some men might say: "I just like girls—all shapes and sizes. I want to hug and kiss them all," which sounds very much like perpetual brotherhood week. So why not treat them as brothers?

Father Gerald Kelly, S.J., in his book *Modern Youth and Chastity*, says: "When even modest signs of affection are frequent and enduring and ardent, there can be no just reason for them. It is based upon the sound psychology that these things invariably arouse physical passion and this cannot be the aim of unmarried people in their demonstration of affection."

It is prudent then to be moderate in this whole area of showing affection through physical contact because things can so easily get out of hand. This is especially true in the young because their emotions are strong and their imaginations are easily inflamed, and the newness of it all should bid them to proceed with caution. If we desire peace of mind and if we wish to avoid anxiety and worry, we should play it a little cool. If we try to walk the razor edge between passion and affection, then there is continual worry and falls are apt to be frequent. Obviously a dedication of one's purity to the blessed Virgin is very helpful.

For women the ideal is not to be a timid woman afraid to use her great capacity for love and affection. Such women do not make ideal wives or mothers or nuns. They are afraid of the gifts God gave them and bury them—so afraid to exercise or use these gifts that they conceal them in a frightened frigidity. Nor is the ideal to be found in a foolish woman—one who carelessly and casually uses the gifts entrusted to her. The ideal is a valiant woman who uses well and generously the tremendous gifts of womanhood entrusted to her by God.

Man's strength should be used, not to dominate, but to protect and cherish. It is immature to use others for one's own selfish pleasure. To do so would make one not the "great lover" but the great self-lover. For the sake of the Blessed Virgin and their own mothers and sisters, men should respect all women—even those who may have lost respect for themselves.

Moods

In the matter of purity there are certain moods which pose a threat, or at least make us more vulnerable to temptation. A mood is not just a passing thought or feeling; it is something which permeates the whole person, body and soul. It colors the imagination and flows over into the emotions. It can even influence the posture of our body. It can direct our thinking so that we consider only a limited aspect of reality. Bright moods can be useful and productive. Dark moods can be deadly. These dark moods often incline the mind and emotions to seek a little immediate consolation and comfort in the area of sex.

One such mood which needs a watchful eye has been classified as the fed-up mood. We may have been doing the same monotonous work day after day. For a student, homework and study with no let up. Or home, office, office, home for the businessman. Scrub, wash, clean, cook, for the housewife. We have had a shoulder to the wheel and a nose to the grindstone just a little too long. Now we have had enough of it! We're fed up—right up to here. Tensions mount. We need a break. "I want out!"

When this mood hits us we generally do need a change of pace, some entertainment, a change of scenery. We need some fun. Reasonably we should take it. The danger is that with this mood in possession we may seek to break the monotony by breaking the commandments. Relief may be sought in sex—alone or with others. This fed-up mood can be observed in soldiers who have been on the line too long or who have had a hard siege of basic training. Sailors, after a long stretch of sea duty, are fed up. Leave time is needed, but the danger is that the sailors may leave the town painted in some rather lurid colors. "The fleet's been in!" Students cramming for exams need a change of pace when the ordeal is over—but there can be danger in the mood. It can easily lead to burlesque shows, or a prowl car, or an armful of girly books and sex novels, or even a lost weekend. The same mood shows up in "tired" businessmen seeking relaxation. So the problem with the fed-up mood is how to break the mood. Obviously this can be done with a little intelligent planning, some prudence, and the help of some good friends. Getting drunk, necking, and so forth show lack of imagination. A good time, a really good time, can be had by all, and the mood can be dispelled once we recognize the mood for what it is and tackle the problem intelligently, gracefully, and prayerfully.

Another mood which is invariably dangerous is the mood of self-pity, feeling excessively sorry for ourselves. Objectively our lives may be very difficult and rugged at times. There can be misunderstandings, lack of love and appreciation where we might reasonably expect to find it. Failure dogs our best efforts. We are misrepresented and misinterpreted, definitely behind the "eight ball." So we find ourselves miserable, empty, and inclined to wallow in self-pity. "Poor Me!" We become a weary burden to ourselves and to others. In this mood the tendency is to seek a little easy consolation wherever and however we can find it— with ourselves or with others. "You are the only one who really understands me," can be famous last words. In this mood sex temptations have a much stronger appeal and seem to offer "surcease from sorrow."

At this point Lucy's advice to Charley Brown, when he was brooding over life and it's difficulties and deep in melancholy, might have a point. She briskly, though somewhat unfeelingly shouted: "SNAP OUT OF IT!" Spiritual writers refer to self-pity as the luxury of melancholy. It is a luxury few can afford since it makes us unfit for effort in every area: business, study, social, spiritual. Melancholy is the source of many faults and sins. That is why some writers have classified it as the eighth capital sin. People who are happy don't go seeking sin.

A third mood, the moonlight and roses mood, also deserves a watchful eye. There is the beautiful girl with her soft, understanding eyes and there is the man, broad-shouldered and masculine and attentive. There is soft music and a June moon and a gently caressing breeze whispering through the trees. There is the murmur of the night and the fragrance of night-blooming jasmine. The mocking bird is going "mock mock" in the trees to say nothing of the nightingale pouring out his heart in liquid melody to the moon. It's the magic of the night. At times all this is real and it can be the atmosphere which leads to a declaration of genuine love. At other times the mood is as phony as the "paper moon in a penny arcade." In either case, when the spell and the mood are broken there is a jolting return to reality. Words and commitments of love, which seemed so natural and so right a few hours earlier, can be as unreal as the blood-chilling horror of a nightmare. "Why did I? I feel so ashamed of myself. How could I have . . . ?" You feel a bit foolish trying to answer such questions in the cold, gray light of dawn and realize that a gently suspicious eye on the moonlight and roses mood might have spared you the effort and the embarrassment.

Heavy drinking in mixed company and the mood of abandon and recklessness that prompt and accompany it are almost too obvious to mention. If we are going to drink we should be rather sure of both our drinking companions and ourselves. You may be under control but can you control another person? Just try to tell a drunk driver that he shouldn't be at the wheel. And Ogden Nash's somewhat cynical and worldly-wise rhyming couplet has some truth in it:

> Candy is dandy.
> But liquor is quicker.

For the young, and even the not-so-young, heavy drinking in mixed company is pouring fuel on a fire already briskly burning, or smouldering and waiting to leap into flame. Father Martindale, S.J., in his little booklet, "The Difficult Commandments" treats these and other moods and their implications with fine insight.

All of this seems to point to the fact that throughout a lifetime we have to be striving for emotional control and maturity. Emotional excesses of any kind can easily have reverberations in the area of sex, which seems to be the Achilles heel of fallen man. So we might take a glance at emotional maturity in general. It is encouraging because it offers the possibility of satisfying growth and is a big part of what makes us well-balanced, mature persons.

We can take it for granted, I think, that we will automatically advance in age. This is simply a matter of the calendar and staying around watching the days go by. We can also be reasonably sure that we will advance in information, not necessarily wisdom, but in information, yes. There is an ever-increasing wealth of facts available. We can even be reasonably sure of advancing in grace if we use even some of the opportunities that Christ offers us so generously: prayer, the sacraments, frequent Communion, the Mass. All of this is to the good and the years that lie ahead offer more of this three-fold growth if only we will grow. But the area of emotional maturity also deserves our attention and requires self-knowledge and self-discipline. And control, naturally, is not something that simply happens when we are born. It must be consciously acquired—worked for.

We are to some degree children of our "advanced" time, and we reflect its moods and values. Our day and age has an abundance of good things and attitudes, but it also has its deficiencies. Critics agree that it is an emotionally and mentally disturbed age; it is undisciplined; and it tends to be intellectually flabby and impatient of authority. And these criticisms point to areas of satisfying growth for us so that while we draw on the strong points of our modern culture, we rise above its weaknesses. Starting with your emotions —are you excessive and unrestrained in the expression of affection, and, childlike, do you use other persons as an outlet? Are you easily and unreasonably irritable and impatient and critical? Are you churlish and ugly at home? And every-demanding, never giving? Do you give way to self-pity? Are you full of unfounded fears and anxieties which cripple many a wonderful person? Emotions are tremendous forces provided to help us achieve and they add immeasurably to our happiness. They should not be crushed. But if they are not disciplined and channeled they can become terrible tyrants in our own lives and in the lives of those who are close to us.

And how is your intellect? Does it jump to conclusions, too impatient to await sufficient evidence for a sound judgment? Are you racially prejudiced? This, in the intellectual order, is simply going from a particular to a universal. Very poor logic. In fact, F minus. It is so unfair. Pretty much like "We'll give him a fair trial and hang him in the morning." Are you willing to spend time to master a subject or a job? Is your theme song, "I'll get by" with a minimum of work and effort? A sense of responsibility as a student, as an employee and as an employer, as a professional man, or as a mother or father shows a maturity devoutly to be prayed for and desired.

How about your memory? Does its current inventory include a generous supply of sex stories and phrases designed to hurt, unpleasant incidents, resentments? Are you willing to make the effort to restock it with worthwhile information, facts, the memory of beautiful music, good poetry, the record of man's achievements? The melody lingers on. Is the memory a storehouse of the good, the true, and the beautiful or . . . ?

How is the imagination? This one can be the menace of the house, the village idiot, and the arch-villain all rolled into one if it is left undisciplined. It is a superb, three-D picture machine for private showings, but the question is "What's on?" Is it continually turning out condemned movies? Or do I just "Dream, Dream, Dream," a briefly satisfying but quite inadequate substitute for the world of reality. Dream we should but dreams alone never got anyone anything. Does the imagination exaggerate fears into giant bogie men ready to strangle any plan of action?

Does it consistently sell the gold brick of pleasure as twenty-four carat happiness?

How is the will? With clear objectives and ends to be achieved, can I keep at a task, confident that with God's help victory can be won? Can I make a mature decision and stick by it?

Obviously these random questions don't constitute an exhaustive treatment of the subject. Some of them may be tellingly appropriate in your case; some of them may leave you wondering who'd be foolish enough to dream them up. And that's where the do-it-yourself part of the retreat comes in. Your own checklist of questions in this vein will be far more practically valuable than any author's book-length treatment. And these few are supplied only to trigger your own thinking. So do-it-yourself! With the self-knowledge that you can thus achieve (Lord that I may know myself) and with the knowledge of God (Lord that I may know Thee) a fuller and happier life awaits us as more emotionally mature adults. This emotional maturity keeps negative destructive moods from crippling the wonderful person God intends you to be. It also adds appreciably to self-control in the area of sex and thus prepares us for a richer, fuller life of grace.

Thoughts

"Blessed are the clean of heart, for they shall see God" (Matthew 5:8)

Even in this life the pure of heart and the clean of mind see God more clearly. The grace is worth praying for. Being clean of heart, however, does not mean being without sex temptations. As a matter of fact only a few of the saints were given the extraordinary gift of being completely free from temptations against purity. One saint, to whom our Lord appeared frequently, complained to Him about the intensity of her temptations and asked: "Where were you, Lord, when I was so sorely tempted?" He told her consolingly, "Right in the midst of your heart." So we cannot reasonably expect to be free from temptation. We are rational animals, not angels, and just as we are tempted to eat too much, or drink too much, we will be tempted to misuse sex. The odds are that temptations of this kind will continue until *rigor mortis* sets in. So don't panic when temptations come. The problem is not that we have temptations but rather how we handle them and reduce them to a minimum. Temptation is not sin. Temptation is allurement to sin. So how do we handle this allurement in the area of sex?

First, it is obvious but useful to recall that it is legitimate to think about sex and its functions. We have to learn about it so we can use well this wonderful, creative gift that God entrusted to us. How would we ever get married if we never thought about marriage with its privileges and duties. If God calls us to a religious or priestly vocation we should know what we are giving up and what we are giving to Him. We need to know the elements involved in a life of perfect and perpetual chastity and how, with God's grace, it can be lived. To repeat, it is legitimate to think about sex. That is why parents should be ready and available to talk it over with their children. That's why there are pre-Cana conferences, counselors, priests, and good books to help you to think clearly and cooly on this very important subject. The information obtained from these sources is much more reliable than street talk and sex magazines that promise to reveal all. Generally the self-styled street corner sex expert is poorly informed. If nothing else, his vocabulary is inadequate; he has to depend too much on four-letter words. If his claim to speak with authority comes from extra-marital experiences you can be sure the source, at least, of your information is contaminated. The sex-magazine that promises to reveal all and tries to do so on the cover is generally not out to instruct you helpfully but to excite you. When accurate, balanced information about sex is sought it is wise to go to the experts not the perverts, to good books not the lurid sex magazines.

Now suppose that I have no good reason for thinking about sex and its functions, but I find my mind full of such thoughts or my imagination is turning out sex pictures in technicolor with myself, perhaps, playing a leading role. When would sin enter in? In the interest of avoiding confusion when we try to answer this question, it is important to recall that we do not have complete and absolute control over our thoughts, imagination, and sensations, and that the control we do exercise is mostly indirect. If we are wise we do not tackle sex head on, as we might some types of temptation. The best technique is to walk away from it. We handle the temptation by trying to turn the mind quietly to something else. We get rid of an objectionable thought or picture by putting a wholesome thought or picture in its place. The mind cannot remain a vacuum. In other words, we treat the temptation as we would treat the unreasonable demands of a little child. The child says, "I want an ice cream cone!" We answer quietly and firmly, "No." The child insists, "I want an ice cream cone!" Instead of arguing the point further (for that can go on endlessly) we say to the child: "Look at the bow-wow, see the birdie, listen to the tick-toc," and the child is distracted at least temporarily. Of course he may be back in five minutes with his demand, "I want an ice cream cone." He doesn't give up the idea of the ice cream cone, but we keep on doing the best we can to distract him. We try the same technique with the unreasonable impure thoughts or imaginations. We try to turn our own minds to something else or we do something to distract ourselves. Naturally, a quick aspiration, a quick call for help is useful; "My Jesus, mercy, Mary help me," a quick Hail Mary. In addition to getting reinforcements from outside time and space, it reassures us that we have set our wills against the temptation. So even though the temptations may continue we are conscious we have tried to dismiss them. We prayed, didn't we? This is about the best we can do. We do not have absolute control in this area. So there is no sin. We can report a victory, hear our Lord's "Well done," and be serene.

Another source of confusion in this matter arises from the fact that impure thoughts, imaginations, and sex sensations are pleasurable. But that doesn't mean that we will to have them. Sin is in consent of the will, not a feeling. For example: I place sugar on your tongue. Sugar is sweet. Will you taste the sweetness?

Yes. Sugar is sweet, I put poisoned sugar on your tongue. Will you taste the sweetness. Yes. Poisoned sugar is still sweet. Will you want the poisoned sugar? No, because it is poisoned. But even as you are rejecting it, trying to spit it out it will still taste sweet and the sensation of pleasure continues. Notice that the human being is now going in two opposing directions. The senses are saying: "I like it. It's sweet." The will is saying: "I don't want it. It's poison." We are conscious of the same ambivalence toward impure thoughts, imaginations, and sensations. The body is finding them pleasurable. Yea hurrah! The will is rejecting this pleasure as forbidden. Boo! So even though the pleasure-giving impure sensation or picture maintains its unwanted presence, that is not sin. Sin is in the will, which in this case has taken its stand and registered its vote, "No!" Even if the "No" must be repeated again there is still no sin, but victory over temptation. The sacrifice made may leave some trace of regret over the pleasure rejected, but the sacrifice is still made. Victory! No sin. On the contrary, an increase in merit.

We find ourselves faced with another confusing situation. For example, a thought or picture might be in my head for a time—unrecognized. Then I become alerted to it. I recognize it as forbidden to me in my state of life. I must now react to it. Responsibility enters at this point. But where does the sin begin? A simple illustration might suggest an easy method for answering such a question.

A man holding a box of strawberries knocks on the door and asks, "Do you want some strawberries?" "No," you shout, and slam the door. Obviously you didn't want the strawberries. A man holding a box of strawberries knocks at the door. "Do you want some strawberries?" He holds them up before your interested gaze. Aren't they luscious? They surely would taste good. You'd like some, but—but, well, no, really, you just can't afford them, and slowly the door shuts out the sight of the berries. No strawberries this time. You didn't really want them, but you hesitated over the "No." You almost lost your sales resistance—but not quite. A man knocks at the door.

"Any strawberries?" "Yes, indeed. Several boxes. Bring them right in. Let's have strawberry shortcake." Obviously you want the strawberries.

Substitute impure thoughts, pictures, sensations for the strawberries and consider the same reactions. At times they are handled with dispatch. "No strawberries." No problem here. We are aware that we reacted to the temptation promptly and did not consent. Also there shouldn't be any problem in deciding when there is obviously serious matter, sufficient reflection, and full consent of the will. "Ah, strawberries! Bring them in. Let's have strawberry shortcake." That's clear! But what about the situation where there is some shilly-shalling? It would come under the heading of carelessness. We spent too long, needlessly, in our reflection but there was no full consent of the will. We did say "No." It might be described in confession as "I had some temptations against purity which I did not handle as well as I might have," or "I had some temptations against purity but there was no mortal sin." It is important to keep serene. A sensitive, clear, accurate conscience is the ideal, not an anxious, worried, fluttery type.

In this whole matter of purity a clean mind is the way to a pure heart. So if we are a little careful about our reading, picture magazines, and entertainment, without being prudish, we save ourselves a lot of grief. In regard to the eyes, it is not so much what we see that causes the trouble, it is what we stare at. Sexy pictures etched into the mind and imagination can come back at us in moments of weakness to harass us. So naturally, blatant sex magazines and entertainments such as burlesque shows and movies condemned for obscenity are deadly enemies of purity. The price for such entertainment is outrageously high. It generally costs us sanctifying grace!

A consoling thought for those who are struggling for purity is that it takes real strength to be pure. Anyone can be impure. It's easy. It takes a strong man and a valiant woman to keep striving for our Lord's blessing: "Blessed are the clean of heart, for they shall see God." There should never be discouragement, no matter how many times we may fail. This is an area of human weakness and the malice in sins of weakness is not vicious. Ultimate victory is assured if only we keep trying and begin again and again with confidence and trust. "Remember, O most gracious Virgin, Mary, that never was it known that any one who fled to thy protection, implored thy help or sought thy intercession was left unaided." Devotion to the Blessed Virgin and frequent, if possible, daily Communion, are obvious spiritual antidotes for disordered sex. The victory can be won if you are patient with yourself, grow in emotional maturity, and are persistent in the use of prayer and the sacraments.

For girls

If we look back into the misty past, it might seem about a hundred years ago, and see ourselves at the age of five or six, we recall that little boys did not care much for little girls and the compliment was returned. Little girls were sissies. Little boys were rough and rowdy. Little girls liked to play house. Little boys liked to play soldiers. Little girls cried. Little boys pulled their hair and dangled worms in front of them just to hear their screams. It was not a mutual admiration society by any means. But even at that age there was a sneaking suspicion that the other race of human beings might prove interesting at a later date. As one little boy, a sophisticated six, said to his younger playmate: "How old are you?" The little fellow answered, "I don't know." "Well do you like girls?" the six-year-old asked, "Do you, huh?" The younger one answered, "No, I don't!" "Well, then, you must be only four years old," was the oldster's worldly-wise conclusion. If we want that particular age and its interests summed up we might say, "Little girls like dolls and little boys like soldiers." Ten years later all this is changed and goes into reverse. The not-so-little girls like soldiers and the not-so-little boys like dolls. What happened? This is a revolution! It deserves a little study.

Taking it from the distaff side, a very profound change has taken place. With physical maturity, for a girl, there comes the tremendous gift of womanhood—a capacity to bring new life into the world.

Accompanying this God-given, life-giving capacity there are equally profound psychological and emotional changes. There is a new and greater capacity to love and be loved, to give affection and to receive it. There is a new capacity for sympathy, and understanding. There is a new capacity for being of service to others. These are tremendous and wonderful gifts which need to be consciously recognized, appreciated, and cultivated. They must be cultivated because they are there only in their beginnings. Obviously a girl will never develop into a good man so she should develop her womanly gifts to their fullness. But these qualities and gifts need working at and are worth the effort knowing that the phrase, "a woman to her finger tips," is quite a compliment.

Every gift that God gives us is meant for our own happiness and is to be used for the service and happiness of others. A musician finds personal satisfaction in his talent and brings happiness and pleasure to his listeners. A doctor finds achievement in the practice of medicine, while his diagnosis, medications, and surgical skill bring health to others. Similarly a woman finds her happiness and completion in using the gifts God has given her. But these gifts are also meant for and can bring happiness to her friends, a future husband and children, and all the people God may send into her life as a wife or professional woman. These talents for love, sympathy, and service can find expression in any of the threefold vocations. We might forget that womanly qualities are needed just as much in the family of the Church as in the family of the home. Imagine a priest or brother teaching kindergarten effectively, or carrying on certain types of social work which obviously require a woman's touch. And as you watch a woman choosing the single, professional life as a career, she is seldom found working as a riveter or construction engineer or foreman of a railroad. She instinctively seeks out areas where her womanly capacities are needed and can express themselves in sympathy, understanding, personal service, love. A woman, it seems, must give herself.

If we consider woman's general role in society, she

is meant to have a gentling and refining influence on a world which may become brutal and crude and feelingless. If a woman were living in a fox hole, in a short time undoubtedly she would have curtains up. It might be a little more difficult getting in and out but it would be more homelike. This gentling, cultural contribution of women to civilization is admirably and dramatically pictured for us in the stations of the cross. For the most part the Passion of Christ is a scene of brutality and cruelty. It is man's inhumanity to man, God become man. The gentling touches in this vicious outburst are found in the fourth station, where Jesus meets His Blessed Mother. Her complete understanding and sympathy make it possible for Him to go on. In the sixth station, Veronica wipes the face of Jesus. She cannot stop the crucifixion but the seemingly futile, feminine offer of her veil to wipe the blood and sweat from His sacred face wins His grateful appreciation and gentles the hearts of all of us. At the eighth station Jesus meets the women of Jerusalem. Their tears and offer of sympathy and the sorrow for His sufferings express the true response of the human heart in the face of human misery; they had compassion. Then there are the women at the foot of the cross. A woman is soft and gentle but valiant. A woman is patient and does not shrink from sacrifice or suffering when she loves. Women are there with their loving care for Him when He is taken down from the cross and lies in the arms of His mother. Faithful unto death, even to death on the cross. Then there is Easter morning and, hoping against hope, they go to the tomb and are rewarded by the risen Christ with one of His first apparitions. "But Mary was standing outside weeping at the tomb . . . Jesus said to her, 'Woman, why art thou weeping?' . . . She, thinking that he was the gardener, said to him, 'Sir, if thou hast removed him, tell me where thou hast laid him and I will take him away.' Jesus said to her, 'Mary!' Turning, she said to him, 'Rabboni!' (that is to say, Master)" (John 20:11 ff.). No comment is needed on this heartwarming scene. Here is Christ and here is woman at her loving and lovable best.

Since this gift of womanhood—to bring life into the world—is such a tremendous gift, God delays giving it until a girl is old enough to appreciate it and use it well. You do not give children an expensive, jewelled watch. They are not able to appreciate it and would misuse it. A little child might even trade it for a bar of chocolate. You do not give a child the keys to a Cadillac. He would wreck it. So this capacity to bring life into the world and its accompanying capacity for loving and being loved is delayed until a girl reaches enough maturity to appreciate it and exercise the self-control and discipline needed to use it well. Consequently there should be a grateful appreciation for the gift of womanhood and insistence that others respect the gift. The protection that God puts around a woman and her capacity to give and receive love is not meant to take the joy and fun out of living. Something as precious as this needs safeguarding. Washington's desk is cherished as an historical monument. People are not permitted to carve their initials on it or casually eat their lunch there. Yet this is only a remembrance of the past. So when God says of the living source of life, "You are so important and precious in my sight that anyone who misuses your gifts and treats you carelessly has offended Me seriously," we can understand His viewpoint. These restrictions are not harsh restraints but loving safeguards of God the Father for His most precious and dearly loved daughters.

What a woman can be in her completion of nature and grace is found in Mary, virgin, mother, widow. She is God's ideal woman and she is ours. We may apply God's beautifully poetic language to her: "And a great sign appeared in heaven: a woman clothed with the sun, and the moon was under her feet, and upon her head a crown of twelve stars" (Apocalypse 12:1).

Do it yourself!

Points for your prayerful thinking (15 minutes)

PREPARATORY PRAYER
See page 18.

Fifteen minutes meditation may be selected from those sections of this chapter which may specifically apply (single? married? engaged? contemplating a priestly or religious vocation?).

Conclude by saying one Our Father, a Hail Mary, and Glory Be to the Father.

The chapter coming up reminds us, who live in the age when man is penetrating outer space and looking forward to interplanetary travel, that another time-space break-through occurred almost two thousand years ago. That break-through came from outside space and time and has changed the thinking, the lives, and especially the hearts of men most profoundly. It was when God broke through from eternity into time and came into this world of ours to raise us up to divinity. And in future ages, when men may take interplanetary travel for granted, God's break-through will still be world shaking. God has become man and dwells among us. Our world will never be the same.

From here on your *DO-IT-YOURSELF RETREAT* is Christ-centered and its direction is growing in personal knowledge, love, and imitation of Him. When meditating on the mysteries of Christ's life, St. Ignatius's suggestion is "to ask for interior knowledge of our Lord, who for me has become man, in order that I may love Him better and follow Him more closely." We can do no better than follow this suggestion and make this our prayer, for He is the way, the truth, and the life.

A more excellent way

I f we look back over the truths we have considered, we can see them as a reasonable, livable, and realistic philosophy of life. They bring out the real good in us. We saw, first of all, that we came out from God by creation, and that it was an act of infinite love. We belong to God, mind, heart, and body, for time and eternity; and we are to spend our lives in His praise, reverence, and service. He has given to each of us a work given to no other. We are unique. In His Fatherly plan we are important. He has destined us to an eternity of happiness with Himself, and our mission in life is to reach that eternity of happiness. This is successful living. "For what does it profit a man, if he gain the whole world, but suffer the loss of his own soul."

We looked at ourselves under the X ray of faith and reason and saw breath-taking beauty and dignity there. We are made in His image and likeness. Further, we share in His divine nature! This dignifies the least actions which we perform and is the basis of our charity and love for one another. We are brothers and sisters in Christ. ". . . as long as you did it for one of these, the least of my brethren, you did it for me."

To live this supernatural life well, God gave us the gift of faith—a light for our minds, so that we can look out on this world and the next and see things as He sees them. This keeps us in touch with reality. We can see life steadily and see it as a whole. "Lord, that I may see." He gave us the promise of divine omnipotence to support our weakness—the gift of hope. Victory is assured. We don't have to do it alone.

We established a principle for using the things of this life. I will use them if they help me to accomplish my mission, to reach an eternity of happiness with God; I will refrain from using them if they hinder me or stand in the way. Logically, too, the more a thing will help me, the more I will use it; the less it will help me, the less I will use it. It is reasonable to give God a reasonable service.

Finally, we saw that there was only one thing that could effectively block us from eternal happiness—mortal sin—a knowing and willing violation of God's law in a serious matter. We learned to hate the disorder and unhappiness that mortal sin brings to all concerned. Then we glanced at the possibility of being an eternal failure—hell. But then we saw reassuringly that between us and that possibility God has placed His infinite mercy and love.

Now, we would think that these truths would be sufficient for us to put order into our lives and live well. But we have a feeling that something is still missing. All this is just a little too abstract. In the process of daily living, these great truths can easily dim out or be forgotten. Christianity is a philosophy of life, but it is something more than that. True, Christianity gives us principles for right living and it gives us commandments and counsels. But Christianity gives us much more than that—it gives us Christ. Christianity is Christ. And until our religion becomes a matter of personal love, attachment, and loyalty to God become man, we have not been really deeply touched. These other truths can hit the mind and bounce off it like marbles off the sidewalk, beebees off a pillbox. But when a person comes into our lives and we begin to love, then we are changed. "Knowledge and love of Jesus Christ goes deeper down than any stoic striving after abstract virtues. Here is flesh and blood giving life and substance, whereas abstract virtue is only dead perfection." When we come to the evening of life, we shall be judged on our love for Christ and to what extent we measure up to His full stature. Knowledge, love, and imitation of Christ is successful living according to God's plan. It brings out the real good in us and draws out the potential for greatness that God implanted.

The desperate need we have for God to become man is felt by all of us. Socrates expressed his longing for something more than a philosophy when he said hopefully, "Perhaps a God will come and teach us." A friend of mine feelingly expressed the same need. We were student priests in theology and we had just finished a magnificent treatise on the unity and trinity of God. We had established God as Uncaused Cause and Unmoved Mover, First Principle, and Final End. We saw that He was Pure Act; His essence was His existence. He was omnipotent, omniscient. There were all those tremendous attributes of the Divinity which fill us with awe and wonderment, but which, at the same time, can so overwhelm the mind that God may seem a little distant or unreal. Just as we closed the book, Father Muldoon, a wonderfully gifted man who sat next to me, leaned over and said, with his usual trace of a stutter: "This is w-w-w-wonderful, but all I've g-g-g-got to say is th-th-thank God for Christmas!" He needed, as we all need, something more tangible than abstract truth. He needed God become man. He expressed our sentiments perfectly: "Thank God for Christmas." Then there is the story of the little girl who was being put to bed by her mother. The room was dark. She was sleeping upstairs by herself for the first time. She was scared. Her mother, to reassure her, said: "Now, Dear, don't be afraid, God is everywhere." "Yes," said the frightened little girl, "but I want someone with a face." Christ fills that need too. The most beautiful of the sons of men! John the apostle put it even better than Father Muldoon or the little girl when, in the last Gospel which we read at Mass every day, he soars up to the eternal Divinity and declares: "In the beginning was the Word, and the Word was with God; and the Word was God. . . . All things were made through him, and without him was made nothing that has been made. . . . And [triumphantly] the Word was made flesh, and dwelt among us. And we saw his glory—glory as of the only-begotten of the Father—full of grace and of truth." God Himself has come to meet our needs, to lead a human life, and to dwell with us.

We live in a very wonderful era, the spacious '60's, in which man has achieved what seemed unreal ten years ago. We've broken through this enclosed little world of ours and plunged into outer space. Gradually we have grown accustomed to astronomical speeds and distances with Sputniks and Explorers in orbit over our heads. The reality of interplanetary travel is taken for granted. We are impressed with these achievements of man, but we are also just a little bit afraid. We wonder what man will do with his new command over nature and its forces. Will it be used for peace or for destruction? We may forget that two thousand years ago there was a time-space break-through much more impressive than what man has accomplished today. Only this break-through came from the other direction. It came from outer space into our little world. It was not man plunging into space. It was God dwelling in light inaccessible who came into the dim light of our earth so that we could see Him. He came out of eternity into time so that we could contact Him more easily. He became man that He might raise us up to divinity. This break-through is the greatest event that ever will happen on the face of the earth. All else pales into insignificance. Yet there is no terror about this break-through. It is the gladdest tidings that God can give to men. ". . . behold, I bring you good news of great joy which shall be to all the people; for today in the town of David a Savior has been born to you, who is Christ the Lord" (Luke 2:10-11).

Successful living according to God's plan is no longer an abstraction. Once God has become man and lived a human life from birth to death, then all sanctity, all human living, must be modeled after Him. He is the Way, the Truth, and the Life. There is no other way, no other truth, no other life. Concretely now, successful living means being Christ-like, and Christ-loving. Our whole life is now directed toward these three things: knowledge, love, and imitation of Christ.

Since our goal and our aim is to be Christ-like, we might find it helpful to study Him lovingly and see what He was like in His human nature. St. Paul gives us the key to our study when he says that Christ is like to us in all things, sin alone excepted. It is good to recall our theology in this matter. The Second Person of the Blessed Trinity, the eternal Son of God, took on a human nature from the Virgin Mary and became the son of man. So there is one person with two natures—the nature of God and the nature of man. Like us, then, He had a created human soul with a finite intelligence and a finite will. He had a human body that was subject to the limitations of time and space and its need for food and rest. He had human emotions and a human heart. God now has a human heart! But there was one difference: His body did not rebel against His mind the way our bodies do. That rebellion is the result of original sin to which He was not subject. But otherwise He was like to us in all things—sin alone excepted.

Now let us study Him in His human nature. Pictures and statues can be a help. Some of them are good and some of them are pretty terrible, but all of them are limited by the artist's ability to sculpture or to paint. Generally they are tinctured by national or racial type and preference. The Japanese will slant His eyes; the Germans will give Him Teutonic coloring; the French will make Him resemble a Frenchman. These representations are a help, but they are limited. Instead of such subjective guides, let's look in the Gospels and discover Him for ourselves. We are on safe ground here. As I briefly trace out the broad lines of our Lord in His humanity (libraries have been written on this), fill in your own picture of what He was like as a man. Get to know Him for yourself.

The first thing we can say with certainty about our Lord is that He was a strong man physically. Now I am not preaching a muscular Christianity, but our Lord must have had strong arms and calloused hands after working as a carpenter for twenty-odd years. If we still wonder about His physical strength consider Him in His public life journeying up and down the length and breadth of Galilee and Judea, at times under a hot sun, his face grown tan, and many times sleeping out at night. "The foxes have dens, and the birds of the air have nests, but the Son of Man has nowhere to lay his head" (Luke 9:58). If we still wonder about His physical strength, think of His Passion. He was scourged with a Roman type scourging—stripes unlimited. Many men had died under such punishment. He was in jail for the night. He went through the emotional and physical ordeal of a trial before Pilate, then before Herod, and back again to Pilate. He carried a heavy cross weighing about 175 pounds, or at least a large section of it, three quarters of a mile to Calvary, where He agonized for three hours before dying. So, our Lord was strong physically. This is just a help in filling in the picture of what He was like as a man.

We can also say that our Lord was a man's man. We can tell that by the way men reacted to Him. On first impact, His divinity didn't shine out; He met them man to man. Men saw Him first as a great teacher or a great prophet. They saw Him and were attracted to Him. It was only after two years or so that Peter made His great confession, "Thou art Christ, the Son of God." Take Peter, or Andrew, His first followers, and their reactions to Him. They were rugged men, fishermen. Not the hook and line type you see along the lake pulling up a perch, but men who earned their living from the inland sea. Our Lord could go up to them and say: "Come, follow me." To be with Him, they gladly gave up what they had. These were capable men with a future, but once they got to know Him, they liked Him and were glad to give up all to work for Him. "And passing along by the sea of Galilee, he saw Simon and his brother Andrew, casting their nets into the sea (for they were fishermen). And Jesus said to them, 'Come, follow me, and I will make you fishers of men.' And at once they left the nets, and followed him. And going on a little farther, he saw James the son of Zebedee, and his brother John; they also were in their boat mending the nets. Immediately he called them. And they left their father Zebedee in the boat with the hired men, and followed him . . . And they were astonished at his teaching; for he was teaching them as one having authority" (Mark 1:16-22). Or take Matthew,

163

who was a tax gatherer. We know that this type of man can be rather hard-hearted and handed, if not by instinct, at least by profession. As Matthew was going about his work, our Lord came up to him and making the same appeal he makes to every man, said: "Come, follow me," and Matthew gladly gave up all to be with Christ. Rather interestingly, it is recorded that he was so happy about this invitation that he had a party and invited other tax gatherers and publicans to be present. When the Pharisees observed our Lord with these men, they criticized Him.

"And it came to pass as he was at table in the house, that, behold, many publicans and sinners came to the table with Jesus and his disciples. And the Pharisees seeing it, said to his disciples, 'Why does your master eat with publicans and sinners?' But Jesus heard it, and said, '. . . go, and learn what this means: "I desire mercy, and not sacrifice." For I have come to call sinners, not the just' " (Matthew 9:10-13).

It fills in the picture of what our Lord was like to see Him at ease with these men and them happy to be in His presence. Or take the Roman centurion, a foreigner, a mercenary soldier. He came to our Lord and said: "One of my men is sick, will you heal him?" And our Lord said: "I will come down to your house, and heal him." But the soldier protested: "Sir, I am a man subject to authority, and have soldiers subject to me. When I tell a man go, he goes; when I tell a man come, he comes. Lord, I am not worthy you should come into my house. Just say the word and my servant shall be healed." This is such a magnificent act of faith in our Lord's authority and power that we make it a part of the Mass, and before receiving Holy Communion, we repeat the prayer of the soldier three times: "Domine, non sum dignus!" "Lord, I am not worthy that you should come into my soul, just say the word and my spirit shall be healed!" All this helps to fill in the picture of what our Lord was like as a man. To know Him was to be attracted to Him.

Take the other end of the social scale, if you wish to call it that. Joseph of Arimathea, a man of political influence and wealth, became our Lord's disciple. When our Lord died, Joseph, who didn't have to go through channels, but could go directly to the top, fearlessly went to the Roman governor, requested our Lord's body, and buried Him in his own rich tomb. Or take Nicodemus, a formally educated, cultured man, a doctor of the law. He came to our Lord at night, questioned Him about His doctrine, and secretly became His disciple. As we observe these varied types reacting to Him, we can see that all kinds of men of good will, meeting our Lord, loved Him and respected Him.

Now our Lord did have His enemies, the Pharisees. But even they said of Him, "Master, we know that thou art truthful." Though they rejected His doctrine and continued their attempts to trap and destroy Him, they said: "The whole world is going after Him." Do you recall the occasion when they proposed a question, charged with political implications? They thought that no matter how He answered, it would put Him in trouble. "Is it lawful to give tribute to Caesar, or not?" they asked Him innocently. Should He say "Yes," He would seem to be siding with the Romans against the Jews. Should He say "No," it would be sedition. Our Lord, knowing their intent, gave them a principle. That principle still holds good for us today. He said, "Show me the coin of the tribute." It was a specially minted coin for taxation purposes. Then He said, "Whose are this image and the inscription?" They answered, "Caesar's." To the Pharisees, and to us, He said: "Render, therefore, to Caesar the things that are Caesar's, and to God the things that are God's." Again, we find these same men defiling the temple, making it a place of business, selling cattle, birds, money changing. Our Lord, in His anger, drove them from the temple with a handful of cords, an inadequate weapon. It was His just anger because they were defiling the house of His Father that put these men to guilty flight. So, as we study the Gospels, we see our Lord in His human nature a little more clearly.

A man's dealings with children are often regarded as a test of him and a revelation of his real self. We see our Lord at the seaside with children flocking around Him. He has them on His knees. He has His arms about them and He gives them His special blessing. Now we know that children are not attracted to a sad-faced, cold, aloof person. It fills in the picture of what our Lord was like to see Him at ease with the children and them happy to be with Him. When the apostles protested that He was too busy and too important to have time for the children, he reprimanded them saying: "Let the little children be, and do not hinder them from coming to me for of such is the kingdom of heaven." Then there is one incident, I think, which brings our Lord directly into our homes. It is a warm and touching incident. An old couple had an only daughter about twelve years old. She sickened and died. Their home was going to be a very lonesome place without their little girl. Our Lord came in upon a scene of mourning and saw their sadness. He gently told the mourners to leave and with the mother and father He went over to where the little girl in her clean, white dress was laid out for the burial. He leaned down and took her cold, white, little hand into His big hand. Our Lord spoke Aramaic, and the exact words are still recorded for us in the Gospel. They sound almost like a caress, "Talitha cumi, Talitha cumi (Little girl, I say to you arise)" (Mark 5:38 ff.). Immediately the color flowed back into her cheeks, her eyes fluttered open, and she looked up trustingly into the face of our Lord. It was a very happy moment for all of them as He gave her back to her overjoyed parents. And what else did he say on that occasion? Did He talk on death, sin, the uncertainties of life? No, He turned to the parents and said simply: "Give her something to eat"; which shows our Lord's knowledge of little girls, and not so little girls, who are able to eat almost endlessly even though they haven't been dead for a couple of days. The humanity and the understanding, the warmth of "Give her something to eat"—we immediately feel at ease with this man.

Another test for a man is his dealings with women. You will see recorded in the Gospels that men did oppose Christ at times, men of ill will; but there isn't one recorded instance of a woman opposing Him. Maybe there were some who did oppose Him, but they aren't in the record. Every meeting with a woman was a happy meeting. It had a happy ending. If the woman was a bad woman, she became good. If she was a good woman, she became better. Think of the lovely women in the Gospels; Mary, His own mother. Recall His loving concern and care for her. Then there were the sisters whose home was always open to him—Martha, to wait on Him and serve Him, and Mary to sit at His feet. Think of the woman taken in adultery, the woman at the well, the women at the foot of the cross, those who followed Him with loving care on Easter Sunday morning. Every meeting was a happy meeting. And here, if you want to speculate (and this is just for the fun of it), I'm inclined to think that women are better fitted for Christianity *by nature* than men are. Notice I stress *by nature*. Why? Because in Christ's teaching, love, self-sacrifice, and self-giving loom very large. And women, possibly because they are destined by nature to become mothers, whether physically or spiritually, have that capacity built into them just a little bit more than men have. But now notice how I defend men. When you find a good man, one who is working at being good you can be sure his goodness wasn't an outright gift by nature. It was worked at and won only with difficulty. But, at any rate, regardless of that type of speculation, we see that Christ in His humanity appealed to all men, women, and children of good will. And it is exactly what we would expect, that when God took on human nature He would draw us all; He would be attractive.

It is consoling to remind ourselves that our Lord has lived our life from birth to death. If there is poverty in our life, we can remember that He was born in a stable. If there is failure: "He came unto his own, and his own received him not." If there is betrayal and false friends: "Judas, dost thou betray the Son of Man with a kiss?" If there is physical suffering, He was crucified. If there is mental anguish: "My God, my God, why hast thou forsaken me?" If there is love and warmth, there were His Mother

Mary and the disciples whom He loved. If there is hard work, He was so tired at the end of a day that He fell asleep in the boat. He walked among men. He heard them talk. He knew their weaknesses and their strengths. He looked up at the same stars we see. He sweated under the same sun we sweat under. That is why He can turn to each one of us now and say: "Come, follow me; I am the way, and the truth, and the life." Sanctity, now, consists in taking on His judgments, His reactions, His actions, and His way of doing things. This is successful living according to God's plan—Christ-likeness. It is that simple. It is no longer a complicated, involved philosophy or abstract virtues. It is simply Christ-likeness. When we come to the evening of life, we will be so judged—how Christ-like are we? Once again we might reflect and apply this measuring rod to the lives of the millionaire playboy, the blind captain, the corporal dead at twenty-three, and our own lives. How Christ-like are they? To that extent they are successful in God's eyes.

Our study of the man who is God become man takes us to the trial for His life. The situation is dramatic. Our Lord is there on the balcony. The Pharisees are whipping the people into a fury. "Crucify Him. He makes Himself to be a king." Pilate, there to safeguard Roman authority, is concerned and seriously asks our Lord: "Art Thou a King?" Our Lord answers: "Thou sayest it. I am a King, but My Kingdom is not of this world." As Pilate studies Him, he sees dignity and a certain calm and majesty. But he wonders, "How could this man be a king?" Caesar, who had given him his appointment, was a king and ruled the civilized world. He had subjects who obeyed him. When Caesar issued an edict, the whole world obeyed it and went to be enrolled. When Caesar demanded taxes, the wealth of the civilized world flowed in. He had an army, the greatest army that tramped this earth, until modern times. Caesar was a king. If this man were a king, where were his followers, his subjects, his power, his authority, the monuments erected in his name? Not seeing any of these, Pilate permitted our Lord to be put to death. In mockery he put over His head: "Jesus of Nazareth, King."

But we say to him: "Now, just a minute, Pilate. You question whether this man is a king and you want to know where his followers are. Well, Pilate, we have the advantage of two thousand years of history over you, and we can tell you that in twenty years you will be dead and so will your Caesar. But in twenty years this man's followers will be so numerous that a hymn of praise to Christ, the King, will be going up from your Roman world. His loyal subjects will become so numerous that your later Roman emperors like Nero, Caligula, and Trajan will try to stamp them out by persecution and the sword. Pilate, did you ever hear of anyone dying with the name of Caesar on his lips, except as a curse? 'We who are about to die, salute thee!' But we can tell you that in your Roman amphitheaters, there will be thousands of 'weak' men, women, children who will find strength to die for love of Christ. There will be little girls like Lucy, Cecilia, Anastasia, Agatha, Catherine, and Dorothy who will gladly lay down their lives, be torn by wild beasts, burned in oil, beheaded. They will gladly die rather than deny Christ as their King. There will be men like Stephen, Lawrence, Peter, Paul, Andrew, Cosmas, Damian, and Polycarp who will count it gain to die for Him. And there will be countless unknown others who will live lives of hidden heroism for His sake. Pilate, if your Caesar could inspire in the heart of one person the love and loyalty which this man will inspire in the hearts of millions, your Caesar would count himself fortunate. And we can tell you that down through the ages the name that millions will breathe out, confidently and trustingly, with their dying breath will be the sacred name of Jesus. In the year 1961, more than five hundred million Catholics will salute Him as their King and declare themselves to be His devoted subjects. He has loyal subjects, Pilate, such as no human king ever had.

"In regard to His monuments, Pilate, we can tell you that there will be statues in bronze, silver, and wood. The greatest artists and sculptors of all time will use their talents to portray Him. These monuments will not be hidden away in museums like the chipped marble busts of your Caesar; they will be raised up and lovingly venerated in public places and homes throughout the world. And, Pilate, much more important than monuments in bronze, silver, and wood will be the monuments of mercy erected under the inspiration of His name—homes for the aged, the blind, the orphaned; schools; universities; hospitals; leprosariums; retreat houses—all staffed and manned by men and women who count it gain to spend their lives in His service. He has living monuments such as no merely human king ever had. Finally, Pilate, that cross—a thing of shame meant to blot out His name forever—will be the first thing a traveler sees when he comes into a little village, or a town, or a great city. The cross of Christ set against the sky line for all to see. Yes, Pilate, all time will be counted and dated from the years before His birth and the years since His coming. He is the pivot of history! He is the center of the universe! He is a King, Pilate, and two thousand years of history prove it. He is the 'King of kings and Lord of lords.' "

Now we find that Man, who is king, turning to each one of us and saying: "It is My desire and My intention, for I am King, to bring the whole world into My kingdom. But to do this I need men and women to help Me. Will you come with Me? Will you labor with Me? Will you help Me to spread My kingdom on earth?" We recognize, with a bit of a shock, that this is truth, not fantasy. Christ did not choose to stay visibly on earth to do the work. He didn't send a band of angels who might be more efficient than we are. He gives the work to men and women. He entrusts the spread of His kingdom to us. He has given to each one of us a work to do, to each a separate and distinct vocation given to no other. Whether His kingdom will be spread, or not spread, depends on each one of us. This is not unrealistic. Study history—what has kept back the spread of Christ's kingdom? It is simply that someone was not doing His work: bad popes, bad bishops, bad priests, bad laity. And what has spread His kingdom? Good popes, good bishops, good priests, and good laity. What if Martin Luther had remained faithful and used his tremendous gifts to reform the Church rather than to revolt? What if Henry the Eighth had chosen to listen to Thomas More?

Our Lord points out that there is a little portion of His kingdom over which you have complete control—your own heart and your own life. He asks: "May I first rule there, as King, with My principles, My ways of doing things, My love? May I be Sovereign, Lord, King of your heart?" We recognize that perhaps this may be the most difficult terrain of all to conquer for Christ, our own hearts. It is encouraging to note that as we establish Christ in our own hearts and life, His work automatically spreads out beyond ourselves. This is the most effective way. Another human life reproducing Christ is the most persuasive argument for Christianity. It reaches out to touch a wide circle of friends, acquaintances, and daily contacts. There is, first of all, our own immediate family. For all practical purposes, whether a family is in the heart of Christ's kingdom or on the fringe, or removed from it entirely, will depend on the mother and father—on their Christ-likeness and their love. And we know that whether we will it or not, we are continually being observed. Even unknown to ourselves we are building or destroying His kingdom in the minds and hearts of others. You can't be in an office, or in politics, or in a university more than a week before they have you stamped as a "Mackerel-snapper." After you've been around awhile, try getting away with eating meat on Friday and they will say: "Did the priest bless the hamburger and turn it into fish?" Or try to miss Mass on Sunday and some acquaintance or friend has a comment. Take a look at the Hollywood stars—and this isn't criticizing any other religion—as soon as a Catholic gets divorced and remarried, the papers say so and so, a devout Catholic, gets married for the third time. So and so, convent-bred, married for the fifth time. They never say, so and so, Holy Roller, married for the third time. It is always "Catholic." Why? Because people generally know what we stand for. We declare our position and, very reasonably it would seem, they measure us by what we believe and hold.

I've had a chance to instruct a lot of people in the faith. I never reached any of them personally. They were all brought to me by somebody else or directed to me. I generally ask these people what made them decide to become a Catholic. Especially in service, the answers would be something like this: "Well, Father, when I was in high school, I used to run around with a couple of Catholics. One or two impressed me; one or two were not so good. Then I went with a Catholic girl for a time. We moved out of the neighborhood and I haven't seen her since. Now I'm in the army and have been buddying around with these fellows, and I've gone to Church with them a couple of times. They seem to have something. I never had any religious instruction. I'd just like to look into it." That, with slight variation, was the usual story. Try and tell those high-school fellows or girls and they'd say: "We forget his name. What year was that?" Tell the girl and she'd say: "Well, you see, we broke up." Tell the fellows in the barracks and they'd probably say, "We're not world-beaters." And yet, that is largely the story of the spread of Christ's kingdom.

And the principles of Christ—honestly, don't they sound odd to us and a little unreal, even though we have heard them all these years? "Blessed are the clean of heart, for they shall see God." Purity of heart, Christ says, even to us who live in a Freudian-Kinzied age that is over-sexed. "Blessed are the poor in spirit, for theirs is the kingdom of heaven." He is asking detachment in regard to wealth and money in an age in which the "quick buck" seems to be the goal in life. "Blessed are the meek . . . ," and our reaction is, "Lord, you don't understand. Step on them before they step on you." Our Lord speaks of humility. Did you ever see that on an application blank for a job—"How's your humility?" As we go through our Lord's suggestions, our first tendency is to say: "But, Lord, You don't understand. All of those are unreal! This is *this* world!" But He reminds us gently: "I have lived your life from birth to death.

I have walked among men. I know their weaknesses and their strengths. I know their temptations. I know time and eternity. I am telling you that I am the Way, the Truth, and the Life. He who follows Me walks not in darkness." So, we say: "Lord, count me in." And His last appeal is, "Do you really want to be counted in?" We answer, "Yes." And He reminds us: "You are following a crucified leader. There will be suffering." At that point, I think that we are all tempted to say, like St. Peter: "Not a crucified leader! That is not the way to spread your kingdom, Christ. No one will follow a crucified leader." Our Lord's rebuke to St. Peter when he said the same thing was: "Get behind me, satan, for thou dost not mind the things of God, but those of men" (Mark 8:33). It is God's way. To the Jews, a crucified Messiah was a scandal. To the Gentiles, it was absurdity and foolishness. To those who know and believe, it is salvation and grace. "And he who does not take up his cross and follow me, is not worthy of me" (Matthew 10:38).

St. Ignatius has said that the attractiveness of this appeal: "Come, follow Me," is that we have a great leader, Christ, who won't ask us to do anything that He hasn't done before us. That is the appeal of a leader. "Come, follow Me." Not: "Go, and do it." "Come, follow Me." The cause is worthwhile! It is the salvation of all souls—our own included—bringing all men into Christ's Kingdom, bringing them to a knowledge and love of Him. The victory is assured! "I'll not lose a single man, and you won't have to do it alone" is our Lord's promise. It will be done through Him, and with Him, and in Him.

As a final help in this whole area of following Christ the King and His cause, there is Holy Communion. Tomorrow when we receive Holy Communion it is not merely getting spiritual food, although it is obviously that, but it is the direct contact with Christ in His humanity and His divinity. Christ, the same yesterday, today, and forever. We are not going to meet a stranger. We are going to meet a man whom we know, a strong man physically. We are going to meet a man of universal attractiveness to men, women, and children of good will; a man who has led our life from birth to death; a man who knows us intimately, knows our weaknesses and strengths and sins, and who still loves us. Communion, then, is a joy which we can look forward to tomorrow morning. Jesus Christ, the Son of God, the son of man, the same yesterday, today, and forever. Thank God for Christmas! Thank God for the Holy Eucharist! Thank God for Christ, our King, who loves us enough to give us a work to do that He has given to no other. With such a leader and such an appeal, no one has the right to take refuge in mediocrity.

Eternal Lord of all things! With Your favor and Your help, I offer myself to You in the presence of Your infinite goodness, Your glorious mother, and of all the saints of the heavenly court. I want and desire, and it is my deliberate determination to imitate You, as another Christ, in perfectly fulfilling the duties of my state of life. I am determined to follow You even though it means hardships and sufferings in Your service, my Lord and King. Grant, O God, that all my intentions, actions, and operations may tend purely to the service and praise of Your divine majesty.

Do it yourself!

Points for your prayerful thinking (15 minutes)

PREPARATORY PRAYER
See page 18.

A more excellent way

1 Christ—true God, true man, like to us in all things, sin alone excepted. God living a human life and therefore the model of manhood. Christianity not just a philosophy—Christianity is Christ. Personal love and imitation of our ideal—life is to be lived "through Him and with Him and in Him."

2 A thumbnail sketch: a strong man, carpenter, outdoor life, sufferings of the Passion. Attracts every type of man: laborer, tax gatherer, Roman governor, centurion, Joseph of Arimathea, children, women. Like us He

slept, He wept, He worked. He had compassion on the multitude. He began to fear and grow sad.

3 Come follow me! I am the way, the truth, and the life. Christ is King—My kingdom is not of this world. Will you join Me? Count me in! A portion of My kingdom —your heart—your family—your friends and business associates—you can win them for Me.

4 In the present crisis no one has the right to take refuge in mediocrity.

Conclude by saying one Our Father, a Hail Mary, and Glory Be to the Father.

NOTE

At this point in the retreat you can see that the emphasis is on love and generosity. These great capacities which we possess are to be centered on a person, and that person is Christ. From here on the retreat is directed toward growth in the knowledge, love, and imitation of Christ. This, then, should be the direction of our whole life and the content of our prayer: "Lord, grant that I may know Thee better, love Thee more, and follow Thee more closely." Archbishop Goodier's expert direction in his little pamphlet "A More Excellent Way" explains why:

"When I was younger, . . . and knew myself less, and knew others less, and was full of high ambitions in the spiritual life, . . . I set virtues before me, and meditated on their beauty, and proposed to myself to acquire them, sub-dividing them, analyzing them, arranging their degrees as the steps of a ladder. This week, . . . I would acquire the virtue of patience; . . . the week after should be given to charity; then should come the spirit of prayer; and in a month or two, perhaps, I might have an ecstasy and 'see the Lord.' But now, when I have grown older, and find myself still struggling for the first of these virtues, . . . and have been taught quite other lessons than I dreamt of, . . . I am convinced that there is one road to perfection better than all else—in fact, that if we neglect this one no other will be of much avail . . . it is not possible to grow in the knowledge, and love, and imitation of Jesus Christ, without at the same time growing in the perfection of every virtue and becoming more a saint every day.

"This, then, if I were allowed to begin my spiritual life over again, is the line along which . . . I would try to lead the lives of any whom God gave into my care . . . When the creature loves, then it is changed, and till then scarcely at all. Thus it is that the knowledge and love of Jesus Christ goes deeper down than any Stoic striving after virtue; it is flesh and blood . . .; it gives life and substance where the other is only dead perfection; the imitation of Jesus Christ includes every virtue, makes them unconsciously our own, produces them from itself, and does not merely put them on from without."

St. John the Baptist had this complete love and devotion for Christ, "the strap of whose sandals," said he, "I am not worthy to stoop down and loose." It is summed up in his heroic and self-forgetful cry, "This my joy, therefore, is made full. He must increase, but I must decrease."

Knowledge, love, imitation of Jesus Christ.

◆◆◆◆◆◆◆◆◆◆◆

G. K. Chesterton was once asked a question which was supposed to be purely hypothetical and speculative. He was asked: "If Christ were here in our world today, what do you think He would do?" With his usual clarity of vision and realism Chesterton answered, "He is present in the world today."

At times the great truth of Christ's real presence in the Holy Eucharist can become a little unreal and unrelated to our daily living. We might even live our daily lives as though we did not believe that "Christ is present, body and blood, soul and divinity, under the appearance of bread and wine." The next chapter reminds us consolingly that Christ is alive and present and active in our world of the sixties. He is still questing men, drawing them to Himself, and moulding them, as He did His apostles, into His image and likeness. He issues daily the same invitation He made in yesteryears:

"Come to me, all you who labor and are burdened, and I will give you rest."

The second part of the coming chapter reminds us that we can give something to God Himself—something that He really wants from us. If given, it is our supreme act of praise, reverence, and service. Naturally it will have to be done "through Him, with Him, and in Him," but we can give God a gift.

Give me Your love and grace,
for this is enough for me.
Suscipe of St. Ignatius

Follow me.
Luke 5:27

Christit with us

There are three qualities present in all of us who are in love. First of all, we have a desire to be with the one we love. It doesn't matter what the setting is; we simply like to be around. Secondly, there is a tendency to share what we have with the one beloved and to give them gifts—flowers on Mother's Day, a diamond ring, birthday remembrances. And a third tendency of one who loves is to give himself totally —mind and heart and body. In human love these three tendencies are perfectly summed up in marriage: two people wish to be together for a lifetime, sharing all things in common, and giving themselves to each other. Love seeks union.

If this is true in human love, we are not surprised to find the same three tendencies manifested, in an even more wonderful and complete way, in God's dealings with men. For God tells us, "I have loved thee with an everlasting love." St. John says simply, "God is love." And so He wants to be with us; He wants to give us what He possesses as far as we can receive it; He wants to unite Himself with us, both for time and for eternity. As we study the great mysteries of the Christian religion, we discover that the key to them is love. A very fine theological thinker, Romano Guardini, remarks that the human mind staggers at such profound mysteries as the Incarnation (God becoming man), the Redemption (God dying for us), and the Holy Eucharist (Christ present with us till the end of time) unless we realize that "Love does this sort of thing." Love breaks the bonds of a purely reasoned syllogism.

With this as a key to help our understanding, let us study the Holy Eucharist. This sacrament has many lovely names, the Blessed Sacrament, Holy

Communion, and the sacrament of love, because in love lies its ultimate explanation. Now it is a very extraordinary thing that we believe about this sacrament. We believe that although it looks like bread, tastes like bread, smells like bread—although it looks like wine, tastes like wine—Christ, in His humanity and His divinity, is really present in the Holy Eucharist. In order to avoid any doubt on this question, the Church spells it out very technically. It almost sounds like a legal document. But the idea behind these carefully chosen phrases is to avoid weasel words and vagueness such as: "Well, if you think Christ is there, you might get a lot out of it." The intention of the Church is to avoid the idea that the Lord's Supper is merely a symbol or memorial. "It's a very nice way of remembering what Christ did for us at the Last Supper on Holy Thursday. If you come to it with faith, you'll have a sense of closeness to Christ." To avoid such vagueness, the Church chooses carefully weighted words: "Christ is present, body and blood, soul and divinity, under the appearances of bread and wine." It isn't just a symbol or a memorial. The whole Christ is there!

Now, this is a tremendous thing to believe. And because the sensory data is to the contrary, we ought to have very good reasons for accepting it. When I say: "This looks like a piece of bread, but Christ is present here," you might reasonably ask: "What makes you think so? Would you please tell me why you believe this?" Now, as we study God's dealings with men, we observe that He never does violence to the human mind. He leads it on gently from one truth to another. So notice, first of all, that Christ has a motive for being so present. Since He loved us, it is conceivable that He would want to stay with us in the Holy Eucharist. Secondly, He has the omnipotence to do whatever He wants to do. It would not even be difficult for God to be present under the appearances of bread and wine. He can't make a square a circle, because that's a contradiction. But there is no great difficulty about being present under the appearances of bread and wine. Thirdly, He has the wisdom, the knowledge, and He can do it. The only real question is, did He do it? His preparations for this great act of love were very elaborate. The first great miracle He worked was at the marriage feast of Cana when He changed water into wine to show that He could do with water and wine what He wished. He was pointing toward the Holy Eucharist and preparing our minds and emotions to accept it. The second great miracle He worked was multiplying the fish and loaves of bread to feed five thousand to show that He could do with loaves of bread what He wished. This miracle obviously points toward the Holy Eucharist where bread is involved. And a third great miracle He worked was walking on the water, showing that He could do with His body things that we can't do with ours. If we tried that sort of thing we would sink. He also raised Himself from the dead, again showing a complete control over His body which we do not possess. These four miracles involving water and wine, bread, and Christ's body are brought together in the Holy Eucharist. So we might take a glance at the Last Supper to see what our Lord did and what He had in mind.

The scene is familiar to us from paintings—our Lord is at table with the twelve apostles. With the clearness of divine vision He knew that in twenty-four hours He would be dead and His body, terribly torn, would be lying in the sepulcher at the foot of Mount Calvary. This was the last meal He was going to eat with His friends. We know how it is when people leave with the possibility of not returning; they will speak out their minds and hearts and affections more openly than at any other time. And so it was with our Lord that night. He called them His little children. He told them to love one another as He loved them. He washed their feet. He told them that He was leaving and they grew sad, but He hastened to reassure them by saying, "I will not leave you orphans." I'm not going to leave you all alone. He hadn't forgotten the promise He had made six months earlier when He had multiplied the loaves of bread. The day following this miracle the crowds came to Him again and wished to make Him king. He told them that they had come to Him because

". . . you have eaten of the loaves and have been filled." Now notice how He used this occasion to lead them on to a higher truth, for He added, ". . . the bread that I will give is my flesh for the life of the world . . . He who eats my flesh and drinks my blood has life everlasting and I will raise him up on the last day. For my flesh is food indeed, and my blood is drink indeed. He who eats my flesh, and drinks my blood, abides in me and I in him. As the living Father has sent me, and as I live because of the Father, so he who eats me, he also shall live because of me." And very emphatically, ". . . unless you eat the flesh of the Son of Man, and drink his blood, you shall not have life in you."

Now these are strong words and they are unusual words. Reading this sixth chapter of St. John, you can see that His audience was somewhat shocked, for they questioned and protested: "How can this man give us his flesh to eat?" Very likely they were thinking in gross terms—eat my flesh, drink my blood. Our Lord dispels this misconception but doesn't retreat from His stand: ". . . unless you eat the flesh of the Son of Man, and drink his blood, you shall not have life in you." Some of the people heard this and were unwilling to await the developments, lacking trust and love. They muttered: "This is a hard saying. Who can listen to it?" And it is recorded, "From this time many of his disciples turned back and no longer went about with him." Our Lord, however, did not give up His divine plan because men could not grasp it fully. He was willing to make an issue of His statement and of this mystery of His love. Turning to Peter and His chosen apostles, He asked them: "Do you also wish to go away?" Peter, generous Peter with his insight and love, answered for himself, and I think for us, when he said: "Lord, to whom shall we go? Thou hast words of everlasting life, and we have come to believe and to know that thou art the Christ, the Son of God" (John 6:26 ff.). He didn't fully understand the mystery, but he had his faith and trust in Christ and His promises. Somehow it would be done. Christ could do it. He would wait and see.

And now, at the Last Supper, in a divinely simple and beautiful way, our Lord fulfills His promise. "Jesus took bread, and blessed and broke, and gave it to his disciples, and said, 'Take and eat; this is my body.' And taking a cup, he gave thanks and gave it to them, saying, 'All of you drink of this; for this is my blood.'" Now if our Lord had wanted to say: "this is a symbol," "this is, as it were," "it is, after a manner of speaking," "it's kind of," "it's sort of my body and my blood," He had those words at His command. We know that He is a master of speech. But clearly and with divine simplicity he declares: "This is my body, this is my blood." Sometimes people wonder what He meant by this. Could it be that He meant what He said? If He didn't mean just that, then He is the only man who ever made such an elaborate preparation for an event, made an issue of it, promised it, did it, and then didn't really expect to be taken seriously.

It takes faith to believe this. By faith, we mean accepting a truth on God's authority. Surely it takes faith, about the same amount of faith, I would think, that the shepherds needed when they came in and adored the infant in Mary's arms. In that instant, divinity was hidden under the white flesh of a child; in this instance, divinity and humanity are hidden under the white circle of the host. About the same amount of faith is required in both cases to make an act of adoration and say, "My Lord and my God."

How did the apostles understand it? If they were laboring under a misconception, surely Christ would have corrected them. St. Paul tells us: "For I myself have received from the Lord (what I also delivered to you), that the Lord Jesus, on the night in which he was betrayed, took bread, and giving thanks broke, and said, 'This is my body which shall be given up for you; do this in remembrance of me.' In like manner also the cup, after he had supped, saying, 'This cup is the new covenant in my blood; do this as often as you drink it, in remembrance of me. For as often as you shall eat this bread and drink the cup, you proclaim the death of the Lord, until he comes.' Therefore whoever eats this bread or drinks the cup of the Lord unworthily, will be guilty of the body and the blood of the Lord. But let a man prove himself, and so let him eat of that bread and drink of the cup; for he who eats and drinks unworthily, without distinguishing the body, eats and drinks judgment to himself" (I Corinthians 11:23-29). You do not use such strong words in regard to misuse of a mere symbol or a picture of a person and say, "You are guilty of His body and blood." It is also interesting to note that the doctrine of the real presence of Christ in the Eucharist was never formally challenged until the eleventh century. Christ is truly present. We are secure in our belief. He loves us and wants to be with us till the end of time. He knows how to do it. He promised it. He did it! We and millions of others down through the centuries believe.

As we study our Lord's purpose in so remaining with us, acceptance of this mystery is made easier and seems most fitting. Every contact our Lord has with us is designed to give us life. "I came that they may have life, and have it more abundantly." We know that a higher form of life can raise up a lower form. We can observe that in nature. Take plants. They draw oxygen out of the air and nitrogen out of the ground, absorb the sun's rays, and drink in the rain. Through photosynthesis they change nonliving matter into a living plant. Quite a mystery, but it goes on before our eyes. A higher form of life raises up a lower form. So it is in every contact that we have with Christ. At Holy Communion the higher form of life, divinity, reaches down, raises us up, and gradually, slowly, His words become verified in us: ". . . he who eats me, he also shall live because of me." As we boldly pray at Mass, "Deign, O Lord, to make us sharers in His divinity, as He hast deigned to partake of our humanity, through Christ, our Lord." What more natural way to be raised up to divinity than by union with the source of divine life. "In Him was Life. And as many as received Him, He gave them power to be made the sons of God."

But we might still have an objection from personal experience. "All of this is true. Christ is present here.

I've been receiving Communion since I was a child, but I can't observe too great an increase in divine life." Obviously, I wouldn't propose the difficulty unless I had a pretty sly answer. Since divine life is internal and invisible, you cannot see or measure the growth, but God can observe it. He observed it in the case of the Blessed Virgin, to whom He said: "Hail, full of grace." You, too, can have the fullness of divine life in you and God can see the growth even though you cannot.

There is a further answer to the difficulty. All life is a gradual growth, whether it be physical life, mental life, or spiritual life. We don't give a baby a bottle and expect him to grow into full manhood overnight. We don't go to school for one day and return home with a Ph.D. We may be expecting too much, too soon, like the little boy who came home from his first day in kindergarten. His father asked him, "Did you learn a lot today in school?" The little boy answered: "No, I didn't; I have to go back again tomorrow." Obviously, he was expecting too much from one day at school. And possibly we're expecting too much from a single Holy Communion. The answer to our problem: "What about my growth?" might well be: "I have to go back again tomorrow," and tomorrow and all the tomorrows of my life. We can be assured that divine life will continue to grow steadily.

Another reason for Christ remaining with us is to make us like Himself. And since successful living is being Christ-like, in what more natural and obvious way could we work toward this success than by personal contact with Him. Constant association with Him enables us to take on more easily and completely His way of thinking. His judgments, His actions, and His reactions. It's a slow, but real progress. Study two people who have lived together happily in marriage, and observe them on their golden wedding day. You'll notice how alike they've become through the years. Certainly, they have still preserved their individuality, but before one speaks the other knows his or her preferences. The woman will say: "You know, I think he's going to tell that joke for the two-thousand-seven-hundred-and-eighty-third time." The husband will say: "Now if I do this, I'll bet she gets sore. She always does." They know and understand each other thoroughly. So, also, by the continued reception of Holy Communion, through constant association, gradually we begin to judge as Christ judges; His values become ours; we act and react the way He does. You could almost prove experimentally that frequent Holy Communion refines a person and gives him spiritual vision. The effect of frequent Holy Communion in gentling and regulating disordered sex tendencies is almost too obvious to need comment. Regular contact with the glorified body of Christ in the Eucharist gradually calms disorderly passions. This strong drive becomes better balanced, controlled, and refined. Ask the man who receives frequently.

I don't know of any surer way to save our souls than by devout, frequent communion. I remember talking to an older priest one time. He was a kind, gentle, foxy-grandpa type. He was just about ready to retire, and I said to him: "Look, Father, you've learned a lot in all these years. Is there any sure way of saving your soul?" "Well," he grunted, "that's the trouble with you younger priests; you're looking for short cuts." But after further prodding, he said: "I figure that if a person went to weekly Communion, it would be very hard for him to lose his soul." That made sense to me. Even as a gambler estimating the odds, you're going to die on Sunday, Monday, Tuesday, Wednesday, Thursday, Friday, or Saturday. Suppose you die on Wednesday. It's only three days since you've been, or three days until you plan to go again. Knowing God's infinite mercy, wouldn't you say that the weekly communicant is pretty secure? Can you imagine Christ saying to us after we've been to communion week after week, and come up for the final judgment: "I know you not." We could protest: "But Lord, I met You a thousand times at Communion. Surely You remember me." This well might be one of the practical resolutions of this retreat, a resolution that gives you every hope of eternal happiness. Weekly Communion!

Involved in frequent Communion are a lot of virtues other than just getting there. First of all, there's faith. A person really believes Christ is present. Then there's a certain amount of love. He thinks it's really worthwhile making this contact, meeting Christ. Then there's humility. If one has committed a mortal sin, he must first go to confession before receiving Holy Communion. So you can see, tied up in this one practice of weekly, or more frequent, Communion are many other virtues, Christ-like virtues, especially love and devotion.

We can recite our belief in the Holy Eucharist by heart: "Christ is present, body and blood, soul and divinity, under the appearance of bread and wine." But, I think, somewhere along the line God moves in a bit and helps us realize, not just know, that these things are true. When that realization comes it changes us profoundly. Here is a real-life story that helped me to realize a little more deeply the real presence of Christ in the Eucharist.

It was told to me by a priest friend of mine. The priest is head of the philosophy department of a large university and the story is about a man who came to him for instruction. The man was a non-Catholic and he said: "Father, I married a Catholic woman; I promised to raise our children in the Catholic faith, and I don't know anything about it. My wife is not practising her faith. Now, I'd like to stick by my promises, so I thought I would look into the Church and see if I could accept it sincerely." The priest gave him thorough instructions over a long period of time and he moved along very nicely until he came to the Holy Eucharist, Christ's real presence. At this point he came to a halt. "This I can't see. I don't get it." There were more instructions, but it was just a dead end. "I don't understand. It doesn't make sense." The priest finally said to him: "I'm sorry, I can't do any more for you. We've gone through the proofs and you've studied and prayed. Why don't you call it off for a while. This is the gift of faith, and I can't give it to you." The man then asked if he could see what was in the tabernacle. Father said: "You'll see something that looks like bread, tastes like bread, smells like bread. That's all that it will look like." The man insisted, "Let me see." The priest, a little impatient, led the man into the sacristy. He took an unconsecrated host and said: "Here, eat it. What does it taste like? Bread? Looks like bread. Smells like bread." The man agreed, but again asked to see what was in the tabernacle. The priest hastily put on a stole, opened up the tabernacle, took the cover off the ciborium, and said: "See!" then put the ciborium back in the tabernacle. The man quietly turned away and went to kneel in the front pew. The priest, realizing that he had been a bit impatient, went up to the man and said that he was sorry for being so irritable. But the fellow just brushed him away. After five or ten minutes, he came into the sacristy where the priest was waiting and said simply and decisively: "I want to become a Catholic." He is now a daily communicant. Father said that he doesn't know what the man saw, but he, himself, saw only something that looked like bread. His point in telling this experience, and mine in retelling it, is this: the man was completely sincere in his efforts in seeking the truth; he needed some special help—psychological miracle—call it what you will, to get over the hump, and God provided what he needed.

We're glad that this man was given that special grace, whatever it was. But what about ourselves who already believe? I think we get a different type of blessing. When St. Thomas, the doubting Thomas, said: "Unless I see in his hands the print of the nails, and put my finger into the place of the nails, and put my hand into his side, I will not believe." Our Lord accepted these conditions and said to Thomas: "Bring here thy finger, and see my hands; and bring here thy hand, and put it into my side; and be not unbelieving, but believing." It was then that Thomas said: "My Lord and my God!" and our Lord replied: "Because thou hast seen me, thou hast believed." Then looking down the years to us, he added: "Blessed are they who have not seen, and yet have believed" (John 20:25). This blessing comes to us especially because of our faith in the Holy Eucharist. We have not seen and yet we have believed.

Give God a gift

We could go on almost endlessly on the Holy Eucharist because it is the sacrament of love—endless love. However, I think it might be useful to turn our attention to the Mass itself. The Mass has always aroused the curiosity of people outside the Church. But notice that the questions people ask about the Mass are always all around the subject; seldom do they get to the heart of the matter. They ask, "Why are the vestments green?" "Why are there three priests up there?" "Why do you stand up and sit down?" "Why is the Mass in Latin?" The questions are in that area. Not too many ask, "What *is* the Mass?" And so it would be useful for us, because we go at least every Sunday, and a help for a sincere inquirer, if we could sum up the Mass in a theologically correct but brief manner.

In this connection I remember a conversation with a non-Catholic major in the Army. "Padre," he said, "you Catholics go to church, but you don't know what it's all about." "What makes you say that?" I asked. "Well," said he, "I'm running around with a Catholic girl, and the other day she got me to go to Mass. I found it very interesting. The priest was up there in those strange robes, and he walked back and forth. The people stood up and they knelt down. The bells rang and they pounded their chests. Then they went up to the front and came back again. I found it very interesting but I certainly didn't know what was going on. I had a lot of questions. So, when we got outside, I said to my girl, starting with something real easy: 'Why do they ring the bells at Mass?' When she told me that she was sorry that she really didn't know, then I figured that if she didn't know that, what did she know? So you see, you people don't know what you're doing."

"Now, Major," I said, "be a little slow to say that. For example, in your outfit you have a lot of mechanics. How many of them fix jeeps and trucks?" "All of them," he said emphatically. "They'd better be able to if they're mechanics in my outfit." "Good," I said, but then asked, "how many of them could pass a written examination in mechanics?" I threw in the word "written" because I knew a few of them couldn't write. He said: "Well, not too many, not too many." "Is there a difference then," I suggested, "between theoretical knowledge and practical knowledge? Your mechanics have practical knowledge, they can fix the jeeps. They lack theoretical knowledge. They couldn't pass a written examination in mechanics. Your girl also has practical knowledge. She always goes to Mass, but she's just a bit lacking in theoretical knowledge. She can't answer all the questions. So be a little slow to say that we don't know what we're doing." I think that defense was correct, but I also wish his girl knew why we ring the bells at Mass.

Is there, then, a simple formula that we can give to a sincere inquirer to let him know what we are doing and that will sum up the Mass for our own thinking and use? The answer is "Yes." It's very simple. We could say to the person, "At Mass, we give God a gift." That is what we are doing, giving God a gift. You might point to the first prayer of the canon which reads: "Most merciful Father, . . . receive and bless these gifts, these presents, these holy unblemished offerings." Then you might continue with some ideas on gift giving.

Did you ever analyze why you give a gift to a person? Why would a man give a girl a diamond ring? Why do we give flowers to our mothers on Mother's Day or neckties to our fathers on Father's Day? One obvious answer is that a gift is an expression of love and affection. A man slips a ring on a girl's finger and even if he doesn't say a word, it means "I love you." A second meaning a gift can have is "thank you." If someone has done a lot for us, instead of writing a formal thank-you note, we might send a little gift, "in appreciation for all you have done," or, "to thank you for a wonderful weekend." If there has been a misunderstanding or a rift in the friendship, a gift can have a third meaning, it can serve as a peace offering. For example, a husband and wife have a quarrel in the morning. That night he comes home with a couple of theater tickets, or a box of candy, or a mink stole if the bank roll can stand it. On the other hand, if the wife was at fault she might have his favorite meal ready and specially prepared. Even if the husband didn't say a word as he put the lovely skins around her shoulders, they mean: "I'm sorry, Dear, let's be friends again." Her extra attention to his likes would carry the same meaning. No one would miss the meaning of such gifts under the circumstances.

You can see this in little boys. They have a fight. Mother wants to make a little gentleman out of Jimmy and tells him to go out and apologize. Jimmy doesn't know how to do that very well, so, instead, he apologizes in his own way. He says to his friend, "Do you want to ride my bike?" or "Do you want a stick of bubble gum?" And that offering is meant to be a peace offering—"I'm sorry"—and as such it is understood and accepted. A final meaning a gift can have is rather on the mercenary side, but legitimate. We can give a gift to someone with the hope of getting something in return. A salesman takes out a prospective client, wines and dines him, and sends a fifth up to his room. Those gifts, obviously, mean "If you get the opportunity and can honestly do so, give me the contract." So giving a gift can be a way of saying: "I love you, I thank you, I'm sorry, please help me," or even all of them at once.

We realize now and again that we do want to say all these things to God. We all love Him and if we had a gift that would express that love, we'd be anxious to give it. We owe God a thank you for the endless litany of blessings that He's given us. We have all offended Him; is there anything we could give Him that would set things right between us? And, we do need a lot of things for ourselves and our families, spiritual favors and temporal favors. Now what could we give God that would dispose Him to pour out His special blessings upon us? When we grope around, we realize that He doesn't need anything. Besides, what could I give Him that is worthy of Him? We are at a loss.

But our Lord arranged for the gift we can give Him at the Last Supper. Now, this is the only technical part, so we might follow it a little closely. Our Lord arranged for the gift when He took bread into His hands, blessed it, and said: "This is my body, which will be broken for you; this is my blood, which shall be shed for many, for the remission of sins." It was Holy Thursday night. He was looking forward to the next day, Good Friday, where on Calvary, in the name of all of us (because He is true man as well as true God), His passion and suffering and death were to be an infinite act of love, thanks, and satisfaction, and an infinite plea for mercy offered to God the Father, to the Trinity. And Christ added and directed at the Last Supper: "Now, do this in memory of Me." So at the Mass, when the priest bends low over the altar and a hush steals over the church as it always does, and the bells are rung to alert us to the most solemn part of the Mass, when the priest speaks those words: "This is My Body; this is My Blood," Christ really becomes present there. When the host is raised up and the chalice is raised up, at that moment we are offering our gift to God the Father, to the Trinity, Christ really and truly present. We are reoffering His infinite merits, passion, and sufferings which say perfectly for us: "I love You; I thank You; I am sorry; please help me." "Wherefore, O Lord, we Thy servants, and likewise Thy holy people, calling to mind the blessed passion of the same Christ Thy Son, our Lord . . . offer unto Thy most excellent majesty, of Thy gifts and presents, a pure victim, a holy victim, an unspotted victim, the holy bread of eternal life, and the chalice of everlasting salvation." And at the same moment God turns to us with a request: "My son, My daughter, give Me your heart." In union with Christ we offer ourselves to God the Father, and to the Trinity, for the duty of daily living, for our observance of the commandments. In union with Christ we offer our whole life, ourselves. "We beseech thee, therefore, O Lord, graciously to accept this oblation of our service, as also of all Thy family." This is the twofold perfect gift we can give to God at Mass—Christ and ourselves—all of us united with one another and united to Him.

193

At the elevation, if you look over the tip of the host and the tip of the chalice, you see behind it, the cross. A symbolic representation of the reality we're offering: Christ's infinite merits, passion, and sufferings. Sometimes in a small chapel when the priest raises the chalice, he can see mirrored in its polished surface miniature reflections of those present. Nothing mysterious about it, just a reflection. But it is a fine picture of the reality, all of us united with one another in Christ, being offered to God, the Father, and the Trinity. How divinely simple the Mass is! It is the perfect gift.

Because we have given God a gift, He wants to give us a return gift. He invites us all up to the Communion rail so He can give us His only begotten Son, Christ, really and truly present, in Holy Communion. And just as in human love, you can not do more than say: "I'm yours, mind, heart, and body," so in this life, God cannot achieve a closer union with us than He does in Communion, while He remains present with us under the appearance of bread and wine. This unseen presence is a pledge of our eternal, visible union with Him in heaven. ". . . he who eats me, he also shall live because of me," and "I will raise him up on the last day." This is our pledge of immortality and eternal salvation.

The Mass is so simple you could explain it to a child. We are giving God a gift, Christ and ourselves. This gift says perfectly: "I love you, I thank you, I am sorry, please help me." And so when you come to the evening of your life, if you wish to count up the great things you've done during your lifetime, count up the number of times you have offered Mass with the priest. You are not idle spectators, as you know; you offer the gift with the priest. It's your offering, too. Take a look at the prayers the priest says: "Pray, brethren, that my sacrifice and yours may be acceptable to God, the Father Almighty." Recall the prayers at the offertory, "Deign to receive, O Lord, these gifts, these presents, which we offer you." Priest and people are offering the sacrifice together.

Now all of this is true. We know and believe that

Christ is present in Holy Communion, and that the Mass itself is the center of our worship. But somewhere along the line I think we get a little deeper insight into these great mysteries of God's love.

Permit me to tell you here of two Army experiences that helped me appreciate more fully the meaning of the Mass. On a particular Sunday I knew I would be unable to get to a certain outfit, largely Catholic. I asked the Colonel if he would send the Catholic men to the nearby German Church — the Catholic German Church. "I'd be glad to, Padre, but what will they get out of it if the prayers are in German, the hymns are in German, and the sermon is in German? I know they don't understand German. Then your Mass is in Latin and I'm sure they don't know Latin, so what in the world will they get out of it?" I tried to explain it to him. "Colonel, if you went to your Church in Germany, and you didn't understand the prayers, or the hymns, or the sermon, you'd show a lot of good will but maybe you wouldn't get too much out of it. But, Colonel, the center of worship in the Catholic Church is not a man preaching, however well or poorly he may preach. It is not a choir singing, no matter how beautifully or off-key they may sing. It's not people getting together to say some prayers to honor Christ. The center of worship in the Catholic Church is Christ being offered at the Mass; Christ being received in Communion; Christ being adored as He is permanently present on the altar. These men will feel just as much at home in their Church in Germany and get just as much out of it as they would back in Holy Name or St. Pat's Cathedral. They'd be as much at ease at Mass in the islands, or in Alaska, or in Spain, as in their parish churches back home. The center of worship is something different. It's the Real Presence versus the real absence."

The other experience that deepened my appreciation of the Mass occurred one Sunday during the war when I was saying Mass on top of a jeep. The men were standing there with their guns slung over their backs and their helmets on. The ack-ack was pecking at the planes upstairs. There was a torrent of rain coming down and a sea of mud to wallow in. So I said, "Don't bother to kneel down." And they didn't—until the Consecration. Then every man went down on his knees in that mud. When they sloshed up to receive Holy Communion, they again knelt down in mud puddles. Maybe these men couldn't define "transubstantiation" in exact words and maybe they couldn't tell why the bells are rung at Mass, and so on, but the Real Presence was visible on their weary faces and in their reverent attitudes. They knew where to go when the chips were down.

At times, I think, we all take the Holy Eucharist and our Lord's Real Presence for granted and even become a little indifferent or unappreciative. Our Lord, being human as well as divine, noticed that growing coldness during the Jansenist heresy which once was so strong. To warm the hearts of men, He broke the silence of centuries by revealing His Sacred Heart to St. Margaret Mary. The Jansenist heresy, with its over-emphasis on the holiness and sanctity of God and the total unworthiness of man, had put up such barriers of fear between man and God that Holy Communion was a dread sacrament. What was meant to be the sacrament of love became the sacrament of fear. Our Lord, pointing to His heart flaming with love for men said, "Behold this Heart, which has so loved mankind . . . And yet it has received in return from the majority of mankind only ingratitude, coldness, and the neglect of me in the sacrament of my love. But what is even more painful to me is that it is hearts consecrated to me which use me thus."

It is the old story. Those who are the closest to us have the greatest power to hurt us. We do not expect too much from total strangers, but those we love can cut us more deeply with a single word than a stranger can by a great act of injustice. Our Lord was commenting, not so much on the indifference of men who did not believe, but on the coldness and ingratitude of those who did believe. "That those who should be most devoted to Me use Me thus."

Now, I think that all of us deeply appreciate our Lord's presence in the Holy Eucharist even though we may get a little thoughtless at times. I think I can prove it. Recall how it is on Good Friday during Holy Week. As you go into church on Good Friday afternoon you begin to genuflect but stop: there is no need to genuflect because Christ is not there. You look up to the altar. The altar cloths are stripped off and the altar is bare. The sanctuary light is snuffed out. The tabernacle door is open and the tabernacle is empty. Christ is not there. The Church seems empty. Life is gone out of it. Now suppose that forever there was no Mass, forever no Holy Communion, forever no Benediction of the Blessed Sacrament; forever no abiding presence of our Lord in the Blessed Sacrament. We realize what an emptiness and loneliness there would be in our lives. Through the years Christ, in His Eucharistic presence, has imperceptibly taken over a considerable portion of our thinking and a large share in our life. What if it was the real absence instead of the Real Presence? What if His love had not prompted Him to remain with us? He would then, indeed, have left us orphans. As it is, "Having loved His own who were in the world, He loved them unto the end."

It is against this background of boundless love and mercy that the great promise of the Sacred Heart takes on new meaning: "I promise you in the excessive mercy of My Heart that My all-powerful love will grant to all those who communicate on the first Friday of nine consecutive months, the grace of final perseverence. They shall not die in My disgrace nor without receiving their sacraments; My divine Heart shall be their safe refuge in this last moment."

Do it yourself!

Points for your prayerful thinking (15 minutes)

PREPARATORY PRAYER
See page 18.

Christ with us

1 One in love wishes to be with the one he loves—share things, give himself.

2 Holy Eucharist—sacrament of love—to be with us—to give us life and grace—to give us Himself. Easy to believe—miracles showing His power over water and wine—over bread—over His own body. "This is my body, this is my blood."

3 How empty our lives would be without Him; no Mass, no communion, no benediction, no abiding presence. I am come that you may have life—higher form of life raises up the lower. You have the Real Presence; we have the real absence.

4 At Mass we give God a gift: "deign to receive these gifts, these presents which we offer Thee." A gift can say: "I love you." "I'm sorry." "I thank you." "Please help me." Gift we offer—Christ, ourselves. Mass often and communion every time I go to Mass.

Conclude by saying one Our Father, a Hail Mary, and Glory Be to the Father.

◆◆◆◆◆◆◆◆◆◆◆◆

Sacrifice, self-giving, and, strangely enough, suffering are the language of love. Our Lord speaks this language eloquently, especially in His Passion. Even a child can understand the meaning of a lance-pierced heart and outstretched arms. If properly understood there is nothing more beautiful than the face of Christ crucified. The next chapter might well bear this inscription:

> That the beauty of His countenance
> Be not hidden from His own,
> That the wounds and woe
> Wherein He wrote His love
> Be known by all the people He redeemed.

And studying these wounds we may learn to speak this language of love, however falteringly.

A mystery of love

It was inevitable, if our Lord were to be our model, that He would be born poor because many of His followers would not have all the nice things of life. If He had had them, we might reasonably say to Him: "You have shown us how to get along with, but how do we get along without?" So, our Lord was born the poorest of the poor in a stable, and throughout His life He had few luxuries. Basic essentials were there but very few comforts. "The foxes have dens, and the birds of the air have nests; but the Son of Man has nowhere to lay his head" (Matthew 8:20). To all His followers He recommends at least the spirit of poverty, an attitude of detachment toward material goods. They are good, but He urges us to sit lightly to them, since He knows that it is so easy for us, sense-bound and earth-bound as we are, to let possessions possess us instead of vice versa. Our Lord asks us to be flexible in the use of the goods of this world, and if He has blessed us with wealth, He looks for humble gratitude and open-handed generosity on the part of His faithful stewards.

It was also inevitable, if Christ were to be our model, that His life would be ordinary because the lives of most of us certainly are commonplace at least externally. There is nothing very glamorous, exciting, or earth-shaking about our daily lives. Therefore our Lord, for some twenty-odd years, lived in a village so small and insignificant that it was an object of ridicule. "Can anything good come out of Nazareth?" (John 1:46) Isn't it amazing that the Second Person of the Blessed Trinity, with all His infinite wisdom, who had come to redeem the world, led this hidden life for nearly three decades? The world had been waiting for His coming for centuries, yet He spent only three years in public life. The rest of His lifetime on earth He spent teaching us by example a lesson that is so hard for us to grasp—that there is sanctity in daily living within the four walls of a home. We find it hard to believe that the work we have to do at home, at the office, at school, although at times boring, is sanctifying. Our Lord showed us by doing and living it year after year; and, I think, may have even convinced us that it is so. "I do always the things that are pleasing to him [the Father]," Christ said of Himself. As we go about our daily routine we can say the same.

In this connection I recall a naval captain who was decorated for sinking a submarine. When he received the award he said, "I don't think I earned it for sinking the sub." Then he added, thoughtfully: "But I do think that the men and I earned it a thousand times over running the routine patrol." He figured that the lonely days and nights up and down the sea lanes in the dark, in the fog, in the stormy weather, with no one to observe or applaud, demanded more in the way of courage and perseverance, humility, and many other virtues, than the occasion on which he "sighted sub and sank same." I think we occasionally get this same insight. On a golden wedding day, as we see two people who have run the routine patrol together through fog, darkness, and storms, we realize that here is true greatness, fidelity. "Well done, good and faithful servant; because thou hast been faithful over a few things, I will set thee over many; enter into the joy of thy master," is one of the highest commendations our Lord can and will give to any of us. When we hear it from His lips it will make us happy for all eternity. In marriage especially, the years "Till death do us part" lived out contain many Christ-like virtues, which, if they were more common, would solve many of the problems rising from poor home situations; for broken hearts and lives often come from broken homes.

It was also inevitable that if Christ were to be our model there would be suffering in His life because in God's fatherly providence, suffering comes to all of us. There are the little daily sufferings and pin-pricks that come from weather, thorny personalities, sick headaches, misunderstandings, failure, financial worries. Then there are the larger sufferings of chronic ill health, crippling injuries, slow-death diseases. There are emotional, mental, physical sufferings that come to us and our loved ones. They come to families, whole nations, and they leave our minds rebellious and our hearts numb and frozen unless there is some understanding and acceptance. Suffering does present a tremendous mystery to the human mind. And any religion or philosophy which does not give some answer to the problem of suffering has left unanswered problems as real as the nearest hospital, funeral home, concentration camp, or a mother weeping at the loss of her only child.

Notice how violent and varied are the reactions to suffering. Some people are so appalled by human suffering and its seeming futility that they attempt to get rid of suffering by getting rid of the sufferer—the mercy killers. "I pumped air bubbles into her veins, she was suffering so terribly," one well-meaning but confused doctor explained. One minister of religion, evidently puzzled by it all, recommended that a medical committee be formed to determine the fate of incurables so that "they could die with dignity." "Come down from the cross," Christ is told, "so You can die with dignity."

One religion, it seems, solves the problem by denying the existence of suffering. "It isn't there. It's all in the mind. No need for a doctor." This is a simple solution—a little too simple. Another attitude, that of the stoic, might be expressed by: "My head is bloody but unbowed under the bludgeoning of a blind, unkind fate. I can take it and I can hand it out, if necessary. Suffering is just one of those things; meaningless, so what can you do about it or with it?"

Another attitude toward suffering is that it is always due to personal sin. This is implied in the reproachful cry we have all heard, "Why has God done this to me? I've been good." Some of the people of our Lord's time had that strong conviction. If you are good, you are wealthy and healthy. If you are bad, you are disease-ridden and poor. With this in mind, the disciples pointed to a man born blind and asked our Lord that same question: "Rabbi, who has sinned, this man or his parents, that he should be born blind?" Jesus answered: "Neither has this man sinned, nor his parents, but the works of God were to be made manifest in him" (John 9:2-3). This answers their question, but it still leaves our minds puzzled about suffering. Here we might recall that the Blessed Virgin, the immaculate, sinless, mother of God, on whom our Lord lavished treasures of nature and grace, was also the Queen of Martyrs and was told: "A sword of sorrows shall pierce thy heart." Sinless, she witnessed her innocent son's execution.

Obviously, there are many different reactions to suffering. We see two people with identical diseases. They are terminal. Before our eyes one becomes audibly rebellious and visibly bitter, hard, resentful. Another will become kinder, more understanding, gentle, patient, and peaceful. What is the difference?

Somewhere in the Passion and death of our Lord on the cross, we should be able to find a better, though not complete understanding of this tremendous mystery. The cross is a fact, so much so that we almost take it for granted and forget its meaning. Little children are signed with it at birth and those in the evening of life leave this world with its blessings. It is flung against the skyline of our cities. It is in our homes. In the public places throughout the civilized world there is "the Man on the Cross." It is here that we must direct our minds and hearts for understanding, for the disciple is not greater than the master.

St. Ignatius suggests that when we meditate on the Passion or recite the sorrowful mysteries of the rosary or make the stations of the cross, we have four or five major thoughts as the background of our thinking. The first truth is that Christ could have gotten out of this suffering. He could have redeemed the world in some other fashion. A single prayer of His had infinite redemptive value. But the eternal and blessed Trinity decreed that the way of the cross was to be the way of redemption. This is the first fact. We may not like the system, but it is the fact. It is God's way. The second truth to keep in mind is that our Lord did not allow His divinity to stand between Him and the pain. It hurt Him to be crucified just the way it would hurt us. It hurt Him to be spat upon, to fail and be rejected, to be scourged, in the way it would hurt us. "He is one tried as we are in all things except sin." In fact, when He was given the mercy potion of myrrh and wine before the crucifixion, a draught designed to deaden the pain: ". . . but when he had tasted it, he would not drink." He took His human suffering straight. We may sometimes think He had such clear knowledge that His passion and death would redeem mankind that, we falsely conclude, it did not hurt. We, too, could know that an operation would be very useful and restore us to health but there would still be the anxious anticipation, the suffering, and the post-operative pain.

Another thought to keep in mind is that since we are so slow to believe God loves us, we find, here in the cross, God's ultimate eloquence that clears away our doubts and insecurities about ourselves. St. Paul, who quite reasonably had some doubts about himself (after all, he persecuted the early Church and was official witness to the stoning of Stephen), looked at Christ on the cross and reassured himself: "I live in the faith of the Son of God, who loved me and gave himself up for me" (Galatians 2:20). Each one of us can say, "This is what I am worth in His sight." Even a child can understand outstretched arms and a lance-pierced heart.

Another thought to keep in mind is that we are not detached spectators at the Passion. This is not simply an historical event, like the Napoleonic wars which we study objectively. We are personally involved. We had a share in this. We helped to cause it. Why? It is true that if you had not been born and if I had not been born, Christ would still have suffered and died for all the others. It is also true that if I had sinned less, Christ would have suffered less. He had to pay up and atone for my personal sins. "Despised and the most abject of men, a man of sorrows and acquainted with infirmity . . . Surely he hath borne our infirmities and carried our sorrows . . . But he was wounded for our iniquities: he was bruised for our sins. The chastisement of our peace *was* upon him: and by his bruises we are healed" (Isaias 53:3 ff.). In this connection, there was a custom in an ancient eastern town in biblical times, that when anyone was murdered the inhabitants were required to pass the body, and place their hands on the wounds of the murdered person and take an oath: "I had no part in this man's death." They did not have the detective devices, lie detectors, fingerprints, and so forth, for tracking down a criminal; but they reasoned that putting a person through the psychological ordeal of facing his victim would make the guilty one confess. If we were asked to pass under the foot of the cross and go through the same ritual, each one of us in all honesty would have to break down and confess: "I had a part in this. I am guilty."

A final thought to keep in mind, since suffering has come and will come again, is that we can watch our Lord, a better man than ourselves, going before us. We can learn how to suffer and possibly something of the why of suffering. So with these major thoughts in mind, let's glance at a few of the highlights of our Lord's Passion, typical situations in which we might find ourselves and in which we might find meaning for ourselves.

Our Lord's words: "This is my body, this is my blood," were still warming the hearts of His apostles when He rose to leave. As He left the warmth and friendship of the supper chamber and went out into the dark and chill of the evening a dread and a fear crept over Him. The apostles observed this change and recorded, "he began to be saddened and exceedingly troubled" (Matthew 26:37). ". . . he began to feel dread and to be exceedingly troubled" (Mark 14:33). Something terrifying and loathsome is clinging to Him and His spirit is striving to throw it off. He leads them toward the garden of olives and tells them: "My soul is sad, even unto death" (Mark 14:34). He is the son of man and like to us in seeking some comfort in His agony as He asks: "Sit down here, while I go over yonder and pray" (Matthew

26:36). And the apostles record: "And going forward a little, he fell on the ground, and began to pray that, if it were possible, the hour might pass from him; and he said, 'Abba, Father, all things are possible to thee. Remove this cup from me' " (Mark 14:36).

In His love for men, He had gladly accepted this mission of redeeming the world, but now that it was upon Him, His human will and feelings shrank from it, the way we would shrink in the presence of imminent danger and pain. He speaks of the chalice, part of the contents of which would simply be the physical suffering that lay ahead. During His lifetime, when He foretold His Passion, He mentioned two or three things that must have stood out in the foreground of His consciousness. He said the Son of Man will be spit upon, mocked, scourged, and crucified; wounds to a man's dignity and person, both mental and physical. Cardinal Newman, who is inclined to think that our Lord's mental sufferings were much more intense than His physical sufferings, eloquently describes them in his sermon on the mental sufferings of Christ. He says sin "which is so easy a thing to us, so natural, so welcome" was to Him "woe unutterable," and "had the scent and the poison of death. . . . Sin is an easy thing to us; we think little of it;" but He knew it in all its hateful ugliness. All sins He bore: the sin that drove our first parents from the garden; the first murder, when Abel lay dead at the hands of his brother, Cain; the lust of Sodom and Gomorrah; the sins of Greece and Rome; the pride and hate and selfishness that have turned our world into a great battlefield. Sins, great and small, the sins of all men: "Of the living and of the dead and of the as yet unborn, of the lost and of the saved," saints and sinners, your sins and mine. His dearest friends are there: Peter, James, and John and add their sins to His burden. A long line of chosen priests and nuns and each one of us come to Him in His agony to add to the weight that presses Him to the ground. "One only is not there," Mary Immaculate. She will be near Him on the cross; she is separated from Him in the garden. This weight and burden of sin was so intense that it forced a bloody sweat from the pores of our Lord's body.

Agonizing He again repeated His prayer, "Abba, Father, all things are possible to thee. Remove this cup from me; yet not what I will, but what thou willest" (Mark 14:36). I think it is good to memorize that prayer. We may have to pray it some day. At some time or other there comes to almost everyone, I think, a mental or physical suffering that is a little more intense than others. We ask that it be removed, but it won't be. Like our Lord, and I say this reverently, we will have to kneel down beside Him and sweat it out. Like our Lord, we will be given grace to bear it out.

And now our Lord is strengthened, just as we will be. "And there appeared to him an angel from heaven to strengthen him" (Luke 22:43). He rises and goes out from under the olive trees, knowing clearly what He's going to meet. In the darkness there is the flicker of pine torches, the murmur of a crowd approaching, and the clash of arms. As He comes out from under the trees, Judas is there. He throws his arms about Christ and says: "Hail, Master." Our Lord's only answer to this kiss of betrayal is, "Judas, dost thou betray the Son of Man with a kiss?" Let us study this betrayal a little because it puzzles us. Judas must have been a rather good man or our Lord would never have invited him to be a chosen apostle; but we are given some little knowledge of a weakness in Judas. We're told that when the woman poured precious ointment on our Lord's feet, Judas complained and said: "This might have been sold for much and given to the poor." And John records that Judas's concern was not for the people, but because "he was a thief." This we know for sure. Theologians also speculate and say that Judas was attracted when Jesus spoke of His kingdom, but when Judas discovered the nature of the kingdom, not one of worldly or political authority—he wanted no part of it. Knowing that the Pharisees were looking for an occasion to seize our Lord when the crowds wouldn't be around, Judas left the supper early and went to them and said: "What are you willing to give me for delivering him to you?" (Matthew 26:15). They gave him thirty pieces of silver. Lest there be any confusion in the darkness, with the other apostles around, Judas arranged for a signal: "Whomever I kiss, that is he; lay hold of him, and lead him safely away" (Mark 14:44). Thus it was arranged and thus it was done. It is also thought that Judas vaguely believed our Lord really wouldn't be seized. He'd seen Him escape from His enemies before; possibly He'd do it again. But now, as Jesus is seized, Judas is overcome with a sense of guilt, which is quite different than sorrow for sin. I can be guilty but not sorry. I can hate myself, but that doesn't mean that I ask for forgiveness. So Judas went back to the high priest and said: "I have sinned in betraying innocent blood"; and, as always, the answer came: "See to it thyself" (Matthew 27:4). And forgetting the story of the prodigal son, Judas went out and hanged himself with a halter. If he had only turned to our Lord, as Peter did, we'd probably be praying to St. Judas. Our tendency when we sin is to run from God. We go off alone by ourselves like a wounded animal and hide. We should run instead to the loving arms of our heavenly Father and the open heart of Christ. Even if we but touch the hem of His garment, we shall be healed.

Our Lord was seized and bound and led off for trial. The trial that took place was a parody of justice. We know enough about the Roman and Jewish law of the time and lawyers studying the case can list a full page of irregularities in the conduct of the trial. For example, it was convened late at night which was illegal; the judges sitting in judgment were not duly authorized; the witnesses openly perjured themselves and still their testimony was accepted. Our Lord didn't even have immunity from physical violence; at one point in the trial an attendant struck Him. Men have killed other men for such a blow, but our Lord's only answer was: "If I have spoken ill, bear witness to the evil; but if well, why dost thou strike me?" (John 18:23) And finally the high priest solemnly asked our Lord a question: "I adjure thee by the living God that thou tell us whether thou art the Christ, the Son of God." Quietly, our Lord answered: "Thou hast said it. Nevertheless, I say to you, hereafter you shall see the Son of Man sitting at the right hand of the Power and coming upon the clouds of heaven." There was awed silence for a minute as the full import of Christ's statement was caught. Then the judge righteously responded, ". . . you have heard the blasphemy." He makes Himself to be God. "What do you think?" They shouted their well-prepared answer "He is liable to death," and they put our Lord in jail for the night (Matthew 26:64 ff.). Men meditating on this scene, have gathered strength to bear some of the injustices that can come through the maliciousness of others or through their thoughtlessness. A better man than ourselves has been unjustly accused and misjudged.

Now these "judges" did not have the authority to impose the death sentence without Roman approval, so they brought our Lord before Pilate the next morning. Only now the accusation is changed; not, "He makes himself to be God," because that would be of no interest to Pilate, just another religious dispute; but a different accusation that would concern Pilate: "He makes himself out to be a king; He rouses up the people; He causes sedition." As Pilate, a Roman with a sense of justice, questioned our Lord, he saw that the trial was fixed. He did not want to condemn the innocent, but he was looking for some other solution than freeing Him outright. That might cause trouble. Pilate loves Pilate—just a little too much. When he realizes that the crowd will not accept his declaration, "I find no guilt in him," he looks for a way out. Knowing that Herod, the tetrarch of Galilee, is in town at this time of the feast of the Passover, Pilate decides to send this Galilean to him for judgment. "And learning that he belonged to Herod's jurisdiction, he sent him back to Herod, who likewise was in Jerusalem in those days" (Luke 23:7).

Herod, we know from way back. He's the man who killed John the Baptist, our Lord's precursor and cousin. John had been jailed for speaking out about the incest going on in Herod's court. When Salome danced for Herod on the occasion of his birthday, he was so pleased that in his drunken stupor he promised her anything she would request. Salome's mother, who was involved in the scandal, told her to ask for the head of John the Baptist, and Herod reluctantly carried out his foolish promise. This is the same man, now, who is going to sit in judgment on Christ. And though our Lord stood in his presence for some twenty minutes or so, He didn't speak a single word to Herod. It was a terrible judgment on the man; but as always our Lord was seeking to win a person back, and the treatment of silence was probably designed to awaken Herod to a knowledge of what he was. But, since our Lord doesn't speak at all, Herod says He's an idiot, a moron, a fool, and orders our Lord to be clothed in the white garment of a fool and to be sent off. As we contemplate the Second Person of the Blessed Trinity, infinite wisdom, declared a fool and so treated by this man and his court, we wonder how far our Lord will go in accepting humiliation. On reflection though, it can give us strength and comfort when we are unjustly accused, criticized, and unable to explain or defend ourselves. ". . . learn from me, for I am meek and humble of heart." And if we think on it a little, isn't it true, that we're regarded as a bit foolish if we take the following of Christ seriously? We're regarded as being a little naïve, perhaps even superstitious, and are advised to smarten up or we'll never really get ahead. But the so-called foolishness of Christ, we know, is preferable to the so-called wisdom of men.

So now back to Pilate. The decision is thrust upon him, and to show that his heart is in the right place, he washes his hands and says: "I am innocent of the blood of this just man," and then permits Christ to be condemned to death.

As the cross falls into place, the first shock almost kills our Lord, but gradually a little strength returns. As He looks down from the cross He sees, off to one side, some soldiers shooting dice for his garments. There isn't much malice there; mercenary soldiers on an execution detail, knowing little or nothing of the merits of the case. The Pharisees are there too, and they are malicious. Christ said to them: "they knew the truth, and perverted it, and led men astray."

And we are there, because we too had a part in this. But, looking down on all of us, our Lord prays: "Father, forgive them, for they do not know what they are doing."

That mercy He prayed for went out to the soldiers, to the Pharisees, and to ourselves. And we once again thank God for His infinite mercy. But, also, it is good to recall that we're asked to pass on this forgiveness to others. We are asked to forgive those who have injured us. In fact, if we don't, it is a little dangerous to say the Our Father, or at least the second part of it which concludes: "forgive us our trespasses, as we forgive those who trespass against us." We are actually asking for forgiveness in proportion to the way we're willing to pass it on to others. This forgiveness of others looms very large in our Lord's teaching. When St. Peter asked Jesus: "Lord, how often shall my brother sin against me, and I forgive him? Up to seven times?" Jesus said: "I do not say to thee seven times, but seventy times seven." If we are mathematically inclined and take things literally, that would be $7 \times 70 = 490$. Four hundred and ninety times we should forgive each man. As we start getting up to that number, and we seldom do, we might recall that what our Lord meant was to go on forgiving indefinitely. However, four hundred and ninety times would do for a start and help form the habit of forgiving.

Even from the viewpoint of mental hygiene, this forgiveness of others is like a breath of fresh air sweeping through a musty garret. If we allow hostilities and resentments to build up through the years, they can twist a personality and harden it and embitter it. Alcoholics, once they have joined A.A., will tell you of their former hostilities, resentments, and self-pity. They could list a thousand people who had wronged them and this injustice always evoked self-pity. One wonderful alcoholic said to me: "Father, when I first joined the program and I'd be at Mass and say that prayer, 'O Lord, deliver me from the iniquitous man,' I could immediately think of thirty, er- uh- undesirable characters, from whom I should be delivered. But now that I've been on the program a few years, I'm a lot mellower, and when I come to that part: 'Deliver me from the iniquitous man,' I can't find too many who were that nasty to me and who did me in." So, forgiveness—a short prayer for those who offended us knowingly or unknowingly—is very Christian and wonderful for mental health.

In the history of Christian forgiveness it is hard to find one who surpassed St. Thomas More, the patron of lawyers. With his fine legal mind, he knew justice and he knew when it had been outraged. Yet after being condemned to death in a trial which was a parody of justice, forgiveness breathed through his every action and word, and his composure and humor stayed with him until the ax fell. As he was being led up rickety stairs to the scaffold, he turned to the lieutenant in charge and said smilingly: "I pray you, Master Lieutenant, see me safe up, and as for my coming down, let me shift for myself." To his executioner: "Pluck up thy spirits, man, and be not afraid to do thy office." He embraced him telling him he bore him no ill-will and would pray for him. He even set aside a certain sum of money out of his diminished resources to be sent to his executioner after his death. And the prayer he composed before his death is the kind of prayer we might want to say ourselves:

"Almighty God, have mercy on N. and N., and on all that bear me evil will, and would me harm, and their faults and mine together, and by such easy, tender, merciful means, as Thine infinite wisdom best can devise, vouchsafe to . . . make us saved souls in heaven together where we may ever live and love together with Thee and Thy blessed saints. O glorious Trinity, for the bitter passion of our Sweet Savior Christ, Amen."

How truly this breathes the spirit of Christ's prayer of forgiveness for His enemies, "Father, forgive them." Perhaps we, too, can learn to forgive more generously and completely.

While our Lord is still on the cross, He wishes to take care of His mother. In His divine providence she is to live some years after His death. Her heart would be in heaven, but He had some further work left for her to do on earth: forming the apostles, His Church, and informing the Church about His early life. She above all knows the mind and the heart of Christ, and she was needed. Often, I think, we recall Mary as the maid of Galilee or the Madonna or the Immaculate Conception or the Mother of Sorrows at the foot of the cross, but may forget that she also lived as an older woman, kindly and gracious in the evening of life. Mary was virgin, mother, and widow.

To provide for His mother during the coming years, our Lord entrusted her to John's loving care. "When Jesus, therefore, saw his mother and the disciple standing by, whom he loved, he said to his mother, 'Woman, behold, thy son.' Then he said to the disciple, 'Behold, thy mother.' And from that hour the disciple took her into his home" (John 19:26-27). In that presentation of Mary to John and John to Mary, we know that she was also given to us as our mother. Because Mary was so intimately identified with the Redemption, she has a heart almost as large as her son's, one that can reach out to embrace each one of us in her motherly, protective love. I don't care how old we get, we need Mary in the picture. I think, too, that she is feminine enough to know and love those who carry her picture or wear her medal. It is one of the strong traditions that those devoted to Mary, the mother of God, do not lose their souls. And obviously a favorite expression of that love and devotion is the rosary. From many of the historic statements that have been made, the rosary, though it may seem to be an inadequate weapon, is one of the most effective means to save our strife-torn world of the sixties. We ought to try then, if we can, to say a daily decade of the rosary— if possible the whole rosary.

I remember that my father, a very kind and wonderful man but still a hard-headed old Irishman (straight from County Mayo—God help us), insisted that we say the rosary at home each night. Not just in October and May, the months especially dedicated to the Blessed Virgin, but he wanted it every night. My brother, sister, and I, deciding that this was much too much (all ten minutes of it) formed a little society to keep father from saying the rosary. We invented delaying tactics. About nine-thirty or ten when my father would say: "Now, we'll kneel down and say the rosary," my brother would protest: "I'm doing my calculus. Could we wait until I finish this problem?" My father would wait about twenty minutes and then repeat his suggestion. But my sister would say: "I'm just writing a poem. You wouldn't want to interrupt that now, would you?" So we'd wait a little longer. Then it would be my turn to throw in a road block. But fathers aren't that stupid and he soon caught on that there was rebellion among the peasants, and said: "Look, if you don't want to be saying the rosary, the five decades, we can say it the way we did in Ireland. There were the joyful mysteries, the sorrowful mysteries, and the glorious mysteries. That's the real rosary, the fifteen decades." He added, "Then, there is the trimmings, five Our Fathers and five Hail Marys for Aunt Bridget (God rest her soul), and five Our Fathers and five Hail Marys for young people to increase their devotion to the Mother of God (Ahem!), and five Our Fathers and five Hail Marys for our holy father, the pope. Shall we say it that way, or shall we kneel down now and say the short rosary?" He had conquered. Unanimously we agreed to say it the short way—the five decades.

I remember one particular Friday night. My brother and sister had escaped but I was there, still stalling. I should have suspected something because he was a little too peaceful about it all. He bided his time and waited until some of the fellows and girls had come over to the house and when they had all arrived he said: "Now, we will *all* kneel down and say the rosary." What a low blow! It certainly brought me to my knees. I figured my social standing was ruined forever. But, as I look back at the whole thing, I think there is truth in the statement: "The family that prays together, stays together." Still, if we can't get the rosary in that way—and it is hard to corner a family in modern times—we can use other moments in a busy day. Instead of sitting on the bus reading

"It keeps you fresh around the clock," over and over again, you can get in a decade of the rosary. It won't be the most devout, recollected prayer, but it is better than reading an advertisement for the one hundredth time. By the end of the day you may have pieced together a whole rosary—a decade here and a decade there. One man who made a retreat decided he was going to say the rosary while driving downtown. The next day he ran an amber light and picked up a ticket on the third glorious mystery. That can happen —but at least his heart was in the right place.

Our Lord saved until the end a suffering which He asks no one else to share. He had often said in His lifetime on earth: "Come to me, all you who labor and are burdened, and I will give you rest." He was strong. What, then, must have been His agony to bring from His lips that cry: "My God, my God, why hast thou forsaken me?" He was united to the Divinity, but there was such a sense of emptiness, loneliness, abandonment, and darkness that it brought that cry to His lips. No matter how deep or dark our lonesomeness may be—we might even teeter on the verge of psychosis—our Lord is there ahead of us. We don't even have to do that alone. In the darkness there is someone beside us. It is Christ. And now, peace comes to Him. "It is consummated!" He had finished the work given Him to do. He had come among men and lived our life from birth to death. He taught us how to live. He established His Church so that we who live in the twentieth century can get His doctrine without error. He instituted the sacraments to communicate to us His divine life. He had chosen to remain with us in the Holy Eucharist until the end of time. He had given us His mother to be our mother. Is there anything more He could do for us? Yes. Bowing His head, He died. We don't even have to do that alone now.

What our Lord's suffering can mean to people! I think Joyce Kilmer groped for that meaning when he wrote the "Prayer of a Soldier in France."

My shoulders ache beneath my pack;
(Lie easier, Cross, upon His back).

I march with feet that burn and smart;
(Tread, Holy Feet, upon my heart).

Men shout at me who may not speak;
(They scourged Thy back and smote Thy cheek).

I may not lift a hand to clear
My eyes of salty drops that sear.

(Then shall my fickle soul forget
Thy Agony of Bloody Sweat?)

My rifle hand is stiff and numb
(From Thy pierced palm red rivers come).

Lord, Thou didst suffer more for me
Than all the hosts of land and sea.

So, let me render back again
This millionth of Thy gift. Amen.

He speaks of suffering as a gift. Suffering, mental or physical, united with Christ is redemptive. It can save our souls, and it can save the souls of others. Christ intends to reproduce Himself in us in every aspect of His life, gloriously reigning with Him, also suffering with Him. To His disciples, who are totally puzzled by His Passion and death, the risen Christ speaks these reassuring words: "Did not the Christ [and we] have to suffer these things before entering into his glory?" (Luke 24:26). Suffering, then, can be a very special kind of gift and a sign of God's special love and regard. Suffering is the language of love. As there is the apostolate of action and there is the apostolate of prayer, so there is the apostolate of suffering. St. Paul tells us: ". . . and what is lacking of the sufferings of Christ I fill up in my flesh for his body, which is the Church" (Colossians 1:24).

And so, Christian suffering is not stupid, wasteful. It is not futile. It is not nothing. It is redemptive. I can save my soul and the souls of others by means of it. For me this truth was summed up by a soldier friend of mine. A shell had landed on the powder bags behind his 105. He was terribly burned and full of wounds. When I went to the field hospital and anointed him and gave him Holy Communion, I kidded him a little (you know at times you could get a purple heart for very minor wounds). Here he was, really shot up, so I thoughtfully remarked that he might just get a purple heart for this. "Yes," he said, smiling a little "maybe I'll get the purple heart. But I have something better than that." He pointed to the Sacred Heart badge on his hospital gown and said, "I've got the Sacred Heart." I think he had grasped in some way the meaning that Christ's lance-pierced heart should have for all of us. Suffering is the language of love.

This incident also reminds me of Dom Thomas Verner Moore's observation: "For every calamity, there are always two ways of looking at it, and we should learn to glean whatever may be humorous and pleasant in our unfortunate circumstances. But should this become too shallow, or wholly impossible in the severe storm that threatens to overwhelm us, then our minds must turn to the cross of Christ."

Do it yourself!
Points for your prayerful thinking (15 minutes)

PREPARATORY PRAYER
See page 18.

A mystery of love
1 Christ could have gotten out of His sufferings. This is what I am worth in His eyes. He delivered Himself for me. I had a part in this. What a terrible thing sin must be!
2 Agony in the garden. Not my will but Thine be done —trial before Herod. A fool—we are fools many think. Crucifixion—Father, forgive them—behold thy mother —why hast Thou forsaken me? It is finished. There is the apostolate of prayer and action. There is also the apostolate of suffering. "The disciple is not above his master. But every one shall be perfect, if he be as his master."

Conclude by saying one Our Father, a Hail Mary, and Glory Be to the Father.

"Of course, I'm working for a reward. I'd be an idiot to work if I didn't hope to get some pay-off." This admission of mine wasn't a conversation stopper, fortunately; but it did surprise my shrewd, agnostic friend who had just leveled an accusation at me. He thought he had me when he said: "We're both selfish—equally selfish. We're both working for rewards, only I'll take mine here because I don't believe in the hereafter."

In fact my friend was so surprised by my admission that he listened while I explained that the difference was not only in when we expected to receive our respective rewards, but in the rewards themselves. "Because I do believe in an afterlife, I'm working to get to heaven, to save my soul. I don't want to go to hell, but that doesn't tell the whole story. It's heaven that's the reward. And heaven, saving our souls, is the possession of God—perfect union with Him in love. He is infinite goodness, beauty, love, and possessing Him is the source of all our happiness. No matter how much we may enjoy the "rewards" in this life, they never completely satisfy. "Our hearts were made for Thee, O God, and they will never be at rest until they rest in Thee." The reward I am working for is not something outside of God, it is God Himself! I thought I did reach my wealthy friend with the parting shot: "You'll have to admit there's a big difference between a woman who loves only your car and bank roll and one who loves you. Think it over."

In this next chapter, we can think over the reward, exceedingly great, that our Lord promised to us so lovingly: "And if I go and prepare a place for you, I am coming again, and I will take you to myself; that where I am, there you also may be" (John 14:3).

Victory with peace

We are approaching the end of the retreat, and I would like to encourage you to keep up your good work. It is worth a final effort because God often reserves special graces and insights for the end, to crown our faithfulness. Then, too, the spiritual exercises are theologically and psychologically progressive. They begin at rock bottom, lay a solid foundation, and build up from there to the very heavens. To put it another way, the mystery story and love story which God writes into the lives of each of us is not complete or even understandable until we reach the last chapter with its happy ending. This happy ending which God plans for us reminds us of the stories we heard as children. Those stories always ended triumphantly. "And they lived happily ever afterward." Then everybody approved, smiled, and clapped their hands. This was the way things should be. For us, God literally translates that familiar storybook ending into "in vitam aeternam per omnia saecula saeculorum." Life everlasting! World without end! And everybody shouts, "Alleluia."

However, before taking a look upward to heaven, the happy ending to our lives, we might take a glance back at the ground we have covered and the progress we have made. This gives us perspective. Recall that we established a basic truth and first principle: Man was created to praise, reverence, and serve God, and by this means to save his soul.

All the other things on the face of the earth are created for man that they may help him to attain the end for which he is created; that is, to save his soul, to reach an eternity of happiness with God.

The "How to" of these great basic truths is concretized for us in Christ, God became man, who led our life from birth to death and showed us how to do it. He is the way, the truth, and the life. Thus to be Christ-like is "successful living" according to God's plan. Our minds and hearts are to be centered on Him. When the evening of life is come, we shall be judged on love. In love and loyalty we devote our energies and talents, our whole lives, to serving Him and establishing His Kingdom in our own hearts and lives, and in the hearts and lives of others. Each one, in his God-given state of life, is to be an apostle. How are we to do all this? "Come, follow me," Christ says. Then, to our surprise and, perhaps, our dismay, he adds: "Take up your cross daily and follow Me." The disciple is not to be greater than or different from the Master. We are to do it His way. We follow a crucified leader. To our timid fearful hearts that naturally shrink at the mention of the cross, He gives this reassurance: "For my yoke is easy, and my burden light." And His heart-warming and encouraging appeal is that of a truly great leader and dear friend. He will not ask us to do anything that He has not done before us. If there is poverty or suffering or labor or failure or contempt involved—things that seem so difficult for us to accept—we can remember that He has experienced them before us to make it easier and less frightening for us. Better yet, He will be with us on our way. We won't have to do it alone. It is to be done "through Him, with Him, and in Him." His faithful promise to those who follow is "Victory with peace." He will not lose a single man. He does not plan to have us shoulder the cross, lead us to Calvary, and then leave us hanging there. He does not bring us to the tomb and seal the door.

His plan is summed up in St. Paul's joyous cry, "But thanks be to God who has given us the victory through our Lord Jesus Christ." Death is swallowed up in victory! "O death, where is thy victory? O death, where is thy sting?" Suffering and labor, then, are only for a little while. "Did not the Christ have to suffer these things before entering into His glory?" Easter follows Good Friday. In the midst of pain and labor we are reassured: "And God will wipe away every tear from their eyes. And death shall be no

219

more; neither shall there be mourning, nor crying, nor pain any more, for the former things have passed away . . . Behold, I make all things new! . . . He who overcomes shall possess these things, and I will be his God, and he shall be my son" (Apocalypse 21:4 ff.). This is the happy ending. Life everlasting!

At this point I think you might be interested in knowing what happened to the blind captain that I spoke of at the beginning and have referred to on other occasions. I mention him here because his story too has a happy ending and psychologically prepares us for the happy ending that Christ promises to all who follow Him. If you recall, the captain, a glider pilot from Texas, was shot down. In the crash his neck was broken, and he went permanently blind. He was held prisoner. When he was at his lowest, physically and emotionally, a hospital nun passed by his bed, noticed the medal around his neck, and began giving him special attention. Slowly he responded. His despair was dispelled and his neck healed, but he remained blind. He was repatriated before the war was over. The townspeople, figuring that he was somewhat handicapped, presented him with the key to a beautiful home, complete with landscaping. He found an interesting and satisfying job. He doesn't need a seeing-eye dog. He wrote happily, "I'm now expecting an all-American end for Notre Dame." I answered back, "How can you be sure it isn't twin girls?" About six months later he announced proudly: "You must have a crystal ball in your room; it is twin girls! Now I'll have to start an hour of charm instead of a football team." He is doing nicely, keeping his fine sense of humor, just as he clung desparately to his faith in his hours of discouragement and darkness. He said: "Being blind isn't too bad. I'm not so blind that I can't find the handle of a beer mug. I don't have to look at women's hats in church, and if I ever lose my present job, I can always become an umpire in the American League."

As we see this happy ending to what looked like unrelieved tragedy, we are reminded that our Lord promised victory to those who follow Him. In this same mood of hope and confidence, we can look heavenward and see what can be said about heaven with certainty, following the clear teaching of scripture and the sure doctrines of the Church. The description is inadequate, but even this glimpse is immensely heartening.

First of all, we can affirm that heaven is a state and place of perfect and everlasting happiness—perfect and everlasting happiness. Now we all know what happiness is, but not perfect happiness. If we were to use words to describe it, we might say: "peace, contentment, security, love, joy, fullness of living." All of these blended might spell out happiness. But for perfect happiness we know that three things would be required. We must have all positive elements of happiness that we can hold in mind, and heart, and in body; there must be no suffering, pain, failure, boredom, weariness, or death; and this blessed state must go on forever. If it didn't go on forever, it would be something like a vacation. "I'm having a wonderful time, but I know it is going to end in a few short weeks and I'll be back at work." The realization that something is going to end dims our present enjoyment. Permanent and secure possession is required for perfect happiness.

Our Lord promised us the fulfillment of these three requirements. All the happiness we can hold. He tells us: "I go to prepare a place for you. And if I go and prepare a place for you I am coming again, and I will take you to myself; and your heart shall rejoice, and your joy no one shall take from you." There is His faithful promise of joy filled to the brim and overflowing. That there will be no suffering, pain, or death, we are told: "God will wipe away every tear from their eyes. And death shall be no more . . . for the former things have passed away." We know that this blessed state will go on forever, because our Lord speaks of "eternal life," and the Church, in the requiem Mass, of "eternal rest." This is rest, not in the sense of inactivity or sleep or oblivion, but of perfect harmony, balance, and peace. Eternal rest. Eternal life. Perfect and everlasting happiness.

We are curious, though, and we want to know how we will be made happy in heaven. Our essential happiness, we are told, will be in the possession of God, the face to face vision of Him. We will, since we share in the divine nature, enter into the inner life of the Trinity. We will know and love and exist with the fullness of life which is the Blessed Trinity. We will share in the divine life of the Father, the Son, and the Holy Spirit to our fullest capacity.

But we are still curious. We want to know how this possession of God will make us happy. Well, we all know, as clearly as we know anything, that our minds are made for truth and knowledge. We want to know. We can see that in the endless questionings of a little child: "Where did I come from? Who is God? Why is the man bald? How far away is the moon? Why do I have to? Why? Why? Why? Why? What? Who? When? How?"—the restless questioning of the human mind for knowledge. We can see that in ourselves. Aren't there a lot of things we would like to know? If only we had the leisure and the talent to investigate! Aren't there a lot of places we would like to visit and explore? Aren't there already a lot of unsolved mysteries in regard to life, its events, God's providence, the problem of suffering—all of which our mind seeks in vain to answer? Aren't there a lot of areas of knowledge that arouse our curiosity: science, medicine, philosophy, art, music, nuclear physics, outer space, the depths of the ocean? Even the most learned man who has spent his whole life in one area of knowledge will honestly and humbly confess that the knowledge he possesses is like a grain of sand compared to the unexplored mountains of truth still about him. The scientists will tell you that the study of the atom, in all its simplicity and complexity, is just beginning. The doctor will admit that medical science is only on the threshold of discovering something about cancer and heart disease. The philosopher will confess that his most profound search for truth leads him on to more mystery. So all of us leave this world with our capacity for knowledge still unsatisfied. But the moment we are in the presence of God we are in the presence and possession of Infinite Truth. And God gives us a share in His own divine knowledge, just as much as we can hold. This great capacity we have for truth finds complete satisfaction. According to our full capacity, we know as God knows. The mind is finally at rest and happy in the possession of the fullness of truth and knowledge.

We also know as clearly as we know anything, that we are made for beauty. We thrill to beauty wherever we see it—sunset at evening, stars seen through the trees at night, the moon on the water, the surf of the seas, a snow-clad mountain peak, a flower, a beautiful woman, the smile of a child, the charm of personality, music that takes us up and out of ourselves, the splendor of form and color in art. Wherever we see beauty, we thrill to it. We want more of it. But at times in this life, there are things which are dull and drab. However, there is also a tremendous beauty in this world of ours, if only we have the eyes to see it. At any rate, we all leave this world with our capacity for beauty still unsatisfied. But the moment we are in the presence of God, we are in the presence of Infinite Beauty. Gather together all the little colored fragments of beauty we see in this life—in people, in art, in nature—God is all these things and infinitely more. And if the beauty we behold here can so seduce and thrill us, what satisfaction and ecstasy there will be in the contemplation and possession of Infinite Beauty, God. St. Augustine cried out: "O Beauty, ever ancient, ever new." Cardinal Newman in his poem, "The Dream of Gerontius" describes the departure of a soul from this life and eloquently pictures it winging past the beauty and splendor and light of the angels, archangels, thrones, dominions, cherubim, and seraphim, but as the soul enters the presence of his God, Newman's eloquence runs out. Like St. Augustine, he simply has the soul exclaiming: "Ah!" Complete breath-taking satisfaction in the possession of Infinite Beauty. Saints Peter and John and James were given a faint hint of this divine beauty at the transfiguration of Christ on Mount Tabor. "Jesus . . . led them up a high mountain by themselves, and was transfigured before them. And his face shone as the sun, and his garments became white as snow. . . . a bright cloud overshadowed them, and behold, a voice out of the

cloud said, 'This is my beloved Son, . . . hear him'"
(Matthew 17:1 ff.). Peter in ecstasy exclaimed:
"Lord, it is good for us to be here." According to our
full capacity we shall behold and possess the splendor
and beauty of the Divinity and exclaim, "It is good
for us to be here." So this great capacity that we have
for beauty also finds complete satisfaction in the
possession of Infinite Beauty.

We know also, as clearly as we know anything,
that we are made for love, and love is one of the
highest forms of living. There is the love of parents
for children, or children for parents. There is the
love of a man for a woman, a friend for a friend,
man for God. Love completes us and fulfills us. It
gives a feeling of warmth, well-being, and joy. When
we love God with our whole heart, our neighbor as
ourselves, we are conscious of a peace within ourselves. And if we are consciously aware that our love
is returned, this is true happiness. But in this life,
even in the most perfect love, there can be misunderstandings and differences. If nothing else, there is
separation from loved ones that comes with death. In
our love for God we do not see Him face to face.
We have to grope to Him through faith. His visible
presence is not there to comfort us. So all of us leave
this world with our capacity for love, both human
and divine, still unsatisfied. But the moment we are
in the presence of God we are in the presence of
Infinite Love. We are conscious of being swept up
into an embrace of infinite love and ourselves loving
back with a completeness and intensity of which
human love in its ecstasy is only a promise and fore-
taste. In heaven, in addition to knowing God, we will
love Him with the love of the Father for the Son, and
the Son for the Father, and their mutual love for one
another, the Holy Spirit. Christ's promises become
fully realized in us, ". . . that all may be one, even
as thou, Father, in me and I in thee; that they also
may be one in us . . . And the glory that thou hast
given me, I have given to them, that they may be one,
even as we are one: I in them and thou in me . . .
thou hast loved them even as thou hast loved me"
(John 17:21 ff.). "God is Love." Love is union. We

are in ecstasy. "Our hearts were made for Thee, O God, and now they are at rest because they rest in Thee."

This opens up possibilities for us. But further, we are promised that our bodies will be restored to us on the last day. We will be men and women in heaven. We affirm that in the Creed at Mass, "I believe in the resurrection of the body!" St. Paul reminds us of the same death-defying truth: "Behold, I tell you a mystery . . . For the trumpet shall sound, and the dead shall rise incorruptible" (I Corinthians 15:51 ff.). "What is sown in corruption rises in incorruption; what is sown in dishonor rises in glory; what is sown in weakness rises in power" (I Corinthians 15:43). The model of what our bodies will be like is the gloriously risen body of Christ as we know it on Easter Sunday morning; bright, beautiful, all deformities and wounds removed, no longer capable of suffering, or pain, or death. On the feast of the Assumption of the Blessed Virgin Mary we are reminded that she, the most beautiful of women, already has her lovely body restored to her. We too shall have our Resurrection and Assumption. St. Paul's words will be verified in us: "Death is swallowed up in victory! O death, where is thy victory? O death, where is thy sting?"

It follows, then, that the social life in heaven will be wonderful. We will not be so preoccupied with the vision and loveliness of God that we won't have both time and the desire to be with those we have known on earth and loved and been separated from by death. Only this difference will exist: people that we never understood or cared for particularly, we will now know, love, and understand. All the deformities and unpleasant habits which distort the beautiful, unique person which God created are removed. Each person stands out in all his completeness, his God-given attractiveness and lovableness. Sometimes people say semi-seriously, "If so and so is in heaven, it won't be heaven for me." Others express some concern about unpleasant memories or relationships in this life projecting them into life hereafter. God promises us, "I will make all things new." It will be heavenly!

Some people regard heaven as being struck immobile, into ineffable ecstasy. But our Lord speaks of heaven as home. Home at last with God, our Father, with Himself, and united with all those dear to us. "In my Father's house there are many mansions. Were it not so, I should have told you, because I go to prepare a place for you. And if I go and prepare a place for you, I am coming again, and I will take you to myself; that where I am, there you also may be" (John 14:2-3). This last phrase should remove the last lurking doubt or suspicion about God really loving us. A suspicious mind might figure that perhaps God would die for us out of a sense of duty. He would do right by us, the creatures He created. But then, having done His duty and taken care of us, He would be done with us. But we notice that there is the same pursuing love, eternally faithful and desiring to be with us. I will that "where I am, there you also may be." This is heaven enough! We are loved and wanted by our Lord forever.

Of course, we will see our Lord in His sacred humanity and be able to say to Him, face to face, all the things we have wanted to say. And when He lovingly reminds us of the little things we have done for Him and says: "Well done, my good and faithful servant. Enter into the joy of your Lord," it will give us a thrill that will keep us happy for all eternity. Also, our Blessed Mother, the most beautiful of women, will be there to show us around and make us feel at home. But really she won't need to make us feel at home because we share in the divine nature, and this is where we really belong. It *is* home. The earth, with its present limitations, isn't quite our home.

What has been said here about heaven is true, but obviously the description is hopelessly inadequate. St. Paul was given a glimpse of heaven's joys and tells us he was "caught up into paradise and heard secret words that man may not repeat." And he said: "Eye has not seen nor ear heard, nor has it entered into the heart of man, what things God has prepared for those who love him." It will be beyond our fondest hopes and imaginings.

Now what should this thought of heaven do for us? First of all, I think it should remove the dread of death. I don't say the fear of death, because God has put into all of us the instinct for self-preservation. We will always put up a struggle to stay alive. This is good. But when, in God's fatherly providence, our work is done and He bids us come, we don't have to be filled with dread. We are not plunging off into the dark, entering an endless, lightless tunnel, or sinking into oblivion and nothingness. The doctor listens for the last, faint flutter of the heart, feels for the pulse, shakes his head, whispers: "He is gone." In that split second, we are in the presence of Christ in His sacred humanity because it has been given to Him to judge the living and the dead. So we are not going to meet a stranger. We have met Him a thousand times in Holy Communion and knowing the infinite mercy and love of His Sacred Heart, we don't have to be filled with dread. One priest put it well. When asked if he was afraid to die, he said thoughtfully: "Afraid— No, I'm not afraid." Then humbly considering how little he had done for Christ, he apologetically added: "A little bit ashamed, but not afraid." He was expressing the same confidence and hope in the Sacred Heart that Claude de la Colombiere, the apostle of the Sacred Heart, counted on: "I shall never lose my hope. I shall keep it till the last moment of my life; and at that moment all the demons in hell shall strive to tear it from me in vain. 'In peace, in the selfsame, I will sleep and I will rest.'"

Also, the thought of heaven should give us courage and strength when the going gets difficult. There are times when the commandments and their observance can be a heavy burden, almost unbearable. Heroic virtue is demanded on occasion. But if we remind ourselves that after a few tears and a little suffering, lonesomeness, labor, and struggle, perfect and everlasting happiness lies ahead, we gather courage and strength to carry on. St. Paul reminded himself of heaven in his moments of darkness. After he had been given a glimpse of heaven, he led a very rugged life. He was scourged three times; he was stoned; he was shipwrecked three times.

". . . a night and a day I was adrift on the sea; . . . in cold and nakedness" (2 Corinthians 11:25 ff.). He was betrayed by friends; he had some personal affliction that so tormented him that three times he asked God to remove it, but three times received God's answer: "My grace is sufficient for thee, for strength is made perfect in weakness." He traveled the civilized world, preaching Christ. At the end of a long lifetime he was jailed and beheaded. We would hardly regard such a life as comfortable. Yet, at the end, looking back over it all, he evaluated it and said: "For I reckon that the sufferings of the present time are not worthy to be compared with the glory to come that will be revealed in us." He knew whereof he spoke, having been given a glimpse of the happiness ahead. We, too, in times of stress and darkness, should lift up our eyes to heaven. If only we do not quit, victory is assured. Just a little more, and the prize is won. "And God will wipe away every tear from their eyes. . . . neither shall there be mourning, nor crying, nor pain any more" (Apocalypse 21:4). This is Christian hope and truth, and this can preserve interior joy even in the midst of suffering and pain.

A third thing that the thought of heaven should do for us is comfort us in the loss of our loved ones. At a Christian death there is pain of loss. There is sadness that someone dear is taken from us, but there is no despair. It isn't the leaden, unrelieved sentence of death. Not, "This is the end." But rather, "I'll be seeing you." It is comforting to recall that Jesus wept at the grave of Lazarus whom he loved. The people standing by said, "How He must have loved the man." So there is sadness, naturally. But the Church reminds us in the requiem Mass for the dead: "Life is not taken away, it is changed. And this earthly abode being dissolved, an everlasting home is prepared for us in heaven." So with the angels and the archangels we say, "Holy, holy, holy. Lord, God of Hosts. Heaven and earth are filled with Thy glory."

The final thing the thought of heaven should do for us is to make us happier people here and now.

In this life there is a Christian joy in living. St. Thomas More died with a jest on his lips. His philosophy of life was, "We can live for the next life and be merry withal." Our solid hope of eternal happiness gives us security. We should not be shattered or broken by the failures and tragedies of this life. With hope strong in us we can preserve our perspective and save our sanity in the crises that arise in human living. It is not Pollyannaism or cockeyed optimism when we say that every life, however tragic, every situation, however desperate, can have a happy ending. Surely we take this life and its duties and responsibilities seriously—but not so seriously that we allow misfortune to destroy us emotionally, physically, or mentally.

We may lose our health, eventually we are all going to die; but there is the resurrection of the body. If we lose our wealth, there is treasure laid up for us in heaven, our Lord reminds us. If there is temporal failure, there can be eternal success. If there is labor, there is eternal rest. If we have sinned and made a shambles of our lives and reputations, there is God's mercy. "If your sins be as scarlet, they shall be made as white as snow." If there is death, there is also eternal life. No Christian in his right mind should plunge from a hotel window or, in despair, reach for a gun or a bottle of sleeping tablets. Christian hope conquers all—even our own stupidity. As Chesterton said: "Wherever a Catholic sun does shine, there is always laughter and good red wine. At least I have always found it so. Benedicamus Domino!"

Keeping this balanced view of time and eternity, a Christian should, I think, be able to plunge into the work of this world with more enthusiasm and energy. He has perspective. Eternity does not so preoccupy him that he forgets or neglects his God-given work in this world. Because an everlasting home is prepared for all of us in heaven, we should not stand by complacently and watch the slums grow up about us. This is God's world and we should make it a better place for God's children to live. Although in heaven God will "wipe all the tears from our eyes," He still expects us to soothe the pain and relieve the poverty of those about us. ". . . out of compassion for them he cured their sick." Because our leader was crucified, we need not go around providing crosses for others to bear. Because we will enjoy the beatific vision, where all truth is opened to our minds, we do not shrink from the labor of scholarship or despise a doctorate in some chosen field. The fact that we will break through time and space into eternity does not mean that we should regard man's conquest of outer space as futile. If we use eternity as a pretext and an escape for getting out of the work of this life, and if we fail to do the work God entrusted to us, then, perhaps, the Communists have a small point when they taunt: "You promise them pie in the sky when they die, but you won't lift a finger to help them here and now." If this were true, then perhaps we would be using religion as "the opiate of the people." This is God's world. It was created by God for His sons and daughters to live in and work in and love in. It should be a better place because we have lived, worked, and loved in it.

In heaven we are told that faith is gone. Faith is that light to guide us here below. In heaven we have come into the all-revealing light of God's own presence. We see face to face, not darkly as in a mirror. So, faith yields to vision. Hope is gone too because hope is the firm trust that God will give us eternal life, and the means to attain it. When we possess the object of our hope, hope gives way to possession, fruition, enjoyment. But we are told that in heaven charity does remain: love for God, love for one another, love for ourselves. If love remains in heaven it must be one of those virtues which, if brought down to earth, can make a little bit of heaven out of our immediate surroundings. This charity then which we should have for one another is a fitting emphasis and conclusion for our consideration of heaven. It brings heaven down to earth.

Our Lord said that love is His special commandment and that this love is to be shown in a new and special way: "A new commandment I give you . . . that as I have loved you, you also love one another." Love even unto death, is Christ's plan. This love was to be the insignia his followers would wear which would single them out and identify them. "By this will all men know that you are my disciples, if you have love for one another."

Naturally this love should go out first to our immediate family. It is not a profound observation that our happiness in this life depends on about five or six people with whom our lives are intertwined in the intimacy of family living. We have tremendous power to hurt or help those who are near us. It is impossible to ignore a person with whom you are living. If there are unhappy people closely associated with us, we might well ask if we are the cause, even partially, of their unhappiness. If we are then we might ask, "Is this pain that I am inflicting necessary?" We can hardly be unaware that we are crushing or violating the personality of those near us, perhaps over-possessing them. The unhappy gift of being able to cut others with the tongue can hardly go unnoticed. A capacity for nagging has to be acquired. A great urge to change and improve others might well yield to a little permissiveness.

Probably our greatest charity will be to bear patiently with one another. Considering the vast amount of unhappiness in this world, wouldn't it be wonderful if we could stand before our Lord and say: "Lord, I have failed in many things, but I never made anyone needlessly unhappy." His answer assuredly would be, "By this will all men know that you are my disciple." This love which we have should go out first to wife or husband, to children, to the immediate family, then to relatives, friends, and a widening circle of acquaintances and ultimately to embrace the whole world. This gives us something of the largeness of Christ's heart. This charity is summed up in a description given of one man, "He loved others with that fierce love with which most men love themselves."

We can get a little insight into how seriously one such man regarded charity by considering a page from his notebook. Cardinal Vaughan was certainly a busy man and had to make many important decisions. Yet he gave this revelation of his major concern in his spiritual notes. "At prayer tonight, very dry; asked God to speak to me. And after awhile I saw clearly what an unchristian *beast* [how very English] I had been today. I saw that N.N. had been a splendid opportunity [to be meek and charitable] and I had lost it altogether. I saw that I might have cheered the tradesman, that I might have been our Lord to Him. Thank God for showing this so clearly. A distinct light such as this will set me on the right track tomorrow. One can represent our Lord and bestow kindness and charity:

1 By a smile, by a bright and sympathetic countenance. This can be bestowed on servants and every one where no words need be uttered. To do so when low and out of humor will be a splendid exercise in the practice of killing my self-love, a thing I am asking for perhaps a hundred times a day.
2 By thinking what pleasant and encouraging thing I can say to so-and-so who has just come to interrupt me, AND SAYING IT.
3 By avoiding any sarcastic remark, and the cold and chilling reception of another's remark, any morose sign of displeasure of ill-humor. Now we'll begin again. And thanks to God for all His kindness."

The Cardinal had evidently thought often of St. James's comments on the tongue and its capacity to scar. "For in many things we all offend. If anyone does not offend in word, he is a perfect man . . . So the tongue also is a little member, but it boasts mightily. Behold, how small a fire—how great a forest it kindles! And the tongue is a fire, the very world of iniquity. The tongue is placed among our members, defiling the whole body, and setting on fire the course of our life, being itself set on fire by hell. For every kind of beast and bird, and of serpents and the rest, is tamed and has been tamed by mankind; but the tongue no man can tame—a restless evil, full of deadly poison. With it we bless God the Father; and with it we curse men, who have been made after the likeness of God. Out of the same mouth proceed blessing and cursing. These things, my brethren, ought not to be so" (James 3:2 ff.).

As you finish reading this, you might say to your wife or husband: "I've just been thinking over the fine things in life and lo and behold! Right here under my very roof—you, the finest!" Of course, you may be immediately accused of having had a few too many or of being sarcastic, but it is worth a try just to see what the reaction would be. Remember in the old days when you figured that you could make any man or woman happy? All of us were going to be great lovers and there would never be a cross word spoken. Never would the sun go down on our anger. Now we wonder, perhaps, if we could make even one man or woman slightly happy. But if we recalled and tried a few of the techniques and thoughtfulness that we employed in the "old days," we might find a response beyond our fondest hopes. Basic needs of men and women do not change because they get married.

I remember one married couple who were really at each other's throat. They could go without speaking for days and they had set up ingenious methods of living in the same house and never being in the same room. I urged the husband to give it another try and pointed out that at least he could up his percentage of happiness from an unbearable ten per cent to maybe thirty, fifty, or sixty per cent. At least he might be able to reduce the tensions of the cold war into peaceful coexistence. He said grimly: "O.K. Father, I'll try. But you don't know that woman. It won't work." So he tried and was as nice as he could be. But she was suspicious and didn't think he would keep it up. She had a backlog of resentments and unpleasant memories. So she literally played it cool. She didn't respond, but she observed. Finally after a month or so, he quit being nice. Just at that point she was saying to herself: "You know, he can be human when he puts his

233

mind to it." She began to be pleasant and considerate. The only difficulty was that he had quit being nice. She went on for a couple of months being nice, while it was his turn to be unpleasant and nasty. It took about a year and a half for both of them to be nice to each other at the same time. Now they're so relatively happy that he will hardly go on a vacation without her. The grass on your side of the fence can be greener if only somebody will be humble enough to prime the pump and water the lawn.

On your mark. Get set. Go! Now all together, "For he (she)'s a jolly good fellow." With the old college try, prayer, humility, and a forgiving, permissive heart, the percentage of happiness can gradually go up, up, up. Surely the other person must have some, even many, admirable qualities or you would not have wanted to marry him. Along with Brotherhood Week, there should be an extension of this spirit toward the rest of the family in their relationship with one another. "Be Kind to Family Week" is another good idea, along with "Be Kind to Husband and Wife Week."

Finally this love we have for Christ, his brethren, his interests, our families, should also go out to embrace the Church. If we don't love the Church, we don't love ourselves because we are the Church. The Church isn't a group of ecclesiastical buildings. Destroy every rectory, retreat house, church, convent, hospital, school, and the Church is still in existence. The Church is people: you and I and the pope, the bishops, the priests. It is people in South America, Africa, Europe, Asia, Germany, Russia, France, and the islands. The Church is people. So, if we don't love the Church, we don't love people— we don't love ourselves. We, in our place, are as much the Church as anyone else. But the Church is more than just people. It is Christ gathering men and women to Himself and communicating to them His divine life so that Christ, describing the union, says: "I am the vine, you are the branches." And St. Paul says: "He is the Head, we are the members." The Church is the mystical body of Christ. So if we don't love the Church, we don't love Christ who is our head, giving life to us His members. The Council of Trent says: "Jesus Christ, Himself, as the head acting on the members and as the vine giving life to the branches, ceaselessly communicates a life force to the justified, and this life force always precedes, accompanies, and follows their every good action. Without it these could in no way be pleasing or meritorious before God!"

At the Last Supper, our Lord lovingly dwelt on this intimate union we have with Him and in Him and through Him. "I am the vine, you are the branches. He who abides in me, and I in him, he bears much fruit; for without me you can do nothing. If anyone does not abide in me, he shall be cast outside as the branch and wither . . . In this is my Father glorified, that you may bear very much fruit, and become my disciples. As the Father has loved me, I also have loved you. Abide in my love. If you keep my commandments you will abide in my love" (John 15: 5-8).

All this sounds good and beautiful, but unfortunately we know that we do not keep Christ's commandments perfectly or keep them all the time. So obviously there is going to be a human element in the Church. This is to be expected—Christ foretold it. Take a look at the limitations of the apostles—Christ's hand-picked and personally-trained disciples. Peter denied Him, but went on to be crucified upside down. Judas betrayed Him. Thomas doubted Him and by his doubt strengthened our faith. All this is an evidence of human weakness, and for us to be unduly upset by it reveals yet another human weakness on our part—spiritual immaturity.

In our charity and love for the Church we bear patiently with the human and thank God for the divine element. But even on the human side, what a glorious host of men and women she has produced. Augustine, Bernard, Francis, Dominic, Benedict, Ignatius. A full roster would sound like pages out of a *World Who's Who*. Think of the glorious popes of our own times, from Leo XIII to John XXIII, who were giants among men and beloved of the world. Think also of the thousands of "unknowns" who lead hidden lives of heroic sanctity. They can be found in every walk of life. They can be found in every parish.

We thank God for the divine element in the Church: her doctrine guaranteed free from error, her life-giving sacraments, and we bear patiently with the human. This attitude is summed up for me rather well in these two little real-life, human-interest incidents which bring out both the human and divine elements in the Church.

An Irishman lay dying in a hospital. He was a good man, but the "creature"—which is Irish for whiskey—had gotten into his life a little too much toward the end. He was a bit alcoholic now. This was the weakness in an otherwise wonderful person. He had pneumonia and was on his way out. His sister, a dark-haired Irish girl, was pacing the corridor and said to me: "I'm just hoping he will get the last sacraments, Father." Finally he regained consciousness and he opened up his big, blue eyes and made a fine confession. He received the sanctifying last sacraments—extreme unction, comforting Viaticum, our Lord to see him on his way—and he leaned back on the pillows with a sigh of contentment and peace. As you might observe, the Irish like to do everything dramatically. So he gathered himself together and, raising himself up from the pillow, said with a smile: "Hurrah for the Catholic Church!" His way of living added a certain human element to the Church, but at least he appreciated the divine element. He had enough sense to cheer for himself and to give a cheer for Christ and the saving sacraments and doctrines which Christ has given to men. "Hurrah for the Catholic Church!" We can all join in that cheer. It is not fanaticism.

Another lad I met in the army humorously brought out another aspect of the Church. He was a sergeant. He was tough—and looked it. He was built like a mack truck—Italian model. He came to me and said: "Father, when I was back home I didn't go to Church much, but now I'd like to become a good Catholic. I want to take some instructions." So I began instructing him.

He was a very interesting fellow; always happy, without any cover up, completely transparent, unsophisticated, and direct in his approach. The first time he came for instructions, I said: "Well, what did you do today?" He said: "I was out directing the target practice and I saw a couple of guys and I said: 'Do you know Father Hogan?' 'Yeah.' And I said, 'Okay, you don't have to do any work.'" This was the type of fellow he was. When he came for the next instruction, I asked: "Well, what did you do today?" I knew it would be something interesting. He said, "I was in the barracks last night arguing religion." (After one instruction, there's enthusiasm for you.) "And some of these guys said to me: 'Why all this religion all of a sudden? What can the Church do for you?' So I said to them, 'Have you guys got a pope in your church?' 'No!' they said. Then I said to them: 'We got a pope, and if you don't like it, come outside and I'll beat you up.'" I think his idea of Catholic action was a few fast rounds in back of the barracks. He was a little misguided in his zeal, but he had caught a great truth about the Church. The Catholic Church has a pope, the vicar of Christ on earth to whom Christ said: ". . . thou art Peter, and upon this rock I will build my Church, and the gates of hell shall not prevail against it. And I will give thee the keys of the kingdom of heaven; and whatever thou shalt bind on earth shall be bound in heaven, and whatever thou shalt loose on earth shall be loosed in heaven." The Catholic Church is founded on a rock which will stand firmly against the storms. Christ has promised to safeguard her from errors in matters of faith and morals. We are sailing in a bark, the bark of Peter, and it cannot be sunk, so hurrah for the Catholic Church! Thank God for Christ! Hurrah for His vicar on earth, the pope! *Viva il Papa!* Hurrah for the Church, and for her authority, and her clear voice speaking out on matters of faith and morals. The truth is inconvenient at times but it is better than doubt, darkness, and uncertainty, especially in our day when the world is full of confusion. It is no exaggeration to say that the words of St. Paul are timely in the sixties. "For there will come a time when they will not endure the sound doctrine; but having itching ears, will heap up to themselves teachers according to their own lusts, and they will turn away their hearing from the truth and turn aside rather to fables. But do thou be watchful in all things" (2 Timothy 4:3-4).

Finally, this love which we have for Christ should be shown, I think, by taking hold of some little area of activity in the Church. Perhaps you can offer your services as an usher, or you might be active in retreat work, offering your organizational ability or your strong back and capable hands. There are also opportunities in the Holy Name Society, Altar and Rosary Society, Christian Family Movement, the Apostleship of Prayer, the Sodality. Obviously, such a great variety offers an outlet for your abilities, whatever they are, and somewhere your love for the Church should find its outlet, lest it become the sterile love of vague thoughts and "sentiments" and not the fruitful love that eventuates in words or deeds.

Do it yourself!

Points for your prayerful thinking (15 minutes)

PREPARATORY PRAYER
See page 18.

Victory with peace

1 Christ leads us beyond Calvary to share in His risen life. Heaven is a place of perfect and everlasting happiness — no suffering — longing for knowledge and beauty and love satisfied — bodies restored — union with loved ones and Christ and Mary.

2 Death is not a terrible thing. The sufferings of this life are nothing.

3 And now there remains charity. Charity — at home — at work in my parish. By this shall men know that you are my disciples that you have love for one another.

Conclude by saying one Our Father, a Hail Mary, and Glory Be to the Father.

◆◆◆◆◆◆◆◆◆◆◆◆

Sometimes it seems like we just can't win. Even priests in their sermons find it hard at times to discover a winning combination. This problem was humorously highlighted by the conversation of two old Irish ladies talking about things ecclesiastical on the church steps. "So you're having a mission at your church this week," said one. "And how is the priest?"

"Well," said the other carefully and charitably, "it's a grand mission he's giving and he's a fine priest, but sure, the way he talks about hell, you'd think he came straight from the hobs of hell himself. He chills the blood in your veins with his talk. And how is the mission at your church?" she asked her friend.

"Ah, it's a fine mission, and he's a fine priest, too," answered her good companion, "but sure, the way he goes on about the love of God is enough to croon you to sleep."

Even St. John the apostle had to cope with this problem of audience reaction. In the evening of life, so the story goes, his disciples thought he was getting rather repetitious, always talking about love—love of God, love of one another, love, love, love. But when his variety-craving disciples begged him, "Tell us something new," he had an answer. He said simply: "There is nothing new. This is the lesson I learned from the Master. Love." Surely St. John should know since he rested his head over Christ's heart on Holy Thursday. And so, I cannot promise anything new in this final chapter. However it should not croon you to sleep as it will show you how, even in the midst of a very active life—which yours undoubtedly is—to find and love God in all things. This is well worthwhile.

You are almost at the end of your *DO-IT-YOURSELF RETREAT*. Congratulations! And keep up the good work, because God often saves until the end some special grace or insight to bless your faithfulness.

Learn to love

The statement "Love and do what you will" of St. Augustine may sound like an oversimplification. It may seem like being handed an endorsed check to be filled out for any amount that our fancies may dictate. Yet, if this statement is properly understood, it sums up life as described by our Lord Himself. When He was asked by a sincere inquirer the secret of life He replied by saying that it was to be found in a triple love:

1   Thou shalt love the Lord thy God with thy whole heart.

2   The second is like to this: thou shalt love thy neighbor.

3   As you love yourself. (This correct self-love is often forgotten. People do not even like themselves in spite of the fact that God loves them.)

If any of these three loves is totally absent the human person is crippled. This crippling can show up in such symptoms as a "sense of emptiness and futility," a certain type of existentialism, or in the beatnik approach to life—hopeless, helpless, calculated confusion. Where any of these three loves is basically weak, it shows up in observable deficiencies.

It is not surprising then, with our Lord pointing the way, that all the saints sum up their teachings in this triple love: love of God, love of neighbor, and love of self. It is also natural that this final chapter of your DO-IT-YOURSELF RETREAT should end with "a contemplation to obtain love" and a few hints on how to grow in love. Love does have to be worked at and learned. It does not come to us instinctively. So here are three approved lessons on how to love taken from the science of the saints. The nice thing about these lessons is that we can begin practicing them right now.

Lesson one

The first lesson on "How To Love God" is to become aware of Him and His loving presence in and about us. It is difficult to love God with our whole heart if we do not know Him well. He cannot become really dear to us unless He is near to us. So all the saints practiced living in His presence and being mindful of Him. This living in God's presence is not something forced or imaginary. For when we find God in all things we are only discovering what is actually there. St. Ignatius, with the simplicity of the mystic he was, sharpens our spiritual vision so we can discover God lovingly present in all things. As a help to this he begins by making observations on love in general.

If we are in love we wish to be with those we love. We simply want to be around, any place, any time. We want to share what we have with the loved one. We want to shower the loved one with gifts and we only wish we had more to give. Not only do we want to give of what we have, but we also wish to give ourselves completely to the other—mind and heart and body. Love seeks union. We can see these three tendencies in human love and they are summed up perfectly in marriage where two people wish to be together for a lifetime, to have all things in common and communicate one to the other mind and heart and body. The saint also adds a general observation that "love is shown more by deeds than by words."

With these clues about the behavior of a lover to guide us, we are now prepared to find God lovingly present in many obvious ways and in a thousand subtle ways which the saints were sensitive enough to perceive. One of these more subtle ways we might miss, and since it comes so highly recommended by all the saints, it is worth pointing out. "Look," says St. Ignatius, "how God dwells in creatures. In the elements, giving them being; in the plants, vegetating; in the animals, feeling; in men, giving them to understand; and so in me giving me being, animating me, giving me sensation and making me to understand; likewise how He makes a temple of me." God has to be present in all things conserving them in being or else they would drop back into the nothingness from which He drew them by His creative act. Ignatius sees in this sustaining presence a fulfillment of the first law of love. God wishes to be with me because He loves me. All the saints were calmly and vividly aware of God's loving presence in and about them. To them God was not a distant God, aloof, disinterested, inaccessible, the god of the Deists. He was not a supervisory deity but a loving Father, guiding their lives with a father's loving providence. They were very conscious of the imminence of God. St. Paul told the Athenians, ". . . he is not far from any of us. For in him we live and move and have our being." He reminds us, lest we miss the obvious: "Surely, you know that your bodies are the shrines of the Holy Spirit who dwells in you." And our Lord Himself tells us: "If anyone love me, he will keep my word, and my Father will love him, and we will come to him and make our abode with him." So, we simply accept this consoling truth. We do not strain our imagination to try to picture it. We just immerse ourselves in it and rest in it, accepting this comforting fact. We can see, too, why St. Theresa of Avila, so aware of God's loving presence, concluded realistically and practically: "Let nothing disturb thee, let nothing afright thee . . ."

Poets, too, have caught God's presence in the most unlikely places. Gerard Manley Hopkins with a poet's insight and a theologian's understanding described his vision of God in all things:

The world is charged with the grandeur of God.
It will flame out, like shining from shook foil;

We may live in the midst of slums and smokestacks where:

. . . all is seared with trade; bleared, smeared with toil;
And wears man's smudge and shares man's smell . . .

But in spite of man's marring of nature, God can be seen. A sunset can be glimpsed between the rows of buildings and the ruined likeness of God in the face of a poor drunken derelict.

And for all this, nature is never spent;
There lives the dearest freshness deep down things;

. . .

Because the Holy Ghost over the bent
World broods with warm breast and with ah!
   bright wings.

This habit of finding God in all things and of living in His presence is not too difficult to acquire and became almost natural to the saints. To them, it would be a matter of "How can we possibly be unaware of Him since He is ever present in nature and especially within ourselves?" Because of this awareness of God they were also able to fulfill the recommendations of our Lord "to pray always." For prayer may be described simply as "being with God" and the saints were with God, more or less consciously, nearly all the time. With practice we, too, can make a beginning in this direction and find that our love for God and intimacy with Him is on the increase. This is one way of growing in love.

This approach to God's love might seem a little subtle but His loving presence is so obviously and dramatically presented in the Incarnation and the Holy Eucharist that no one can miss it. "For you know the graciousness of our Lord Jesus Christ—how, being rich, he became poor for your sakes, that by His poverty you might become rich." ". . . Christ Jesus, who though he was by nature God, . . . emptied himself, taking the nature of a slave and being made like unto men." "And the Word was made flesh, and dwelt among us." There we have God's love for us and His desire to be with us eloquently expressed through the Incarnation. In the Holy Eucharist too, the only ultimate explanation of His abiding presence with us is love. ". . . having loved his own who were in the world, loved them to the end." To me, these same tendencies of love "To be with the beloved and give self" are heart-warmingly highlighted in this simple story.

It was Christmas eve during the war and a gray,

shadowy troop transport nosed into New York harbor with a boatload of returning GI's. By good fortune many of them would be home for Christmas. Pfc. James Mahoney was especially happy. He was sure to be home for midnight Mass and the celebrations with his young wife. He lived in the Bronx! As he was hastily processed he realized with a sinking feeling that he did not have anything worthwhile to give his wife. He had gotten orders unexpectedly. There had been no time to buy her a gift. It was late. The stores would be closed or the remnants left on the counters would be pretty shoddy. This gift had to be something special for a very special person. Then, time entered the picture. At last a brilliant idea lighted up his face, and he hurried to the corner drug store a couple of blocks from his home to make a quick purchase. He mounted the steps to his apartment, pounded on the door, and as his wife opened it, she looked up into his grinning face. Tied around his neck was a red ribbon and hanging from it was a printed greeting card hastily inscribed, "From Jim to Mary with all my love." As Mary nestled into his arms both realized without words that this was the best gift of all—himself. Beside this, all else was unimportant.

So also for us, above the crib at Christmas and above the tabernacle in the church, as clearly as if it were spelled out on a greeting card, there is the message: "From God the Father, God the Son, God the Holy Spirit, with all our love." And although Christ comes to us on Christmas and in the Eucharist bringing gifts of light and life, mercy and grace, the best gift of all is Himself, and beside this all else is unimportant.

Reflecting on this tremendous lover and His tremendous love for us, we naturally ask ourselves what shall I give Him in return. What else but ourselves? We don't need a red ribbon to tie around our neck, but almost instinctively we want to give Him ourself. "To God the Father, God the Son, God the Holy Spirit with all my love." St. Ignatius in his famous Suscipe makes this offering of self to God. We might like to make his words our own:

Take, Lord, and receive all my liberty,
My memory, my intellect, and all my will,
All that I have and possess.
Thou gavest it to me,
To Thee, Lord, I return it.
All is Thine.
Dispose of it according to all Thy Will.
Give me Thy love and grace,
For this is enough for me.

Lesson two

The first lesson, then, is to find God lovingly present in all things and give Him a return of love. The
second lesson on how to learn to love is very simple
and easy. We fill our hearts with gratitude to God
for benefits received and move on from gratitude to
love. We lovingly count up God's gifts to us the way
we might recall the list of gifts given us by a loved
one. "He gave me flowers; he gave me this lovely
ring; he gave me his love and his heart. Isn't he wonderful! He is so generous and thoughtful! He is kind
and so good! I love him. I love him." St. Ignatius
suggests the same approach to our love of God.
"Bring to memory," he suggests, "the benefits received
of creation, of redemption, and particular gifts, pondering with much feeling how much God, our Lord,
has done for me, and how much He has given me of
what He has; and how the same Lord desires to give
me Himself as much as He can according to His
divine ordination." He feels that this consideration
will fill us with such gratitude that we will "be able
in all things to love and serve His divine majesty."
This is the simplicity and the realism of the saints
who see God ever present in all things; ever loving,
ever laboring for us, ever communicating, ever seeking union, ever giving of what He has and giving of
Himself just as much as we will open our heart to
accept. In return they and we try to imitate God in
His loving and generous ways and return love for
love, gift for gift. We try to live always in His presence; we use our God-given talents to labor for Him;
we seek total union with Him imperfectly, it is true,
in this life but perfectly in the world to come.

245

This approach from gratitude to love should come rather easily and naturally because in daily life we certainly say "thank you" or its eq̲u̲i̲v̲a̲l̲e̲n̲t many, many times. "Have a cigarette?" "̲T̲h̲a̲n̲k̲ ̲y̲ou." "Thank you for your time." "Than̲k̲ ̲y̲ou." A man opens a door for a woman, h̲e̲ ̲p̲u̲l̲l̲s̲ back her chair, and "thank you" ̲i̲s̲ ̲s̲p̲o̲ken or by a glance of appreciatio̲n̲ ̲o̲r̲ ̲c̲o̲mmon courtesy. It would be conserva̲t̲i̲v̲e̲ ̲i̲n̲ ̲o̲ur society "Thank you" or its ̲e̲q̲u̲i̲v̲a̲l̲e̲nt more than ten times a day. Transf̲e̲r̲ ̲t̲h̲i̲s̲ ̲g̲r̲a̲ti- tude and courtesy to God ̲b̲y̲ ̲l̲o̲o̲k̲i̲n̲g̲ ̲a̲round with the eyes of the heart ̲a̲t̲ ̲t̲h̲e̲ ̲m̲i̲l̲l̲ions of blessings and gifts, ̲a̲n̲d̲ ̲t̲h̲i̲s̲ ̲w̲i̲l̲l bring a spontaneous lift̲i̲n̲g̲ ̲o̲f̲ ̲t̲h̲e̲ ̲h̲e̲art and eyes to God the give̲r̲.

Take the variety o̲f̲ ̲g̲i̲f̲t̲s̲:̲ ̲h̲e̲alth; music; success; suf̲f̲e̲r̲i̲n̲g̲ ̲w̲h̲i̲c̲h̲ ̲i̲s̲ ̲better than health; sanc̲t̲i̲f̲y̲i̲n̲g̲ ̲g̲r̲a̲c̲e̲;̲ ̲the Mass; heaven; M̲a̲r̲y̲;̲ ̲t̲h̲e̲ ̲s̲a̲c̲r̲a̲m̲ents; of faith; the infi̲n̲i̲t̲e̲ ̲l̲o̲v̲e̲ ̲o̲f̲ ̲t̲h̲e̲ ̲Sacred Heart; the smi̲l̲e̲ ̲o̲f̲ ̲a̲ ̲c̲h̲i̲l̲d̲;̲ ̲and the warmth ̲o̲f̲ ̲a̲ ̲f̲r̲i̲e̲n̲d̲ ̲a̲n̲d̲ ̲a thousand oth̲e̲r̲ ̲g̲i̲f̲t̲s̲,̲ ̲a̲n̲y̲ ̲o̲n̲e̲ ̲of which alone dese̲r̲v̲e̲s̲ ̲m̲o̲r̲e̲ ̲t̲h̲a̲n̲ ̲t̲h̲e̲ ̲"Have a cigarette ̲o̲r̲ ̲t̲h̲e̲ ̲c̲o̲u̲r̲t̲e̲s̲y̲ ̲o̲f̲ ̲a̲ ̲birth- day card ̲w̲e̲ ̲s̲o̲ ̲r̲e̲a̲d̲i̲l̲y̲ ̲a̲c̲k̲n̲owledge. the words o̲f̲ ̲t̲h̲e̲ ̲p̲r̲e̲f̲a̲c̲e̲ ̲a̲r̲e̲ ̲true: "It is truly fitting ̲.̲ ̲.̲ ̲.̲ ̲f̲o̲r̲ ̲o̲u̲r salvation, at all times a̲n̲d̲ ̲g̲i̲v̲e̲ ̲t̲hanks to You."

What a terrible tragedy it w̲o̲u̲l̲d̲ ̲b̲e̲ if, after a long lifetime of benefits received, God ̲w̲e̲r̲e̲ ̲t̲o̲ ̲face us and say: "After all I did for them, t̲h̲e̲y̲ didn't even say thank you. They didn't even acknowl̲e̲dge the wonderful gifts I gave them." The lament of̲ Christ in revealing His Sacred Heart was man's ingrat- itude. "It is the ingratitude of men which hurts Me more than all the sufferings I underwent during My Passion." "If they gave Me a return, then all that I have done for them would appear but little to My love."

How myopic and cold a person would be not to see

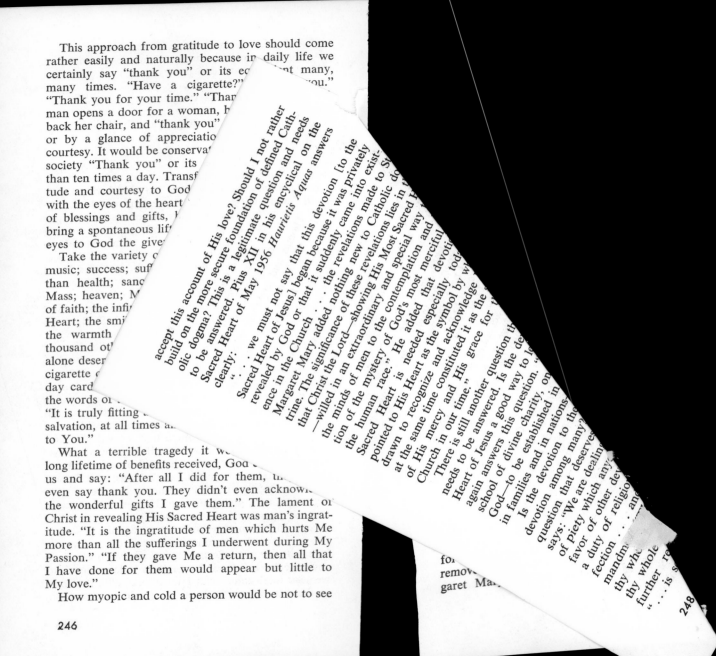

246

accept this account of His love? Should I not rather build on the more secure foundation of defined Cath- olic dogma? This is a legitimate question and needs to be answered. Pius XII in his encyclical on the Sacred Heart of May 1956 *Haurietis Aquas* answers clearly:

"... we must not say that this devotion was privately revealed by God or that it suddenly came into exist- ence in the Church ... the revelations made to St. Margaret Mary added nothing new to Catholic doc- trine. The significance of these revelations lies in this, that Christ the Lord—showing His Most Sacred Heart —willed in an extraordinary and special way to invite the minds of men to the contemplation and venera- tion of the mystery of God's most merciful love for the human race." He added that devotion to the Sacred Heart is needed especially today. "We are pointed to His Heart as the symbol by which we are drawn to recognize and acknowledge the greatness of His mercy and His grace for the Church and at the same time constituted it as the pledge and sign of Church in our time." Is the devotion to the Sacred Heart of Jesus a good way to love God? Pius XII again answers this question. Devotion to the Sacred God—to be established, one the ... in families and in nations.

Is the devotion to the Sacred Heart a devotion among many? ... question that deserves ... says: "We are dealing ... of piety which any ... favor of other devotions ... a duty of religion ... mandment ... thy whole ... further re ... "... is

for ... remove ... garet Ma ...

248

far as practice is concerned, the perfect profession of the Christian religion."

I have spent some time on this documentation even at the risk of beating the obvious to death because this retreat is suggesting that the center and core of our spiritual lives be love for the Sacred Heart of God become man. God has a human heart! This recommendation and strong emphasis would be imprudent if He were not the throbbing heart of Christianity or if this were just "another devotion."

The fact is that mankind seeks for love and will find it at its height and depth in the heart of God become man. And, it was to set our cold hearts on fire and win a return of love that Christ broke the silence of the centuries and made the revelations of His Sacred Heart to St. Margaret Mary. Christ makes His reasons for these revelations clear. St. Margaret Mary tells us, ". . . it was the great desire He had to be perfectly loved by mankind that had made Him form the design of revealing to them His Heart, and of giving them in these latter times this last effort of His love. This He would do by proposing to them an object and a means calculated to win them to love Him." "He assured me," the saint continues, "that He took a singular pleasure in being honored under the representation of this heart of flesh. This was in order, He said, to touch the unfeeling hearts of men."

In a single sentence our Lord summed up the deep and all-pervading reason for these remarkable revelations: "It is the ingratitude of men which hurts Me more than all the sufferings I underwent during My passion." And if, Christ told Margaret Mary, "they gave Me a return, then all that I have done for them would appear but little to My love." As we listen to the further details of what Christ revealed to her, there is a warmth and divine simplicity to it. As we read, we feel like the discouraged disciples on the way to Emmaus to whom our Lord appeared and with whom He conversed. Having listened to Him talk, they said: "Was not our heart burning within us while he was speaking on the road and explaining to us the Scriptures?" (Luke 24:32). Our cold hearts may also "burn within us" as we listen to the story of His love.

Christ told Margaret Mary: "My divine Heart is so full of love for men, . . . that it is unable to contain within itself the flames of its burning love. It needs must spread them. . . . and so manifest itself to men to enrich them with the treasures this Heart contains. I discover to you the price of these treasures. They contain graces of holiness and salvation which are necessary to draw men from the abyss of loss." The saint describes what she saw: "The divine Heart was represented to me as upon a throne of fire and flames. It shed rays on every side brighter than the sun and transparent as crystal. The wound which He received on the Cross appeared there visibly. A crown of thorns encircled the divine Heart, and It was surmounted by a cross." This symbolism even a child readily understands. Christ's heart was all aflame showing how intensely He loved men. Above His heart was a cross showing that He loved men enough to die for them. On the heart was the wound of the spear. From this wound Christ gave the last drop of His blood for men. Twisted painfully around the heart was a crown of thorns showing how painful to Him was man's lack of love and gratitude for all He had done for men. "Behold this Heart which has loved men so much!"

Then there was the most memorable of the apparitions of His Sacred Heart. What has made it of lasting memory has been the introduction of the great feast of the Sacred Heart which our Lord explicitly called for. On the day in question (June 16, 1675) Margaret Mary was kneeling on the flagstone a few feet from the altar. Her eyes were fixed upon the tabernacle. Suddenly our Lord appeared above the altar. With His eyes upon the kneeling figure, He pointed to His Sacred Heart flaming with love and spoke the words which have been quoted with loving repetition since that precious moment: "Behold this Heart, which has so loved mankind that it has spared itself nothing, even to being spent and consumed to prove its love for men. And yet it has received in return from the majority of mankind only ingratitude, coldness, and the neglect of Me in the sacrament of My love. But what is even more painful to Me is that it is hearts consecrated to Me which use Me thus."

What does our Lord, the victim of unrequited love seek in return? He seeks a loving consecration of ourselves to His Sacred Heart, a consecration that is lived out daily. He asks, too, for a reparation of love for the coldness and ingratitude of so many, perhaps ourselves. Pius XII explains these two very important elements of devotion to the Sacred Heart.

"Among the different practices which directly accompany devotion to the most Sacred Heart, assuredly the foremost is the act of consecration by which we offer to the Heart of Jesus both ourselves and all that belongs to us, recognizing that all we have comes to us from the infinite charity of God." Consecration, then, is giving ourselves lovingly to God. But Christ also asks for reparation which is simply making up to Him for what we and others have failed to give Him. ". . . if this same Uncreated Love has either been passed over through forgetfulness or saddened by reason of our sins, then we should repair such outrages . . . Ordinarily, we call this duty, reparation. . . . We are held to the duty of making reparation by the most powerful motives of justice and of love; of justice, in order to expiate the injury done God by our sins and to reestablish, by means of penance, the divine order which has been violated; and of love, in order to suffer together with Christ . . . insofar as our human weakness permits . . ."

The characteristic love, confidence, and trust that are part of the devotion to the all-merciful and loving heart of Christ and which should be a strong emphasis in our spiritual life are eloquently expressed by Leo XIII. This stout-hearted warrior standing alone in the center of his generation, aged and spent by over twenty years of crowded action governing the Church and fighting for basic human rights, wrote in his encyclical *Annum Sacrum* on May 25, 1899:

"When the Church, in the days immediately succeeding her institution, was oppressed beneath the yoke of the Caesars, a young emperor saw in the heavens a cross, which became at once the happy omen and cause of the glorious victory that soon followed. And now, today, behold! Another blessed and heavenly token is offered to our sight: the most Sacred Heart of Jesus, with a cross rising from it and shining forth with a dazzling splendor amidst flames of love. In that Sacred Heart all our hopes should be placed—and from it the salvation of men is to be sought with confidence."

We in the '60's, sick in mind and emotions as we are, desperately need the same reassuring love of Christ's Sacred Heart. We need the same trust, the same hope. We are a generation that is insecure and anxiety ridden; afraid to love and afraid that we are not loved; afraid to give love and suspicious of accepting it. In the midst of unparalleled advances in science and knowledge we are sick at heart and sick in our emotions. Christ in the revelation of His Sacred Heart meets the needs of modern man. He warms our hearts first and assures us of our worth in His sight by pointing to His lance-pierced heart flaming with love and saying simply: "Behold this heart that has loved men so much." This is unsophisticated and direct. It is as uncomplicated as "I love you." It brushes aside our protests of unworthiness and wipes out the doubts and insecurities and feelings of inferiority and guilt which we may have about ourselves. If we protest "Lord, I am not worthy," Christ's answer would be, "I didn't say you were. I said I loved you." Now having been loved first, we can begin to like ourselves and be patient with our inadequacies. We need not be continually fighting ourselves. Now we can begin serenely and genuinely to love our neighbor because we are supposed to love our neighbor as we love ourselves. Now, too, loving our neighbors, we can begin loving God more completely, with our whole heart, for as St. John reminds us: "How can we love God whom we do not see when we do not love our neighbor whom we do see." Thus it is that we who are sick at heart can begin to love. The threefold love which makes for balanced and complete living grows through devotion to the Sacred Heart. Above all, it makes us like God, because "God," St. John tells us, "is love."

Since this is a do-it-yourself retreat, here is a simple plan which will bring this triple love—love of God, neighbor, and self—into daily practice and into daily living.

APOSTLESHIP OF PRAYER
AS A WAY OF LIFE

1 "It is not possible to grow in the knowledge, and love, and imitation of Jesus Christ, without at the same time growing in the perfection of every virtue . . . When the creature loves, then it is changed, and till then scarcely at all" (Goodier).

2 The Sacred Heart is the road which will most surely lead us to know intimately Jesus Christ and will cause our hearts to love more tenderly and to imitate Him more generously than we have hitherto done (Pius XI, Miserentissimus Redemptor).

3 The Apostleship of Prayer is a way of life by which the Christian learns to unite his daily life in a spirit of love and sacrifice with the Sacred Heart of Jesus for his own salvation and that of the whole world. Pius XI said of the Apostleship of Prayer, "It is the most perfect form of Christian living . . . a perfect form of devotion to the Sacred Heart."

PRACTICES OF THE
APOSTLESHIP OF PRAYER

1 The Morning Offering—said each morning on arising. A daily practical consecration of the day to the Sacred Heart.

2 Frequent Mass and fervent Communion—always on First Friday—in a spirit of reparation.

3 A daily decade of the rosary.

A brief glance at this program which is within the capacity of all and brings love into daily living is worthwhile. The Morning Offering is the only required practice of the Apostleship of Prayer. A familiar form of the offering follows. Prayerful study will show its worth and depth. It is not just a prayer, it is a loving consecration of this day to His Sacred Heart.

O Jesus through the Immaculate Heart of Mary,
I offer you my prayers, works, joys and
sufferings of this day.
For all the intentions of Your Sacred Heart,
in union with the holy sacrifice of the Mass
throughout the world,
in reparation for my sins, for the intentions
of all our associates
for the reunion of Christendom,
And in particular for the intentions of the Holy
 Father.
(The particular intention for the month is selected
by the pope and varies from month to month.)

This simple offering, said and lived, reduces to daily practice the triple love which Christ said was the heart of Christian living. Christ loved us, "Behold this heart that has loved men so much." We accept His love for us. In return we love Him and those He came to save. With the instinct of love we identify with the interest of His Sacred Heart, the salvation of souls, and we give Him what we can give, "The prayers, works, joys, and sufferings" of the day. It is our life broken down into the manageable unit of this day which He has given us. We give our offerings to Him and say, "Use them for Your Heart's desire." His desire is the salvation of souls and He uses our offerings for that purpose. Our day becomes apostolic. We join with Christ in saving souls. This is truly Christian and immensely satisfying. It is a return of love for love.

According to Pius XI, the Mass is the perfect act of reparation. "We must always remember that the expiatory value of our acts depends solely on the bloody sacrifice of Christ, which is renewed without interruption on our altars in an unbloody manner." It is the Mass that matters and for this reason we unite our day with this unending sacrifice and try to be present at Mass as often as we can.

A Communion of reparation is the fervent reception of Holy Communion to make up to our Lord especially for the sacrileges, the irreverence, the coldness, indifference, and ingratitude with which He is treated in the Holy Eucharist, the sacrament of His love. Our Lord, Himself, asked for this.

We make reparation for our neglect and that of others by fervent preparation and reception and by adequate thanksgiving. It is estimated that Christ remains sacramentally present for about ten minutes after we receive Holy Communion.

A daily decade of the rosary keeps our Blessed Mother in our life. Pius XII said: "That graces for the Christian family and for the whole human race may flow more abundantly from devotion to the Sacred Heart, let the Faithful strive to join it closely with devotion to the Immaculate Heart of the Mother of God. By the will of God, the most Blessed Virgin Mary was inseparably joined with Christ in accomplishing the work of man's redemption, so that our salvation flows from the love of Jesus Christ and His sufferings, intimately united with the love and sorrows of His Mother."

Of this way of life just proposed, Pius XII has said, "The daily offering of self is the essence of the Apostleship of Prayer . . . All the sacred practices of which the Apostleship of Prayer makes use to round out and perfect this oblation, taken together, *contain the sum total of Christian perfection*."

A MORE DETAILED WAY OF LIFE

The following practices of the spiritual life, which include those of the Apostleship of Prayer, present a more detailed way of life and may be described as the Sodality way of life. It brings love and the supernatural life to a glowing white heat.

1 Morning Offering said each day upon arising, along with acts of faith, hope, charity and three Hail Marys.
2 Mass and Communion daily if possible.
3 Spiritual reading for an average of fifteen minutes a day. (Excellent preparation for step four)
4 Fifteen minute person-to-person talk with Christ daily.
5 Daily rosary.
6 Weekly or bi-monthly confession to a regular confessor.

7 Nightly examen of conscience.

8 Working in some parish activity.

9 Doing the job in factory or office or school and in the home so that by example, word, and deed, people might be drawn to Christ's Heart and Church.

10 Annual retreat.

Note: As a help to step four, daily mental prayer, see page 259 for different methods of praying.

You have done-it-yourself. God and you. Congratulations! But far more important than these words of congratulation would be the commendation of our Lord Himself, His "well done, good and faithful servant" carries with it a blessing that will last through your lifetime and follow you into an eternity of happiness with Him.

In praying for all of you who have made this retreat my petition will be that of Cardinal Newman:

> May He support us all the day long,
> Till the shadows lengthen,
> And the evening comes
> And the busy world is hushed,
> And the fever of life is over,
> And our work is done!
> Then in His mercy
> May He give us a safe lodging,
> And a holy rest,
> And peace at the last!
> May our Lord be with us all the days of our life.

Planning for life

I t is useful to make a plan for the year ahead—to give our spiritual lives a definite direction. A general resolution: "I'll be good," is a little too vague. Our aim is to find God and lead a fuller, happier life in union with Him. That is, I want either to decide my vocation, or decide upon the means I should adopt to take disorder out of my life and to advance in the perfection of my present state of life. This is done by growing in the knowledge, love, and imitation of Christ. "The knowledge of God without a perception of man's misery causes pride, and the knowledge of man's misery without a perception of God causes despair. Knowledge of Jesus Christ constitutes the middle course, because in Him we find both God and our own misery."

METHOD

1 The desire to choose and use the necessary means to order my life and free myself from sin must come from God. So I should pray to the Holy Spirit for light and the desire to follow God's will.
2 Using a projective technique, I place myself in the position of a man who is giving advice to a person whom he does not know but who is asking for help to serve God more perfectly. I then follow the advice I would sincerely give this person.
3 Another way of obtaining objectivity and detachment is to look at the matter from the point of view I shall have at the moment of death. Let me do now what I shall then wish to have done. This should not be a grim, ghoulish affair. The viewpoint of eternity helps to sift out the nonessential and, as St. Thomas More shrewdly observed, "We can live for the next life and be merry withal."

4 I offer my resolutions to God. I ask Him to accept them and to give me the courage and strength to keep them.

RECOMMENDATIONS

1 I decide upon a few efficacious means that will remove disorder from my life.
2 I choose something that will improve my daily habits: prayer, family life, work, social contacts.
3 I keep before my eyes motives strong enough to make me carry out my resolution. For example: I will be happier, closer to God, surer of salvation. I will be using my God-given talents.
4 I begin at once to put my resolutions into practice, having written them down for daily, weekly, and monthly review. I will use the form given below as the basis for my written retreat resolution. I will keep the paper upon which I have written my resolution in my missal where I can review it periodically.

My retreat resolution

1 I choose as a way of life
   a the Apostleship of Prayer (page 253).   ( )
   b the Sodality way of life (page 255).   ( )
   c a combination of both.   ( )

2 I wish to make the following particular resolution(s).
   a _____
   b _____
   c _____

I promise You, Lord, that on each Sunday at Mass I will glance over this decision, and if I have not carried it out I will begin again.

Signed_____

Prayers and examen

At times the set forms of prayer, such as the Our Father, the Hail Mary, and the Creed, which we say so frequently can become quite routine, sometimes almost meaningless. Here is an approved method for putting new life into jaded prayer. You might like to try it. With a little practice—do-it-yourself—I think you will find this method easy, interesting, and rewarding. Let's take the Our Father as an example.

Begin by saying the preparatory prayer on page 18. Kneel or sit, as may be better suited to your disposition and more conducive to devotion. Keep your eyes closed or fixed in one position without permitting them to roam. Then say, "Father," and continue meditating on this word as long as you find meanings, comparisons, and consolation in the consideration of it. The same method should be followed with each word or phrase of the Our Father, or with any other prayer which you wish to use.

Continue for fifteen minutes in the way described going through the whole Our Father word by word. Or, if in contemplation you find in one or two words abundant matter for thought and consolation, you should not be anxious to go on, even though the whole fifteen minutes is taken up with what you have found.

When the fifteen minutes is over say the rest of the prayer in the usual way. You will find it is beginning to take on new meaning and depth for you.

If you have been occupied with one or two words of a prayer for the full fifteen minutes, when you wish to pray on another day say those words in the ordinary way. Then begin to contemplate with the words that follow immediately after, thus eventually completing the whole prayer in this meditative fashion.

At the end of your fifteen minute prayer you should turn to the person to whom the prayer is directed and ask for the virtues or graces which you need most.

As you can see, this method is good for enriching any set form of prayer. For example, take the Creed. "I believe . . . in God . . . the Father . . . almighty . . . Creator . . . of heaven . . . and earth."

Even at a glance the rich possibilities of this form of prayer are evident. Try it for fifteen minutes and see what happens. Prayer should be varied to meet our changing needs, and prayer can be kept interesting. Consequently you could, if you wished, try this method on the great Principle and Foundation of St. Ignatius on page 62: "Man . . . was created . . . to praise . . . reverence . . . and serve."

The problem of communication between persons of varied backgrounds and experiences is always an interesting challenge. To establish effective communication with God who has such a "different background" from ours is always interesting and rewarding because God the Father, God the Son, and God the Holy Spirit are the most interesting persons in this universe. They, of course, created it. They, on their part, are also most eager to communicate with you whom they also created so lovingly.

Here is still another method of praying. For this method it is useful to choose and to arrange the subject of your meditation beforehand. Then you choose a scene or a picture which you should try to keep before your mind during the meditation. Next, you petition for what you want to get out of the meditation. And finally you bring your spiritual faculties into play:

1 *Memory*

Recall the point on which you want to meditate, helping yourself with the questions: Who? What? Where? When? How? Why?

2 *Understanding*

Ask yourself: What truth is to be considered here? What practical conclusion should I draw? What motives are there for following this conclusion—becoming, useful, easy, pleasing, necessary? How have I observed this up to the present? What must I do in the future?

260

What obstacles must I remove? What means must I employ?

3 *Will*

Make repeated acts of the virtue you wish to acquire. (O my God, I believe in You.)

The next step is to make a practical resolution based on your meditation which is suitable to your present state. This should be followed by a heart-to-heart talk with our Lord, our Lady, etc. Say a vocal prayer in conclusion.

Night prayers

In the name of the Father, and of the Son, and of the Holy Spirit. Amen.

Eternal Father, I offer You the Sacred Heart of Jesus, with all its love, all its sufferings and all its merits, to make up for all the sins I have committed today and during all my life. May His sufferings and merits bless the good I have done in my poor way today and during all my life. May they make up for the good I ought to have done and neglected today and during all my life.

Glory be to the Father, and to the Son, and to the Holy Spirit. As it was in the beginning, is now, and ever shall be world without end. Amen.

ACT OF CONTRITION

O my God, I am heartily sorry for having offended You, and I detest all my sins above every other evil because they displease You, My God, who are perfectly good and so deserving of all my love. I firmly resolve by Your holy grace never more to offend You, and to better my life. Amen.

Help me right now to make a good, practical resolution for tomorrow. (*Pause here to decide on that resolution.*)

My Lord God, even now I accept at your hands, cheerfully and willingly, with all its anxieties, pains, and sufferings, whatever kind of death you decree for me. Amen.

Jesus, Mary, and Joseph, I give you my heart and my soul.

Jesus, Mary, and Joseph, assist me in my last agony.

Jesus, Mary, and Joseph, may I breathe forth my soul in peace with You. Amen.

Bless, O Lord, my family, my relatives, living or dead. Take under Your protection all who are near and dear to me, and all who wish me to pray for them. Bless our Holy Father, our bishops, and priests. Bless the labors of missionaries in pagan lands and spread Your holy Church over the whole earth.

Divine Heart of Jesus, convert sinners, save the dying, and deliver the holy souls in purgatory. Amen.

May the Lord Almighty grant us a quiet night and a perfect end. Amen.

Eternal rest grant unto them, O Lord, and let the perpetual light shine upon them. May they rest in peace. Amen.

Visit, we beseech You, O Lord, this home and drive from it all the snares of the enemy. Let Your holy angels dwell here to keep us in peace. May Your blessing be upon us always, through Christ, our Lord. Amen.

OFFERING

O divine Jesus, dwelling tonight in so many tabernacles without visitor or worshipper, I offer You my heart. May its every beat be a prayer of love to You. You are ever wakeful under the sacramental veil; in Your love You never sleep and You are never weary of Your vigil for sinners. O dear Jesus, may my heart be a lamp, the light of which shall burn for You alone.

Watch, sacramental Savior, watch for the weary world, for the erring soul, and for me Your son.

Angel of God, my guardian dear,
To whom His love commits me here,
Ever this day be at my side,
To light and guard, to rule and guide. Amen.

Jesus Christ, my God, I adore You and thank You for all the graces You have given me this day. I offer You my sleep and all the moments of this night, and I beseech you to keep me without sin. I put myself within Your sacred side and under the mantle of our Lady, my Mother. Let Your holy angels stand about me and keep me in peace, and let Your blessing be upon me.

May the most just, the most high, and the most lovable will of God be in all things done, praised, and evermore exalted.

Morning prayers

In the name of the Father, and of the Son, and of the Holy Spirit. Amen.

O Jesus, through the immaculate heart of Mary, I offer You my prayers, works, joys, and sufferings of this day, for all the intentions of Your Sacred Heart, in union with the holy sacrifice of the Mass throughout the world, in reparation for all my sins, for the intentions of all our associates, for the reunion of Christendom, and in particular for the intentions of this month.

Our Father, who art in heaven, hallowed be Thy name. Thy kingdom come, Thy will be done on earth as it is in heaven. Give us this day our daily bread and forgive us our trespasses as we forgive those who trespass against us; and lead us not into temptation, but deliver us from evil. Amen.

Hail Mary, full of grace, the Lord is with thee! Blessed art thou among women, and blessed is the fruit of thy womb, Jesus. Holy Mary, mother of God, pray for us sinners, now and at the hour of our death. Amen.

ACTS OF FAITH, HOPE, AND CHARITY

O my God, I firmly believe that You are one God in three divine persons, Father, Son, and Holy Spirit. I believe that Your divine Son became man, and died for my sins and that He will come to judge the living and the dead. I believe these and all the truths which the holy Catholic Church teaches, who can neither deceive nor be deceived.

O my God, relying on Your infinite goodness and promises, I hope to obtain pardon for my sins, the help of Your grace, and life everlasting, through the merits of Jesus Christ, my Lord and Redeemer.

O Christ Jesus, I love You above all things, with my whole heart and soul, because You are all good and worthy of all my love. I love my neighbor as myself for the love of You. I forgive all who have injured me, and I ask pardon for all whom I have injured.

TO CHRIST THE KING

O Christ Jesus, I acknowledge You to be the king of all the universe. All that has been made is created for You. Exercise over me all Your sovereign rights. I hereby renew the promises of my baptism, renouncing Satan and all his work and pomps, and I engage myself to lead henceforth a truly Christian life. In a special manner do I undertake to bring about the triumph of the rights of God and Your Church, so far as in me lies. Divine Heart of Jesus, I offer You my poor actions to obtain the acknowledgement by every heart of Your sacred kingly power. In this way may the kingdom of Your peace be firmly established throughout all the earth. Amen.

TO THE BLESSED VIRGIN

My Queen, my Mother, I give myself to you, and to show my devotion, I consecrate to you my eyes, my ears, my mouth, my heart, my entire self. Therefore, O loving Mother, since I am your own, keep me, defend me, as your property and possession. Amen.

TO GOD MY FATHER

My gracious God, You see me here in Your presence more clearly than I see myself. You know me through and through, my good qualities and bad. You are my real and loving Father. I know you are, and I gladly profess that I am Your son.

You are giving me today, not as a trial but as an opportunity, another chance to know You and myself a little better. Help me, Father, to live this day of my retreat as You want me to live it. Teach me how to see You in all the people around me. Help me to be a pillar of strength and encouragement to them, as You, my God and Father, are to me. Amen.

PRAYER OF ST. FRANCIS OF ASSISI

Lord, make me an instrument of Your peace. Where there is hatred, let me sow love; where there is injury, pardon; where there is doubt, faith; where there is despair, hope; where there is darkness, light; and where there is sadness, joy.

O divine Master, grant that I may not so much seek to be consoled as to console; to be understood as to understand; to be loved as to love; for it is in giving that we receive; it is in pardoning that we are pardoned; and it is in dying that we are born to eternal life.

Thanksgiving after Communion

Soul of Christ, be my sanctification.
Body of Christ, be my salvation.
Blood of Christ, fill all my veins.
Water from Christ's side, wash out my stains.
Passion of Christ, my comfort be.
O good Jesus, listen to me.
In Your wounds I fain would hide.
Never to be parted from Your side.
Guard me should the foe assail me.
Call me when my life shall fail me.
Bid me come to You above,
With all Your saints to sing Your love, world without end. Amen.

I THANK YOU

Lord Jesus Christ, present in my heart, I thank You for all You have done for me. Surely I am one of Your favorite children. My life has been a succession of gifts from Your loving hands: my birth in a Catholic home; my adoption in baptism as the child of Your heavenly Father and as Your brother; the care and protection and love that surrounded my infancy; the health and soundness of my mind and body. How can I thank You, dear Lord, for the joy of my first Holy Communion, the numberless Holy Communions since then, and especially for my Holy Communion this morning. Would that I had the same eagerness in receiving You that You have in coming to me.

For all Your goodness I am most grateful. But this morning I thank You especially for these favors: *(Here pause and think of some favor recently received by yourself, your family, a close friend).*

I AM SORRY

Yet, in spite of Your great generosity to me, dear Lord, I am deeply conscious of the fact that I have been ungrateful and ungracious and very sinful. By my sins I have used Your gifts of mind and heart, tongue and hands to offend You. I know very well that I have deserved to be punished, perhaps in hell, certainly in purgatory.

But not so much for any of these reasons do I tell You my sorrow. I am sorry, above all, because Your gifts have failed to win my heart. I am sorry because You have been so good, and I so thoughtless and ungrateful. One look at the crucifix and I need nothing more to convince me of Your love.

This morning I want to tell You my sorrow especially for these things: *(Here beg pardon for some recent personal sin, for a sin of your past life, for some sin common in the world today which you have committed).*

I ASK YOU

Never during Your life here on earth blessed Savior, did you refuse any request. You are no less kind in the Blessed Sacrament. I have many requests to make of You. Better than I, You know my many needs, those of my family, of the Church, of the sinful world. If the fulfillment of these needs is for our good, grant it, O Lord.

Especially I beg to be whole hearted in making this retreat. Help me to make a good one. You are much interested in me during these days. Help me to be mindful of this, and keep in close touch with You. Make this retreat have lasting results. Watch over my life that I may live it in accord with Your teachings and Your wonderful example, dear Lord.

Here are some special favors I want to ask this morning: *(Ask for some favor for yourself, your family, our country).*

MAY I TALK IT OVER WITH YOU

Blessed Savior, to us life seems very complex. From Your point of view there are not too many things that really count. There are You, and myself— especially my soul—there are creatures and sin, and at the end death and heaven or hell. All the things of which the world makes of so much account, what value have they for our real life in eternity! Only by taking Your point of view can we find the true answer to our difficulties.

You, dear Lord, understand all my difficulties. There are so many temptations and occasions of sin, arising from association with people, from misunderstanding, from unpleasant dispositions; I know well how You want me to meet them. There is only one question I must consider: Does my way of deciding help me to save my soul, or does it not? Give me the courage always to make this the rule of my life.

In all this I need Your counsel and guidance, Your help and support. Now that You are in my heart I can talk over my problems with You. Today I wish to consult You about these things: *(Discuss some personal trouble and how to overcome it, some problem connected with the family, with your work).*

I PROMISE

Lord, Jesus Christ, in the past I have often disappointed You. I have failed again and again because I tried to work alone, without You. Problems came up and I did not think of coming to You for guidance and help. But the strength and light gained from this Holy Communion gives me hope for the future. Stay with me, dear Lord, and I shall not fail again. I promise from now on to live my life with You. I want to go back to my daily tasks carrying You with me in my heart. Let me take You with me into my home, to my work and amusements, among my friends. I am convinced that this retreat must better my whole life. To make sure of this, dear Lord, I promise especially to improve in these particular matters: *(Make a promise regarding some sin and its occasion, regarding your home life, your work).*

And while You are still close to me in my heart, I promise also to keep myself in the atmosphere of the retreat. I will make the effort as reparation to Your Sacred Heart for all the sorrow I have caused You by my sins. Heart of Jesus, I implore, that I may love You ever more and more. Amen.

PRAYER BEFORE A CRUCIFIX

Behold, O good and sweetest Jesus, I cast myself upon my knees in Your sight and with the most fervent desire of my soul, I pray and beseech You to impress lively sentiments of faith, hope, and charity with true repentance for my sins and a most firm desire of amendment upon my heart. While with deep affection and grief of soul I consider within myself and mentally contemplate Your five most precious wounds, having before my eyes that which David, the prophet, long ago said: "They have pierced my hands and feet; they have numbered all my bones."

Examination of conscience

Imagine that you are on Calvary in the presence of the crucified Jesus.

O my God, I thank You for the benefits You have given to me. You loved me from all eternity. You created me to Your own image and likeness. You died on the cross to redeem me. You made me a member of Your Church and gave me a share in Your sacraments, in the holy sacrifice of the Mass, in

Holy Communion whereby You become the food and drink of my soul. I thank You for all these blessings especially for the opportunity I now have of making this retreat, to know You far better and follow You more closely. And I thank You too, dear Lord, for the many blessings that will be mine in heaven, if I am faithful to You here on earth. In thanksgiving I offer You all that I am and all that I do. And to make my thanksgiving more pleasing to You, I offer it through the immaculate heart of Mary.

PETITION

O my God, give me the grace to see sin in the light in which You see it. Let me understand something of the real meaning of sin as You understood it when You were forced to cast the angels into hell and drive our first parents out of paradise—for one sin. Give me something of Christ's understanding of sin as He knelt in the garden of olives pleading with You to take away from Him the chalice filled with the bitterness of our sins. I ask You also for light to know and understand my own sins and to be sincerely sorry for them. More especially, give me now the grace to see whether I am in any way failing to make this retreat well, and how I can make it better.

EXAMINATION ON THE RETREAT

Am I trying to make a good retreat? Am I keeping the recollection expected so that I may hear the voice of God? Have I frequently asked God to help me by being generous in my prayers and little sacrifices? Am I jotting down the thoughts which appeal to me or which impress me in a special manner? Do I spend time in profitable spiritual reading or prayer?

THE GENERAL EXAM

How do I regard sin? Do I realize what sin is? Let me remember that it is only because of Christ's death on the cross that I can hope to attain eternal life after being sorry for my sins. Do I try to do better? Am I avoiding the occasions of sin or am I halfhearted in my endeavors to keep from sin? Is my soul at this moment, perhaps, stained with mortal sin because of some person, place, or unbridled passion, drink, gambling, or lust? Have I tried to use my free will as a real hero and not as a weakling? Do I indulge in sinful thoughts that prepare the way for sins of act? Sin does exact its penalty even in this world. I have only one soul and only one life in which to save my soul.

FIRST COMMANDMENT

Do I deliberately entertain doubts about faith? How many things I take for granted on human testimony! Shall I believe man rather than God? Do I read or spread irreligious books or writings? Do I allow myself to become disgruntled, discouraged, even distrustful of God if things do not go my way? Am I superstitious? In time of temptation do I pray, make acts of faith? Do I murmur against God, His Church, priests, religious? Have I received any sacraments unworthily?

SECOND COMMANDMENT

How have I used the name of God? Do I dishonor Him by cursing, swearing, using His name when angry or without good reason? Do I utter the holy name with reverence? Am I careful at home about my language? How quickly can I become the cause of serious scandal by using improper language before children! Why not make reparation and join the Holy Name Society at your local parish?

THIRD COMMANDMENT

Do I attend Mass on Sundays and holidays of obligation? The greatest devotion of the Church is the devotion of the fifty-two Sundays! Do I consider it manly to go to church? The active athlete makes many sacrifices and is trained in his bearing and actions. How do I kneel while attending Mass? Am I distracted, half-asleep, or inclined to gaze around while at Mass? A missal, prayer book, or rosary would help keep your attention fixed. Do I participate actively in the Mass by receiving the Holy Eucharist frequently? Give your children the example of seeing you receiving Holy Communion frequently on Sundays, on the first Fridays, on the first Saturdays (and every day, if possible); and don't forget to spend some extra time in making a suitable thanksgiving after Holy Communion. Do I perform unnecessary servile work on Sundays? Do I keep holy the Lord's Day? Not merely the little time that I spend while at Mass? What about the manner in which I take my Sunday recreation?

FOURTH COMMANDMENT

Do I fulfill my duties toward my family? Am I helpful around the house? Do I have time for my family? Do I insist that the adolescent children keep regular hours? Am I watchful over their companionship and amusements? There may be grave danger in being too lavish in giving them spending money and thus creating in them a habit of undue self-sufficiency and independence of parental authority. Do I allow them uncontrolled use of an automobile? Much child delinquency springs from carelessness on the part of parents. Do I try to make my home a home dedicated to our Lord and His Mother? The practice of making the family join in the family rosary would help to make your home life a happy and blessed one. It takes only ten minutes or so to say it. Ask yourself if after coming home from work and feeling tired you find yourself pushing your family around, even out of the house, because you are not tolerant with them? Have your children enjoy their home and your company! Am I giving my children a Catholic education even though this may require a great sacrifice?

For children

Am I obedient even when some things become irksome and the folks just don't seem to understand? It is well to remember that our Lord during those many years "was subject to them." Do I consider myself too important to help my parents or the younger members of the family? Am I the sort who only offers his help when he expects a return? Do I come home at a reasonable hour, recalling that my parents are answerable to God for their watchfulness over me? Are my companions of high principles? Am I dating a Catholic girl or boy? One who can later teach my children according to Catholic principles? Am I working or studying as I should? Am I trying to be as congenial and kind a son or daughter as Christ was? Do my actions and words, at play and at work, clearly stamp me as a cultured, Catholic gentleman or lady? You should try and enter into the Catholic life of your parish by actively participating as a member of Church societies.

271

FIFTH COMMANDMENT

Do I control my temper at all times or do I easily fly into a rage? Have I injured others physically by striking or wounding them? Have I injured or exposed my health and life by keeping late hours? By intemperance, in eating and especially in drinking? Am I a reckless driver? Have I by my sinful life been a source of scandal or even induced others to sin? Have I respected the life and health of others? Even the unborn?

SIXTH AND NINTH COMMANDMENTS

How have I watched over my purity in thought, word, and deed? Have I allowed myself to become a victim of some habit of impurity? Am I careful to repel all impure thoughts and desires, realizing that I cannot play with fire? Am I careful about my amusements, so that they may not be a source of sin? What about movies, dances, companions? Do I guard against temptation when "keeping company"? Am I careful about my reading? Do I realize that the Church's laws about marriage, birth control, abortion, divorce are God's laws? Am I shrewd enough to realize the devil may make it all appear so innocent and so harmless until it is too late? The greatest help is derived from frequent Holy Communion. I need God's help, as I cannot do it by mere human strength. Let me not forget that mortification is necessary and that the Church wisely gives me such opportunities by her laws of fast and abstinence. Do I allow the devil to keep me away from confession if I have fallen into sins of impurity? Have I even made bad confessions because of these sins? It is only by frequenting the sacraments that the victory can be won.

SEVENTH AND TENTH COMMANDMENTS

Have I deprived others of their possessions? Have I ruined the goods of others? Do I pay my bills? Have I cheated others? If I have been entrusted with the goods of others, either in a private or a public capacity, I must realize that I am accountable to God for the proper use or misuse of any funds, property, possessions, or trusts. Do I contribute to the support of parochial needs, bearing my share of the cost of maintaining church buildings, property, and Catholic education? Am I trying to make necessary restitution for anything which I have stolen, mutilated, spoiled, or injured?

EIGHTH COMMANDMENT

Do I tell the truth, or do I exaggerate, side-stepping the truth? Have I injured the good name of others? Do I try to make amends if I have hurt their good names? Am I open with those at home or do I conceal what they should know or what should be discussed? Let me be honest with God, especially in the great sacrament of penance.

CONTRITION

I am sorry, dear Sacred Heart, because I have crucified You by my sins. My sins of the flesh have scourged Your back; my sins of the mind have crowned You with thorns; my sins of tongue have cried aloud for Your crucifixion; my sins of pride have put a red rag upon Your shoulders and a reed into Your hands; my sinful loves have driven the lance into Your side; my dishonesty has nailed Your hands to the cross; my venial sins slapped You in the face and covered you with spittle. My God, I am sorry. Forgive me for what I have done to You.

AMENDMENT

O my God, I do not want to commit any sins again. I certainly do not want to repeat my former ingratitude and selfishness. With the help of Your grace, I promise to improve my life in the manner which Christ, my leader and king, is pointing out to me in this retreat. From now on I will be more faithful in living up to my obligations toward You, my God, toward Your Church, my family, my neighbor, and myself. I promise especially, if perhaps I have failed, to enter more wholeheartedly into the spirit of the retreat by keeping in closer touch with God, and by observing better silence. I will try to do better. To my efforts and good will add the support of Your grace. With these two I know that I cannot fail. Christ crucified, help me. Amen.

The angel of the Lord declared unto Mary,
And she conceived of the Holy Spirit. Hail Mary . . .
Behold the handmaid of the Lord.
Be it done to me according to Your word. Hail
Mary . . .
And the Word was made flesh,
And dwelt among us. Hail Mary . . .
Pray for us, O holy Mother of God,
That we may be made worthy of the promises of
Christ.
Let us pray. Pour forth, we beseech Thee, O Lord,
Your grace into our hearts, that we to whom the
Incarnation of Christ, Your Son, was made known
by the message of an angel, may by His passion and
death be brought to life everlasting. Amen.

May He support us all the day long,

till the shadows lengthen,

and the evening comes

and the busy world is hushed,

and the fever of life is over,

and our work is done!

Then in His mercy

may He give us a safe lodging,

and a holy rest,

and peace at the last!

May our Lord be with us

all the days of our life.

Cardinal Newman

About this book

William Nicoll of EDIT, INC., designed *A do-it-your-self Retreat*. It was set by the TAMWILL CORPORATION. The text is 9/10 Times; the reduced matter 8/9. The chapter transitions are set in 9/11 Futura Medium.

The text display type is 14 Futura Demi and 9/10 Futura Bold. The titles on the cover and title page are in 48, 36, and 30 Times.

The book was printed by PHOTOPRESS, INC., on 60-pound Montgomery Offset and bound by A. C. ENGDAHL AND COMPANY, INC.